Staging Systemic Violence

Methuen Drama Engage offers original reflections about key practitioners, movements and genres in the fields of modern theatre and performance. Each volume in the series seeks to challenge mainstream critical thought through original and interdisciplinary perspectives on the body of work under examination. By questioning existing critical paradigms, it is hoped that each volume will open up fresh approaches and suggest avenues for further exploration.

Series Editors
Mark Taylor-Batty
University of Leeds, UK
Enoch Brater
University of Michigan, USA

Titles in the series include:

*Contemporary Drag Practices and Performers:
Drag in a Changing Scene Volume 1*
Edited by Mark Edward and Stephen Farrier
ISBN 978-1-3500-8294-6

Performing the Unstageable: Success, Imagination, Failure
Karen Quigley
ISBN 978-1-3500-5545-2

Drama and Digital Arts Cultures
David Cameron, Michael Anderson and Rebecca Wotzko
ISBN 978-1-472-59219-4

Social and Political Theatre in 21st-Century Britain: Staging Crisis
Vicky Angelaki
ISBN 978-1-474-21316-5

Watching War on the Twenty-First-Century Stage: Spectacles of Conflict
Clare Finburgh
ISBN 978-1-472-59866-0

Fiery Temporalities in Theatre and Performance:
The Initiation of History
Maurya Wickstrom
ISBN 978-1-4742-8169-0

Ecologies of Precarity in Twenty-First Century Theatre:
Politics, Affect, Responsibility
Marissia Fragkou
ISBN 978-1-4742-6714-4

Robert Lepage/Ex Machina: Revolutions in Theatrical Space
James Reynolds
ISBN 978-1-4742-7609-2

Social Housing in Performance: The English Council Estate
on and off Stage
Katie Beswick
ISBN 978-1-4742-8521-6

Postdramatic Theatre and Form
Edited by Michael Shane Boyle, Matt Cornish and Brandon Woolf
ISBN 978-1-3500-4316-9

Sarah Kane's Theatre of Psychic Life: Theatre,
Thought and Mental Suffering
Leah Sidi
ISBN 978-1-3502-8312-1

For a complete listing, please visit
https://www.bloomsbury.com/series/methuen-drama-engage/

Staging Systemic Violence

British Theatre 2010–2019

Alex Watson

methuen | drama
LONDON • NEW YORK • OXFORD • NEW DELHI • SYDNEY

METHUEN DRAMA
Bloomsbury Publishing Plc, 50 Bedford Square, London, WC1B 3DP, UK
Bloomsbury Publishing Inc, 1359 Broadway, New York, NY 10018, USA
Bloomsbury Publishing Ireland, 29 Earlsfort Terrace, Dublin 2, D02 AY28, Ireland

BLOOMSBURY, METHUEN DRAMA and the Methuen Drama logo are trademarks of Bloomsbury Publishing Plc

First published in Great Britain 2024
This paperback edition published 2025

Copyright © Alex Watson, 2024

Alex Watson has asserted his right under the Copyright, Designs and Patents Act, 1988, to be identified as author of this work.

For legal purposes the Acknowledgements on pp. xi–xii constitute an extension of this copyright page.

Cover image © Helen Murray / ArenaPAL

All rights reserved. No part of this publication may be: i) reproduced or transmitted in any form, electronic or mechanical, including photocopying, recording or by means of any information storage or retrieval system without prior permission in writing from the publishers; or ii) used or reproduced in any way for the training, development or operation of artificial intelligence (AI) technologies, including generative AI technologies. The rights holders expressly reserve this publication from the text and data mining exception as per Article 4(3) of the Digital Single Market Directive (EU) 2019/790.

Bloomsbury Publishing Plc does not have any control over, or responsibility for, any third-party websites referred to or in this book. All internet addresses given in this book were correct at the time of going to press. The author and publisher regret any inconvenience caused if addresses have changed or sites have ceased to exist, but can accept no responsibility for any such changes.

A catalogue record for this book is available from the British Library.

ISBN:	HB:	978-1-3503-8727-0
	PB:	978-1-3503-8728-7
	ePDF:	978-1-3503-8729-4
	eBook:	978-1-3503-8730-0

Series: Methuen Drama Engage

Typeset by Integra Software Services Pvt. Ltd.

For product safety related questions contact productsafety@bloomsbury.com

To find out more about our authors and books visit www.bloomsbury.com and sign up for our newsletters.

Contents

Content Warning		ix
List of Acronyms		x
Acknowledgements		xi
Introduction		1
Staging Systemic Violence: Context and Methodology		4
A Brief and Partial History of Onstage Violence		8
The Representation of Violence in 2010s British Theatre and *Mr Incredible*		17
Overview of the Chapters		20
1	Violence	23
	The Critique of Violence and *Escaped Alone*	25
	Making Invisible Violence Visible	31
	Violence and 'Truth'	37
	Conclusion	42
2	Performativity	45
	Violence and Performativity	47
	The Violence of Performativity and *Some People Talk About Violence*	50
	The Performativity of Violence and *A Very Very Very Dark Matter*	58
	Conclusion	64
3	Protest	65
	Protest, Theatre and (Non)Violence	67
	Witnessing Black Witnessing in *ear for eye*	76
	Conclusion	85
4	Climate Crisis	87
	The Violent Performativity of Resource Exploitation in *Oil*	88
	Performative Taxonomical Violence and *The Children*	94
	Conclusion	102

5	Neoliberalism	103
	Theatrical Visions of Neoliberal Dystopia and Apocalypse	104
	Cross-Cultural Dramaturgies of Violence and *Three Kingdoms*	113
	Conclusion	122
6	Racism	123
	Europeanness and the Other in *Lampedusa* and *How to Hold Your Breath*	125
	Racism and British Identity in *Fall of the Kingdom, Rise of the Foot Soldier*	135
	Conclusion	143
7	Gender	145
	Gender, Violence and the Fourth-Wave Onstage	146
	The Performative 'Reality' of Gender-Based Violence in *Bird*	151
	Breaking (Violent) Form in *seven methods of killing kylie jenner*	157
	Conclusion	167

Conclusion: Theatrical Critiques of Violence	169
Final Remarks	175
Notes	177
Works Cited	184
Index	205

Content Warning

This book – being concerned with issues, theories and representations of violence – frequently references theoretical, invented and real instances of violent conditions, acts and assaults. These include, but are not limited to, gendered violence, gender-based violence, queerphobic violence, racism, race-based violence, murder, war, terrorist attacks and physical assaults. The author has attempted, wherever possible, to write about and cite references to these descriptions and examples in a manner that is not explicit, egregious or graphic.

List of Acronyms

BLM - The Black Lives Matter movement

Fringe - The Edinburgh Fringe Festival

GBV - gender-based violence

NT - The Royal National Theatre, London

RE - The Royal Exchange Theatre, Manchester

RC - The Royal Court Theatre, London

YV - The Young Vic Theatre, London

Acknowledgements

This book would not have been possible without Royal Holloway's Department of Drama, Theatre and Dance, where I was granted the space to shape and grow not only this research but my own academic and pedagogic practice. Especial thanks to the students who engaged with some of the case studies explored here, and the ever-friendly staff who were consistently helpful and generous with their knowledge, including Lynette Goddard, Chris Megson, Liz Schafer, Bryce Lease, David Bullen and my exemplary tutor Dan Rebellato.

Thanks to those in the world of theatre and performance studies more widely who gave me further opportunities and encouragement to develop this research: such as Kevin De Ornellas, Kélina Gotman, Jacqueline Bolton, Alan Read, Nicholas Holden, Élisabeth Angel-Perez, Catriona Fallow, Clare Finburgh Delijani and Vicky Angelaki. All my best to the staff and students of ICTheatre Brighton – with my time here seeing the evolution of this research from a postgraduate thesis to a fully realized book. Thank you also to those fellow early-career researchers with whom I had (and will undoubtedly continue to have) many invaluable conversations, not exclusively including Lisa Moravec, Clio Unger, Milo Harries, Grace Joseph, the wonderful Lianna Mark (and the whole *Platform* editorial team), Corrie Tan, Hannah Greenstreet, Tim Cowbury and Florence Platford. To you all, and to those not mentioned here, my utmost appreciation and solidarity.

I have found working on my first book a rewarding, though initially apprehensive, experience. However, this was very much quelled by the friendliness and professionalism of the Methuen Drama Engage publishing and editing staff. Thank you to the series editors Enoch Brater and particularly Mark Taylor-Batty for answering my initial enquiries, not to mention Aanchal Vij and Anna Brewer who remained constant sources of assistance throughout.

My warm appreciation also goes to those friends who often took a leap of faith with my taste for good theatre – and were even sometimes rewarded – such as Katie Porsch, Kate Wood-Hill (shout out to the Hello gang), Mia Micozzi and Rachel Seymour. My gratitude to the staff of No. 32 Clapham and Jackson & Rye Richmond (RIP) for working around my postdoctoral, teaching, and writing schedules, particularly Jess (and Jeff!), Alexis, Elina, the ever-supportive Sean Connolly and Alvaro Garcia – who perhaps has the best understanding of philosophy in the entire British service industry. Thanks for the many invaluable on-shift chats on thinkers from Bauman to Bacon, sometimes while even serving bacon (sorry).

Love to my family and, especially, my parents: thank you for never once batting an eyelid at my pursuit of drama – and even actively encouraging me to do so! Finally, the greatest of thanks to both Tom Quilty who witnessed the bulk of this research come together while stuck together during the national lockdowns (and remained on hand to provide much-needed downtime); and to my brilliant partner Kit Narey to whom this book is dedicated, whose own research in violence studies will undoubtedly prove far more significant than anything gleaned in this book. Thank you both for your unfailing belief, advice and support.

Introduction

The man standing in front of us does not look or sound like a perpetrator. He is by turns charming, emotional, funny, relatable, remorseful and disarmingly 'normal'. In this play, he tells us about his family, about his desire to have children, his distaste for the impersonal nature of dating apps, and how sad he is about Holly, his ex-girlfriend, leaving him. We sympathize with him – perhaps we even empathize with him. The playwright, Camilla Whitehill, even notes that some of her male friends 'felt compelled' to state that they recognized 'parts of themselves' in Adam (2016a), played here by Alistair Donegan. However, by the end of this performance of *Mr Incredible* at London's 2016 VAULT Festival, Adam will reveal that, at the end of their relationship, he sexually assaulted Holly. As we reconcile this reprehensible act to this seemingly 'nice guy', we also discover that Adam has been talking to us, the audience, as if we were his lawyer: the office-like set suddenly makes sense.

The cognitive dissonance of this perpetrator's 'relatability' had, for Whitehill's friends, 'kind of freaked them out' (2016a). Yet, the knowledge of his perpetration underlines some issues that may have been gleaned in Adam's recollections throughout – was he really that 'nice' or was he, in fact, coercive and controlling? When we look a bit deeper into his socially normative statements and behaviours, might we see something that could be called *violent*? The production concludes with Adam being acquitted of his actions, thanking his lawyer: 'it was good you mentioned that we'd been out, and she'd been drinking' (Whitehill 2016b: 88), relating to a culture of 'victim-blaming' in British society.[1] Did the same structural misogyny which enabled Adam to be cleared of charges in a court of law obscure our recognition of the violence in his words, behaviours and actions?

Mr Incredible is, in many ways, typical of how new writing in British theatre over the course of the 2010s represented and articulated violence: namely, not as something explicit or spectacular – but offstage, on the peripheries of dialogue, permeating implicitly but almost intangibly through the action and dramaturgy, or in the atmosphere between the performers and the audience. In other words, it was invisible, yet there – and asking the audience to perceive it was arguably central to the socio-political objectives of many theatre-makers. This approach to representing violence was informed by the wider social context of 2010s Britain: a decade where understandings of violence in public discourse advanced beyond standard, obvious ideas and images like combat, fights and war. Acknowledgements of institutional, hegemonic, systemic and structural violence – or, violence that could not traditionally be 'seen' – became more widely disseminated. Although such theories have existed for decades, social movements through the 2010s attempted to alert the public to them. Among the most prominent of these were Occupy, who opposed socio-economic inequality; the various members of the Climate Justice Alliance, who urged a response to environmental crisis; Black Lives Matter (BLM), which sought to combat racial inequality and oppression; and #MeToo, that looked to widely alert the public to the extent of societal misogyny and sexual harassment.

The Royal Court's artistic director from April 2013 through the rest of the decade, Vicky Featherstone, responded to the latter of these in the British theatre establishment by releasing an industry 'Code of Behaviour' (2017a).[2] Towards the end of the decade, she stated of the movement's effect on playwriting that: 'It's not only people writing with more freedom or more analysis post-MeToo. It's also going, "that doesn't feel appropriate any more". We normalise things so quickly […] [but] we don't need to do that. We have a vocabulary now' (Thompson 2019; see also Fallow and Mullan 2021). Such 'vocabulary' is more widely applicable to how the form and content of British theatre was influenced by, and reflective of, emergent conceptions of violence in the 2010s. Namely, violence was increasingly distinguished by redoubled attempts to identify it within cultural norms and the otherwise invisible or banal.

The violence that movements like BLM and #MeToo resisted often manifested in immediately apparent and reprehensible acts, yet the roots of these acts lie deeper, entrenched in culture and society – and might even lie within the everyday behaviours, assumptions, gestures, language and acts of the citizenry that might otherwise be judged as 'normal'. Therefore, I contend in this study that the concept of performativity is essential to the understanding of systemic violence, and particularly regarding its representation in theatre. Performativity is the effect that words, actions, behaviours and gestures have on (our) reality, that they can 'do things', especially when ritualized or repeated over time. And as the influential philosopher Judith Butler contends, just as performativity establishes reality, so too can it change it: 'the task is not whether to repeat, but how to repeat' (2007: 202–3). Performativity is the (changeable) process of reiterating 'the way things are'. So, the assault perpetrated by Adam in *Mr Incredible*, for example, is an explicit act of violence; but the attitudes and dialogue he espouses must be examined to understand where this act comes from – what performatively motivates and authorizes it. British theatre in the 2010s, then, was responsive to ideas about violence that were increasingly being disseminated in public debate. This Introduction continues with four sections: the first outlines the considerations of this study; the second offers a brief history of onstage (proto-systemic) violence; the third returns to *Mr Incredible* to offer an opening analysis of staging systemic violence; and the last section overviews the chapters ahead.

Staging Systemic Violence: Context and Methodology

The rationale for the subject matter of this work is informed by several considerations. The specific time-period of the 2010s follows from the historicization of (particularly post-war) British theatre through decades – seen most notably in the *Modern British Playwriting* series (2012–13) edited by Richard Boon and Philip Roberts. They 'recognize that there is an inevitable danger of imposing a spurious neatness' in their decade-oriented classification of British theatre from the 1950s to the 2000s, therefore 'some account is given of relevant material from earlier years' (Boon and Roberts 2013: vii), which is an approach I follow here: the influence of earlier work from Caryl Churchill and Sarah Kane, for example, recurs throughout the study. Furthermore, at the time of writing, there is little scholarship that specifically examines new writing in British theatre in the overall context of the 2010s. There have been accounts of twenty-first century work in the Methuen Drama Engage series from scholars such as Vicky Angelaki (2017), Clare Finburgh Delijani (2017), and Marissia Fragkou (2018) which have served as useful touchstones, but due to the time of their publication do not provide studies of the whole decade.

As Boon and Roberts mention, the categorization of decades does suggest a certain temporal and historical 'neatness', yet the 2010s can be understood as a period between two prominent global crises – with crises being, as Angelaki states, organized around 'three interconnected primary areas: political, environmental, financial' (2017: 1), as well as being central to historicizing and contextualizing time periods and their culture. Alongside Angelaki's work, Anja Hartl too contends that '[a] sense of crisis has pervaded both politics and the arts since the end of the twentieth century', identifying 'postmodernism, the demise of socialism and the global spread of neoliberalism' as factors (2021). In terms of the 2010s, the decade began as much of the world was still reeling from the 2007–9 Great Recession and ended with the discovery of the COVID-19 virus. The crises (the latter being political, environmental *and* financial) have both been global in scale and had specific impact on British society. These phenomena will have lasting ramifications, and both have influenced public perceptions of violence – the former through the financial inequality and often-indirect violence of neoliberalism, the latter more literally demonstrating the catastrophic injurability of that which cannot be tangibly seen.[3]

This exploration of socio-cultural understandings of violence is legitimized by the material conditions of the medium under discussion.

As Finburgh Delijani writes, theatre 'has a tradition of taking the pulse of society, politics, economics, culture and history' and, comparative to 'most cinema and television […] it can be realized within modest means […] [and] respond rapidly to current affairs' (2019: 5). These characteristics certainly continued through the 2010s, with those movements listed above finding rejoinders, support and responses from British theatre. Moreover, theatre is generally better positioned to represent systemic violence than cinema or television. Like these mediums, contemporary theatre is predicated on the visual – but not nearly to the same extent, with liveness and audience-performer proximity generally seen as distinguishing factors of the form, even if this has been troubled by the necessities of theatre's adaptation to the COVID-19 pandemic. Generally speaking, cinema and television have more danger of slipping into 'spectacularization', of creating enthralling, absorbing images of violence. This is not to say that such spectacle is always uncritical of violence,[4] rather, the proliferation of such images can have a habit of 'running away' from the message: appearing out of context. Finburgh Delijani, whose work explores 'watching war' onstage, contends that theatre can alternatively offer more of a critical distance, drawing attention to how 'what we watch is framed as spectacle, and how those spectacles might seek to impose certain ideologies on us' (2019: 12); a contention developed in the first chapter here. It so follows that British theatre – distinguished in the 2010s by its rapid response to social issues and its proxemics over visuals – serves as a more adept medium for representing 'invisible', socially maintained forms of violence.

As for exploring theatre from Britain specifically, this stems from personal and political considerations, as well its ability to quickly comment on contemporaneous issues. The rapid response to 'current affairs' in theatre is heightened by Britain's continual supply of new writing (Sierz 2011) – especially, for example, in relation to its close geographical neighbour France which had a relative dearth of new writing (Danan 2013) and Britain's linguistic neighbour the USA, 'where theatre is very much a minority art' (Finburgh Delijani 2019: 6). As mentioned, Britain faced the global crises of the 2010s at a distinct national level as well as contending with more region-specific examples of relevance to performativity and systemic violence. Chief among these was the 2016 referendum to exit the European Union (EU) – otherwise known by the portmanteau Brexit – which was intertwined with issues of structural racism as explored in Chapters 5 and 6. In terms of practical and personal considerations, Britain was also my chief place of residence through the 2010s: being the society I am most familiar with and the theatre of which I attended most. Adhering to Boon and Roberts' series, I have also elected to explore British rather than UK theatre, with the theatre of

Northern Ireland implicated in that region's formal, cultural and material ties to theatre of the Republic of Ireland; increased debates on its status as part of the UK in the context of Brexit; and its historical colonization and factional violence different to the experiences of the rest of the UK (Phelan 2016). That said, the classification of 'British theatre' here has not been dogmatically narrow – with Chapter 5, for example, exploring mainland European theatre that played on British stages.

Some geographical and representational limits were present in this research and its purview. The majority of theatre I witnessed in the 2010s was in London and, consequently, of the sixteen plays highlighted here, eleven opened in the capital. Although this betrays my address for much of this decade, it also demonstrates London's continued status as the theatrical centre of Britain particularly regarding new writing, informed by a continuation of major cultural inequality between British regions: even adjusted for tourism, 'London has more theatre visits per person by a factor of around nine' compared to the rest of the UK (Rebellato 2018: 20). The Royal Court (RC) remained vital for new writing, debuting five productions closely analysed here – while four more opened at smaller, fringe venues such as the Gate Theatre and the Ovalhouse. Other productions explored in this study have played in Edinburgh, Warwick, Manchester, Aldeburgh, Stratford-upon-Avon, Cardiff and Liverpool; as well as internationally in cities including New York, Tallinn and Munich. It could also be said that the characteristic of 2010s British theatre representing systemic violence took some years into the decade before it was firmly established: three of the productions explored here debuted between 2011 and 2014, whereas thirteen were released in the latter half of the decade – meaning that the temporal spread of the plays here is somewhat uneven.

Additionally, the 2010s British theatre industry was still predominantly made up of white, cis-males – as Whitehill puts it, '[i]f men are in charge of 85% of an industry, it will not always be pleasant for those of us in the minority' (2017). The perpetuation of this structural inequality has resulted in some of the most urgent, articulate representations of systemic violence coming from the new writing of female playwrights: of the sixteen playwrights explored here, ten identify as women, five as male and one is non-binary. Four of the playwrights are Black British, one is of Irish descent, and one is of Jewish descent, while one is Scottish, one is Welsh, eleven are from Southern England, and three are Northern.[5] These numbers, while symptomatic of the prominence of white, English, London-based theatre-makers in the industry, reveal some effort on my behalf to include a range of backgrounds among the playwrights explored, especially with my identity as a white cis-male and in the context of work that explores structural oppression of certain identity groups.

This study focuses on new writing, which means that revivals, versions, adaptations and new stagings of pre-2010s texts are not examined in detail here. Although the contemporary direction and dramaturgy of a canonical text can certainly demonstrate relevant issues – with updates of ancient Greek plays or new Shakespeare productions, for example, being a barometer for the issues or styles of the day – new writing still arguably offers more contemporaneous perspectives on social, political and cultural phenomena. Furthermore, with 2010s British theatre providing so many productions that engaged with (systemic) violence, the limits of this work dictate that not all areas could be provided in detail, such as the representation of war. Although Britain was directly involved in the Libyan Civil War (2011), Operation Shader (2014–) and the Persian Gulf Crisis (2019–21), these were not as prominent in the cultural landscape as the Iraq War (2003–09) and the war in Afghanistan (2001–21, with British military personnel withdrawn in 2014). Theatrical representations of war were therefore more common in the 2000s and, although proceeding by established systemic violence, can be considered as more of an explicit example of subjective violence. Furthermore, detailed studies of British theatre and war have already been offered by Jenny Hughes (2011) and, as mentioned, Finburgh Delijani (2017). Other areas not extensively included are mental health, ableism and disability, homophobia and sexual orientation-based violence, classism, and the struggles of Welsh and Scottish national identities; although most of these are, at least, touched on. Again, there is existing scholarship on these topics, as well as definite scope for further research to explore the representation of systemic violence in these areas.

A Brief and Partial History of Onstage Violence

The representation of violence has arguably always been a concern of Western theatre – as has the choice to *not* make violence visible onstage. A retroactive exploration of the canonical drama generally accepted as the 'lineage' of contemporary British theatre can reveal dramatic methods and narratives as sharing commonalities (or alike ideas) to theories and representations of systemic violence. Therefore, as a historical and contextual ground for the study that follows, I offer here a whistle-stop overview of some significant, relevant moments along the canonical timeline of British theatre and its predecessors. That said, the subject of violence in theatre history is so vast and complex that it defies easy summary, and so I would invite those interested to seek out specific studies on respective time periods or movements – of which some good starting points are referenced throughout this section.

To begin at the contested 'origin' of Western drama, the theatre of ancient Athens saw many narratives depicted onstage that were shaped by both legendary and historical violent events, from the aftermath of Xerxes' failed invasion of Greece in Aeschylus' *The Persians* (472BCE) to the titular character's frenzied familicide in Euripides' *Heracles* (416BCE). The conventions of ancient Greek theatre demanded that depictions of death, blows, or other physical violence were not witnessed by the audience (Sommerstein 2010) – these ostensibly took place 'offstage'. That said, the violence inherent in much of ancient Greek myth means that it is reductive to state that violence was practically absent on its stages: not only would it be present in the imaginations and contextual understanding of the audience but could be said to be represented differently to our contemporary, realist-informed conventions of how theatrical violence is normatively represented (Deacy et al. 2023). For example, H. D. F. Kitto writes of Aeschylus' *The Suppliants* (*c.* 468BCE) that as the Danaids refused to yield to the pursuant Egyptians: 'we must imagine the orchestra filled with wild movement, violence made manifest. For the moment, the dance and music are more important than the words' (2011: 12). This stretch of the imagination (often the case with Kitto) nevertheless reminds us that text was not the primary representational factor in ancient Greek performance, and that violence may have been 'present' onstage in ways a contemporary British audience would not grasp.

Still, it is certainly true that mimetic acts of violence were not 'realistically' physicalized onstage by our current standards. Although it would be contentious to suggest that this dramaturgical rule was to better alert the audience to the structural violence of Athenian society, the fact that any physical violence that happened during the duration of the plot would not be seen – even if the audience would be well aware of what such acts generally 'looked like', being composed of many who had experienced battle first-hand – likely downplayed visceral spectacle in favour of moral questioning. The Roman theatre that emerged from ancient Greek culture was less modest, with the plays of Seneca drawing on the same legends but not shying away from explicitly dramatizing Medea's killing of her children or Thyestes eating the remains of his son, for example. This was likely affirmed by the sanguine nature of other Roman cultural events such as gladiatorial contests, though Seneca's plays have been argued as demonstrative of socio-cultural fragmentation as well as the ethical ambiguity of violence and power (Remshardt 2016). Still, practitioners and theorists including Antonin Artaud have perceived Seneca's use of represented violence as gesturing towards the inherent chaos of the universe (Crewe 1990) rather than, for example, used for specific critiques of the structural issues of his contemporary society.

During the medieval period, early theatre across the island of Britain also featured the onstage representation of violence – as gleaned from the records of the mystery and saint or miracle plays. Despite the emergence of these performances to better educate the common populace on Christian tradition and morality, they often revelled in drawn-out spectacles of suffering, like the Crucifixion. Sid Sondergard writes that the Cornish *Ordinalia* mystery play cycle (attributed to the late 1300s) 'reflects an increasing dramaturgical awareness of the sheer entertainment value of amplifying stage representations of violence' as it seemingly encouraged 'audience participation in graphic spectacle rather than in contemplative meditation' (1985: 169). Understanding how it was depicted and interpreted will only be partial due to a lack of documentation, as Clifford Davidson states (2001: 292), though in the case of the saint plays he argues that these representations were necessary to demonstrate the stories of martyrs – who would often endure great feats of suffering – rather than, as Jody Enders contests (1999), the plays being 'carnivalesque' precursors to Artaud's Theatre of Cruelty (2001: 314). What can be surmised is that the violence of the mystery and saint plays was likely not used to inspect the structural issues of feudal society, other than perhaps a surface-based urging that it should better adhere to Christian doctrine, regardless of whether the depictions of violence were for revelry or spiritual contemplation.

During the Early Modern period, around the time of the English Renaissance, Seneca had a profound influence in theatre as recognized, notably, by T. S. Eliot (2015). The approach to onstage violence gleaned in Seneca's surviving texts can certainly be detected in works like Thomas Kyd's *The Spanish Tragedy* (*c*. 1582), Christopher Marlowe's *Tamburlaine* (*c*. 1587), John Ford's *'Tis Pity She's a Whore* (*c*. 1626), and infamously so in William

Shakespeare's *Titus Andronicus* (*c.* 1588). The numerousness of these tragedies gesture to the appetite among Elizabethan–Jacobean audiences for violent spectacle (Hiscock 2022), and the intertwinement of 'staged violence' with absolutist power as Michel Foucault argues of public executions, for example (1991). There were, however, theatre-makers who offered social commentary of hegemonic structures, such as the interludes or *anterliwtau* performed and published as pamphlets (1739–1810) by the Welsh dramatist Twm o'r Nant. Shakespeare's works, too, appear to have shifted over time from prioritizing spectacular violence to moral anxieties around its use, particularly by those in positions of power (Cohen 1993; Foakes 2002). Tragedies such as *Hamlet* (*c.* 1600), *Macbeth* (*c.* 1606) and *King Lear* (*c.* 1606) show immoral or poorly informed decision-making from leaders as contributing to a more widespread socio-cultural violence and chaos across their domains: plot elements perhaps informed by the rulers of these plays forgoing the ideals of the Tudors and Stuarts' absolutist belief in the Divine Right of Kings.

Something approaching structural or systemic violence might be said to exist in the History Plays. Jan Kott, who offered a revised perception of Shakespeare in post-war Europe and in the context of movements like the Theatre of the Absurd, characterized these plays as being akin to a revolving wheel of power (1990) in which characters ascend or fall but essentially fulfil the part of various cogs in a machine, locating this especially in *Richard III* (*c.* 1592). The violence of the History Plays still erupts into representations of torture, murder and battles – arguably in both supportive and critical showings of Foucault's absolutist power – but the dynastic struggles across their plots give a palpable sense of an invisible mechanism at work. Likely understood by Shakespeare's contemporary audiences as fate, divine guidance or the inevitability of history, this could retrospectively be perceived as alike to structural violence. Kim Solga, too, examines the politics of violence's visibility in theatre of this time: specifically, that done against women, which she describes as 'both visually stunning and culturally invisible' (2009: 4). This is drawn from the work of feminist historians on 'the "effacement" of violence against women, particularly rape, in Renaissance English culture' (8), as well as theoretical explorations of performance and absence (which I return to in Chapter 1). Rather than see 'Shakespeare and his fellow Renaissance men [as] our "contemporary", as Jan Kott does, Solga asks 'what it means to claim their work as "ours"[?]' (2009: 28). Although we see the effects of extreme cultural misogyny in their plays, its invisibility in historical context when combined with the discussion of these issues in our current time might throw up questions of how we recognize (systemic) violence now.

By the first felicitous translated performance of Henrik Ibsen's *A Doll's House* (1879) at London's Novelty Theatre (1889), the rise of naturalism was in full effect on the British stage. With it came the depiction of types of violence that had not heretofore widely been considered as such, as well as social issues that had not yet been widely represented onstage. For example – continuing Solga's contentions – whereas gender-based violence was 'effaced' in Renaissance culture, there was a widespread discussion of women's rights at the turn of the twentieth century. This was due in great part to the establishment of the middle class through the Industrial Revolution, with the rise of the suffrage movement and the phenomenon of 'the New Woman' who had greater autonomy and education: among whom Ibsen's Nora became an important theatrical figurehead. Indeed, the prominence of the #MeToo movement on the 2010s stage seemingly invited theatre-makers to revive Nora's presence, with adaptations and versions from Zinnie Harris (Donmar Warehouse, London, 2009), Carrie Cracknell and Simon Stephens (Young Vic, London, 2012) and Stef Smith (Young Vic, 2020); with Tanika Gupta's transplanting of the action from Norway to colonial India (Lyric Hammersmith, London, 2019) speaking to how British imperial violence was similarly effaced from Victorian and Edwardian society. The symbolism of Ibsen's naturalism, which deviated from the strict study of 'real life' defined and championed by Émile Zola (1881; 2001), became more popular on the British stage as seen, for example, in George Bernard Shaw's use of melodramatic techniques such as farce and denouement, as well as the high symbolism of the dream sequence of *Man and Superman* (1903), seen during the 2010s in a rare staging by Simon Godwin (NT, 2015).

The intervention of such symbolist techniques into naturalist form invited audiences to participate in the moral questions asked by Shaw's work, for example, or perceive Halvard in Ibsen's *The Master Builder* (1892) and Torvald in *A Doll's House* as being hegemonic symbols made impotent by the narratives' moral denouncements against patriarchal oppression. Mads Bunch similarly writes of August Strindberg's male protagonists that they are mostly 'trapped in the very rigid, masculine, and authoritarian structure[s] of the late nineteenth century' (2012: 53), although the playwright seems to place the blame of this impotence on the intervention of the New Woman into traditionally male areas of the public sphere. Strindberg's misogynistic tendencies did not sit well within the landscape of 2010s British theatre, as reflected in revisions of *Miss Julie* (1888) by Katie Mitchell (Schaubühne, Berlin, 2010), David Eldridge (Royal Exchange, Manchester, 2012), Yaël Farber (Fringe, 2012), Polly Stenham (NT, 2018) and Amy Ng (Southwark Playhouse, London, 2021), with Farber and Ng again inserting intersectional issues of colonialism. Strindberg's critical depictions of women's place in society often worked alongside representations of psychological violence and the deleterious effect of 'unseen' theatrical devices: such as the overbearing, offstage patriarchal menace of the Count in *Miss Julie*. Strindberg's misplaced judgement of women for the psychological violence done against men made to feel powerless in disenfranchising social structures (not dissimilar from anti-feminist male sentiment in the 2010s) arguably proves that he did not grasp a comparable theory to systemic violence. His works do, however, effectively demonstrate the performativity and coercion that socio-cultural structures have on individuals.

In the context of mass warfare and shifting social attitudes, many of the avant-garde theatrical experiments around 1890–1950 comprehended these structures with contempt: with many European theatre-makers finding their works staged in Britain or maintaining rich dialogues with British artists (Warden 2012). For example, Alfred Jarry's *Ubu Roi* (1896) reduced the pretensions of patriarchal rule to primal gluttony; Tristan Tzara's anarchic *The Gas Heart* (1920) offered a Dadaist destruction of theatre – a medium connected to the bourgeois structures that sanctioned the madness of the First World War (Cardullo and Knopf 2001: 265-7); and Artaud's Theatre of Cruelty similarly sought to deconstruct traditional theatre, reveal 'cultural hypocrisies', and confront audiences with 'the cruelty of existence, of humans' precarious position in the universe' (ibid.: 375). This last objective is a central feature of the Theatre of the Absurd which, as defined by Martin Esslin (1980), offers something of a theatrical response to Albert Camus' articulation of the meaninglessness of life in the context of a post-war, increasingly atheist and disillusioned Europe. Samuel Beckett's works certainly give a sense of oppression and confusion, with characters pitifully set against forces beyond their comprehension. Although the disdain of hegemony and perception of oppressive systems might encourage an easy equation of the subject and intent of these avant-garde works with the representation of systemic violence, the anti-establishment convictions of figures like Jarry and Tzara were fixed more on critiquing social norms and the elite rather than the specific systems of power structures, whereas the oppression of the absurd relates to a feeling of wider human meaninglessness rather than the socio-cultural specificity of systemic violence.

This said, some 'absurd' dramatists certainly touched on similar ideas to the theory of systemic violence, or issues relevant to it. Jean Genet's *The Blacks* (1959; first British performance: RC, 1961), for example, locates the illusion of racial superiority and the control it seeks to justify within 'performance': such as the staginess of the establishment and the criminal justice system, parodied by Black cast members using Whiteface. The viral fascism symbolized in Eugène Ionesco's *Rhinoceros* (1959, first British performance: RC, 1960) can be retroactively perceived as how systemic violence innocuously works through the actions and behaviours of citizens: with this ideological embodiment being defamiliarized through Ionesco's animal transformations. Additionally, as I argue elsewhere (see Watson 2021a), the work of Harold Pinter could be considered a precursor to representations of systemic violence in 2010s British theatre; emerging as it did around the same time of Johan Galtung's theory of structural violence – the origin of contemporary understandings of systemic violence. Here, I compare the literal and social structural issues of *The Caretaker* (Arts Theatre, London, 1960) to the layers of racism in debbie tucker green's *ear for eye* (RC, 2018), as well as the similarities of invisible menace created by offstage elements and enmeshed onstage behaviours between *Party Time* (Almeida Theatre, London, 1991) and Mark Ravenhill's *The Cane* (RC, 2018), concluding that Pinter's influence 'has set a precedent for British playwrights to stage the systemic violence of our contemporary society [...] revealing the unseen violence in urgent need of address' (Watson 2021a: 154).

However, the post-war British playwright who could perhaps best be accredited for the identification of a proto-theory of systemic violence is Edward Bond. In an author's note for a collection of his plays, entitled 'On Violence' (1977), Bond contends that 'violence is contingent not necessary, and occurs in situations [...] in which people are at such physical and emotional risk that their life is neither natural nor free', with human nature 'created through our relation to the culture of our society' (11–12). This contextualizes the shocking representation of violence in his most famous work, *Saved* (RC, 1965), in which disenfranchised lower-class male characters stone a baby in a pram to death on an apparent whim for entertainment. 'Capitalism has made violence a cheap consumer commodity' (15), as Bond continues: that those made abject and 'lower-down' in the hierarchies of capitalist societies may turn to violence and prejudice due to the conditions forced on them by systems of power. Due to the near-total pervasion of capitalism into British society, he concludes that violence inherently exists within it: 'whenever you walk quietly down the orderly street of a capitalist society you are surrounded by the hidden debris of waste and destruction and are already involved in a prolonged act of communal violence. Violence is not a function of human nature but of human societies' (17). This remarkable perception demonstrates an understanding of an invisible network that encourages other forms of violence: a theory very similar to systemic violence. However, Bond's works arguably failed to depict this onstage. Although the violence of *Saved* gestures to the wider socio-political conditions that allowed it to happen, the shock of the represented subjective violence (a common feature in Bond's plays) detracts from this invisible network of the violence of capitalist society: the spectacular violence that Bond critiques as 'very readily available on TV' (15) shifts audience perception away from the root causes.

Of course, other post-war British playwrights beyond Pinter and Bond interrogated traditional power structures and normative social relations. To name just a few, John Osborne infamously railed against the vestiges of Edwardian ideals in *Look Back in Anger* (RC, 1956), helping to bring 'kitchen-sink-realism' to the British stage. John Arden and Margeratta D'Arcy meta-theatrically platformed the brutalities of the hushed imperial violence Britain still participated in with *Serjeant Musgrave's Dance* (RC, 1960), as well as the violence and tension brought by unreconciled social and class divisions (similarly to *Saved*) in *Live Like Pigs* (RC, 1958). And Caryl Churchill, whose more recent work is explored in Chapter 1, began a storied playwriting career of political work with plays like *Owners* (RC, 1972), which illustrates the violent effects of wealth and property disparity, and later her seminal, anti-Thatcherite exploration of neoliberalism's intertwinement into 'feminism', *Top Girls* (RC, 1982). Churchill, like many British playwrights since the 1950s, was influenced by the work of Bertolt Brecht, who became well-known among theatre-makers following the Berliner Ensemble's influential 1956 tour to Britain. His famous *Verfremdungseffekt* (the distancing/alienation effect) combined with the violence in plays like *Mother Courage and Her Children* (1939, first British performance by Joan Littlewood's Theatre Workshop, 1955) and *The Resistible Rise of Arturo Ui* (1941, first British performance: Glasgow Citizens, 1967) asked audiences to think beyond the actions represented onstage. Though Brecht does not appear to have demonstrated comparable ideas to violence in the same capacity as Bond (who developed his own political theatre counter to Brecht's), the critical eye his dramaturgy demands is reflected in *Serjeant Musgrave's Dance*, *Top Girls* and many British plays since – with his influence still very much alive in contemporary British theatre (Hartl 2021) and in how systemic violence was depicted onstage in the 2010s.

With the abolishment of censorship in British theatre through the 1968 Theatres Act, productions in theory now had permission to represent anything within legal limits onstage. Although different forms of censorship still existed – such as the conservative activist Mary Whitehouse's infamous campaign of 'gross indecency' against Michael Bogdanov's staging of Howard Brenton's *The Romans in Britain* (NT, 1980) – new playwrights in the 1990s were emerging in a theatre landscape where representational restrictions were, generally, a thing of the past: meta-textually referred to in Anthony Neilson's *The Censor* (Finborough Theatre, London, 1997), for example (Gilleman 2010: 89–90). The 'in-yer-face' movement was defined among new 1990s playwrights which, as its coiner Aleks Sierz states, 'affronts the ruling ideas of what can or should be shown onstage' (2001: 4). Although the term has been troubled and critiqued for being reductive (Reid 2012: 140), it captures something of the experiential aspirations of many playwrights and directors in the 1990s.

In-yer-face, as a term, tends to signify images of onstage gore – like the murders, rape and evisceration of the final scene in Sarah Kane's *Phaedra's Love* (Gate, 1996) or the blood-stained games and exploitation of Mark Ravenhill's *Shopping and Fucking* (RC, 1996) – and indeed such scenes were, as Sierz writes, sometimes 'truly distressing' (2012: 57). Such tactics were historically informed by the more overt violence of Seneca and his Renaissance admirers (*Titus Andronicus* saw a surge in popularity during the 1990s), as well as the unsettling surrealism of modernist writers like Artaud, Jarry and Strindberg – not to mention the more recent deployments of visceral representations like *Saved* and *The Romans in Britain*. In-yer-face's continuation of the 'shock' techniques established through theatre history continued into the 2000s, where the often-televised and spectacular violence of 9/11, 7/7 and the wars in Afghanistan and Iraq further informed these formal experimentations with showing violence – the human rights violations in Abu Ghraib, for instance, being reflected in Dennis Kelly's *Osama the Hero* (Hampstead Theatre, London, 2004) and Simon Stephens's *Motortown* (RC, 2006). Although both productions avoided literal representations of violence, they still conveyed very discomforting representations to their audiences through prolonged torture scenes.

The language of many of these plays, too, was often shocking. One example, touted as the first in-yer-face play, is Philip Ridley's *The Pitchfork Disney* (Bush Theatre, London, 1991), with especially uncomfortable extended, evocative monologues. As a character recounts of a nightmare: 'The whole world is on me [...] They start to flay me. Peeling my skin to reveal blood. Muscles. Veins. The blood makes me slippery' (Ridley 1997: 76). Although visual images and verbal descriptions cannot be easily equated – and certainly are very different sensory and imaginative experiences – Ridley's horrific imagery troubles any easy equation of explicit, onstage representations as being 'more violent' than spoken dialogue. Tim Crouch's *The Author* (RC, 2009) plays on this false dichotomy, in which performers sat among the audience and recounted their experiences of working on a fictional production resembling an in-yer-face play. As the play's eponymous author (played by and 'as' Crouch himself) narrates their suicide after being exposed as a paedophile, Dan Rebellato describes that 'the lights began to dim and most of the speech was delivered in the dark [...] We were, so to speak, directly confronting our own imaginations' (2013: 141). This greatly affected the audience – with walk-outs, tears, heckles, vocal anger and fainting (139). As *The Pitchfork Disney* and *The Author* show, diegetic approaches cannot be claimed as inherently less violent, visceral, or more 'in-yer-face' than physicalized mimesis.

What *Phaedra's Love*, *Shopping and Fucking*, *Motortown*, *The Pitchfork Disney*, and *The Author* share in their varied representations is a preoccupation with what the philosopher Slavoj Žižek calls subjective violence (2008: 1). It is characterized by 'obviousness', by clear violence being done on subjects; perhaps confusingly, it is what might 'objectively' be called violence. These representations are placed within specific contexts: but, as mentioned above regarding spectacularization, the foregrounding of these acts can threaten a fuller comprehension of the context behind them. Rebellato writes of *The Author* that it 'provocatively suggests that realistic representation may be an act of violence in itself, one that degrades the imagination' (2017: 17). As Chapter 7 shows, this has been contended by feminist scholars, and in a similar vein to this argument I suggest that the very foregrounding of the violent act – whether it is realistic, narrated or surreal in its representation – can be something of a 'misdirection': a platforming of a specific event, rather than the structure it is symptomatic of. This is supported by the cultural theorists Brad Evans and Henry A. Giroux, who state that 'the alienating cultural, social, and political climate achieved through spectacle [...] normalizes violence, terror, and insecurity, while editing out the human realities of suffering in order to cauterize social conscience and incapacitate political responses' (2015: 31–2), and that spectacles of violence have 'infected our very ability to perceive and ethically interpret and respond to the destruction being waged around us, upon us, and even within us' (160).

The representational downplaying of violence as a spectacle can allow a better consideration of its relationship to spectatorship, politics, ethics and affect – whereas subjective spectacles can neuter these responses. Both *The Pitchfork Disney* and *The Author* are sophisticated texts because, like the plays explored throughout this book, they challenge their audiences to consider that which they might not normatively perceive: in the former, the commodification of violence; and in the latter, challenging the very perception and imagination of the audience. But both plays' use of subjective acts of violence to convey affect can hamper perceptions of wider systemic violence: the horror of what they describe can 'get in the way' of their gestures towards larger structural issues in society. Although I contend that 2010s British theatre deviates in its representation of violence comparatively to theatre that has come before it, its dramaturgical approaches are as much a response to contemporary socio-political issues as they are to its theatrical heritage: from the dialectics of 'Greek' vs 'Roman' onstage violence, to the spectacles of medieval and Renaissance drama, the social issues of naturalism, and the more recent touchstones of Brecht, Bond, the Theatre of the Absurd and in-yer-face theatre.

The Representation of Violence in 2010s British Theatre and *Mr Incredible*

My contention, then, is that much 2010s British theatre that represented violence did so through dramaturgical methods that did not foreground central acts of subjective violence – if such 'obvious' acts were present, they were significantly downplayed: visually, descriptively and referentially. This allows audiences to find a sense of systemic violence: the fundamental representational puzzle of which is its intangibility, its difficulty to be perceived. *Mr Incredible* is exemplary of this approach. Adam's rape of Holly is not explained in detail, and though the revelation of the act certainly creates affect (if not to the same extremes as *The Author*), this reinforces the glimpses of systemic violence in the earlier dialogue – and likely encourages audience members to proactively perceive this. The rape is not positioned in the production, for example, to shock the audience into affirming that 'sexual assault is bad', but to underline the central systemic violence that runs through the dialogue: the normative assumption of male dominance, or hegemonic masculinity.

The sociologist R. W. Connell describes hegemonic masculinity as the ideological dominance of men – though 'not a fixed character type' (2005: 76), hegemonic masculinity allows 'the majority of men [to] gain from its [...] overall subordination of women' (79). Adam expresses significant anxiety at failing to live up to a version of hegemonic masculinity, transferring his feelings about his father leaving to a near-obsession with becoming an idealistic family man: 'I'm desperate to have kids [...] It's quite a feminine attribute isn't it?' (61). When it becomes clear to Adam that Holly neither shares his desire for a family nor wants to be with him any longer, his rape of her comes as a violent reaction to his lack of control; as well as the questioning of the dominance of his performed hegemonic masculinity and as a 're-gendering' of Holly into conforming with traditional gender roles by – as Lisa Fitzpatrick states of sexual violence – 'imprinting her' as a 'feminine victim' (2018: 14).[6] The manner in which the crime is revealed adheres to this 'inscription' – he can tell his side of the story, she cannot. The representation of this subjective violence, then, sublimates into the dramaturgical concern of the systemic violence of hegemonic masculinity.

This specific representation – and those of rape in 2010s British new writing more generally – demonstrates this turn in how violence was shown and theorized onstage: 'The effectiveness of violence may be measured by its capacity to instil fear in its object and in those who witness its ravages. If rape is to be understood primarily as a method of demonstrating and perpetuating patriarchal power, then its capacity to instil fear in all women is key to its efficacy' (ibid. 27). This relates to issues of spectacularization mentioned above: that the image of violence, especially out of context, perpetuates the ideology and oppression that specific acts of violence can enforce. Essential to this is the concept of performativity: as Lucy Nevitt writes, it informs how 'representation[s] of violence can reiterate or challenge normalised social structures' (2013: 29). She uses the example of Theseus' rape of Strophe in a specific production of *Phaedra's Love*, in which 'all the choices made about the woman's part in this image drew on familiar, normalised assumptions to performatively reiterate the sexual oppression of women' (34).[7] The simulation of a subjective act of violence – with the portrayal of Theseus depicting controlled, aggressive power and Strophe's being one of passivity and subjection – not only spectacularizes this act but reasserts the normative power structures that shape such violence. This is not to say that the audience will be moved to leave the theatre and perpetuate what they have witnessed. Rather, what they have witnessed has not challenged the standard ways in which violence is understood: the act is shown, yet the conditions and systems that motivate it remain hidden.

Understanding performativity, then, can allow theatre-makers to portray violence in ways which do not reaffirm but potentially challenge structural violence. For example, while Strophe's rape spectacularly reasserts the existence of gender-based violence (at least in the production critiqued by Nevitt), the incident recalled in *Mr Incredible* exposes and questions its normalization – using the 'every-day' characterization of Adam in Whitehill's dialogue and Alistair Donegan's performance to illustrate the commonplace presence of hegemonic masculinity, gender-based violence and sexual assault. As Connell states, such violence 'is not an individual pathology but a logical consequence of men's collective privilege' (2005: 245). This is arguably what occurs in *Mr Incredible*: Adam does not appear to have a violent pathology, yet when his presumed dominance is threatened, he resorts to the 'script' of rape to reassert his privilege. He utilizes the violent tools of a hegemonic system that has hitherto dictated that his normative desires be fulfilled when that system is made unstable by Holly's self-determinacy. As developed further in Chapter 2, performativity shows how 'normal' behaviour – such as that exhibited by Adam – perpetuates and maintains structural violence. Additionally, the performativity of *Mr Incredible*'s production, where subjective, spectacular acts are significantly downplayed to the audience, does not proliferate a spectacle of women being scripted as oppressed victims.

This is not to say that all representations of violence in new work of 2010s British theatre adhere to this approach. For example, Gary McNair's

Locker Room Talk (Traverse, Edinburgh, 2019), which had a cast of four female performers reciting verbatim, highly misogynistic dialogue, is troubled by Effie Samara's analysis that there was 'a consensus' among reviewers that it was 'shocking, if little else beyond that', as '[l]ine after line of dialogue denotes womanhood to essentialist imbecility underserving of full subjecthood enacting, to all intents and purposes, a performative process of dehumanization' (2021: 56). This, then, supports Nevitt's contention that such representations should not seek to reproduce oppressive cultural assumptions. *Mr Incredible*, like many other examples of 2010s British theatre, instead alerts audiences to better understand how violence exists not in spectacular acts but in the 'normal functioning' of society. This said, *Mr Incredible* does annex the experiences of the victim of rape to the narrative of the perpetrator, a representational pitfall identified by Fitzpatrick (2018: 2). Despite Alistair Donegan's performance – which certainly depicts a character with the insecurities and anxieties of a sensitive person attempting to hold themselves to the (here, violent) standards of hegemonic masculinity and socio-cultural norms – and Sarah Meadows's direction, which sees Adam in a space of constant interrogation where he is never fully at ease, the play never has Holly onstage.[8] Whitehill considers that 'I wanted to talk about male entitlement and I felt the best way to do that would be to examine a man', but questions the approach 'given that the play is in part about sexual consent' (2016a). Still, she arguably does this in a way that places the untrivialized sexual assault in a wider context of systemic violence and questions the audience's normative responses to Adam's story.

Similar articulations of sexual assault and domestic violence were seen in Cordelia Lynn's *Lela & Co.* (RC, 2015), where the titular character narrates her experiences as she is trafficked by family members and prostituted by her 'husband'. Adapted from a survivors' testimony (possibly from the Iraq War), Lynn calls the play '*a monologue*' (2015: 1) despite the fact a male performer, playing various men through Lela's life (the eponymous 'Co.'), persistently interrupts, silences or alters her story. Additionally, Dennis Kelly's *Girls & Boys* (RC, 2018) features one extended monologue of a grieving mother whose ex-husband's feelings of inadequacy lead him to commit filicide and kill himself.[9] Like *Mr Incredible*, the violence of these plays is not visualized onstage outside the dialogue – which leans more into the trauma and experience of the survivors rather than an intimate description of the acts themselves. Although I return to a more in-depth overview of representations of gender-based violence, these productions evidence a commitment to placing such acts in a network of wider, systemic violence without resorting to spectacularization – a hallmark, as the case studies inspected throughout this work show, of the depiction of violence in 2010s British theatre.

Overview of the Chapters

In my exploration through this work of 'staging systemic violence', I explore five main areas. These are protest, climate crisis, neoliberalism, racism (these last two areas within the context of Brexit and national identity) and, lastly, gender-based violence – specifically, misogyny and transphobia. These are all examined through the two central concepts of violence and performativity, the latter being essential to the representation and conceptualization of violence in 2010s British theatre as it serves to demonstrate how attitudes, behaviours and actions constitute a socio-cultural reality of violence. These concepts are introduced and explored in further depth through the first two chapters to illustrate my theoretical approach, as well as the necessity of these theories for thinking through systemic violence on the 2010s British stage and, arguably, in general.

Like similar studies of twenty-first century British theatre, each themed chapter explores one to three separate productions. To cover as much scope as possible, none of these productions are from the same playwright. Each of the plays are closely read through a mixture of textual analysis, performance response, theoretical illustration, audience affect (gauged first-hand or through mainstream and more fringe reviews) and material considerations of the production. Additionally, a more general survey of other 2010s British plays connected to the respective subjects is included in the last five chapters, which help to contextualize the plays more closely examined, as well as offer something of an index of numerous 2010s British plays. Due to the extensive body of writing on the central concepts of violence and performativity, the work of cultural theorists, philosophers, sociologists, historians and others are deployed here contextually or in synchroneity with these productions' analyses. Among these, of chief importance are Butler, Žižek, Balibar, Evans and Giroux. Selected mostly from publications contemporaneous or close to the 2010s, their work is of specific relevance to the concerns and productions explored here and serves as a theoretical spine through which to trace the issues in the selected plays.

The first chapter analyses Caryl Churchill's *Escaped Alone* (RC, 2016) by situating it in Churchill's wider oeuvre and applying it to several established critiques of violence. I then approach the production through three theoretical aspects of violence: its definition (informed by Hannah Arendt and Susan Sontag), its visibility (through Evans, Giroux and Žižek), and its relationship to 'truth' and reality (with Butler and Jean-Luc Nancy). Chapter 2 begins with an overview of performativity and its connection to violence through the work, predominantly, of Butler and Étienne Balibar. Lulu Raczka and Barrel Organ's *Some People Talk About Violence* (Fringe, 2015) is then explored through the potential of performative 'injurious speech' informed by Pierre Bourdieu's concept of symbolic violence; followed by a reading of Martin McDonagh's *A Very Very Very Dark Matter* (Bridge Theatre, London, 2018) through theories of interconnected, structural violence. These two parts of the chapter, though disparate in their approaches, both establish the relevance of considering concepts of violence and performativity together in relation to these 2010s British plays. The next five chapters then overview specific areas represented by 2010s British theatre in which violence and performativity intersect.

Chapter 3 continues by exploring the relationship between theatre and protest in the 2010s with particular focuses on its relevance in the public sphere, challenged by Christopher Balme, and the 'dramaturgical' use of nonviolence in protest to generate public support touched on in Chris Thorpe's *There Has Possibly Been An Incident* (Fringe, 2013), before closely analysing debbie tucker green's *ear for eye*, which dialectically poses the justification of revolution or progress in the context of continued structural racism. Chapter 4 looks at complications of perspective in Ella Hickson's *Oil* (Almeida, London, 2016), which uses magic realism to take a more 'zoomed-out' approach to the climate crisis, before inspecting classifications of disposability in Lucy Kirkwood's *The Children* (RC, 2016).

Chapters 5 and 6 are 'twinned' in their inspection of Brexit and its related structural issues. Chapter 5 traces how neoliberal ideology was critiqued and depicted in British theatre, the first section exploring productions that did this through apocalyptic or dystopian aesthetics such as Alistair McDowall's *Pomona* (Gate, 2014), while the next looks at how cross-cultural British-European theatre depicted neoliberalism on each other's stages, taking the European plays produced by the Royal Court International Department on its London stages and Simon Stephens's collaborative *Three Kingdoms* (Teater NO99, Tallinn, 2011) as case studies. Chapter 6 then looks at Brexit and racism, with an additional focus on the performative construction of European and British identities in contexts of structural violence – particularly against those deemed 'Other'. The first section overviews theatrical responses to the Mediterranean refugee crisis such as Anders Lustgarten's *Lampedusa* (Soho Theatre, London, 2015) and Zinnie Harris's *How to Hold Your Breath* (RC, 2015); before the second section reads Somalia Nonyé Seaton's *Fall of the Kingdom, Rise of the Foot Solider* (RSC, Stratford-upon-Avon, 2016) as a retort to Brexit and its implication in British structural racism.

Chapter 7 continues from this Introduction in its focus on articulations of gender-based violence in 2010s British theatre. It also advances the notion of continuum-thinking regarding violence from theorists including Rebecca Solnit: applied to Katherine Chandler's *Bird* (Sherman, Cardiff, 2016), before

Jasmine Lee-Jones's *seven methods of killing kylie jenner* (RC, 2019) is argued to use practices of performative re-inscription and formal experimentation to 'break' violent continuums. The conclusion of this work then illustratively presents Travis Alabanza's *Burgerz* (Ovalhouse, 2018) to assert three main contentions developed through the research of the seven chapters outlined here: that violence can be understood through 2010s British theatre as a continuum, that continuums of violence performatively maintain structures of violence, and that non-normative ways of seeing and comprehension are essential to recognizing this violence.

1

Violence

Resting on a saucer against a plain background, a white teacup is full to the brim with a black, bubbling liquid like oil or tar, with thick rivulets dribbling down its side. This is the Royal Court's striking promotional image for Caryl Churchill's *Escaped Alone* (2019), an image which Angelaki describes as an 'imaginative metaphor' regarding the play's form and content, and for how 'Churchill's playwriting in the 2000s and 2010s overbrims with political potency' (2017: 22). It also speaks to how this most 'British' of objects – the cup of tea – is infused with a history of exploitation and imperialism (Rappaport 2018). Similar images created by Root Design were used alongside other 2015–16 Court plays, including a suspended pair of formal shoes; a butterfly caught in a jar; and a cracked, precariously held-together ornamental swan figurine. With the subjects of institutional punishment in Martin McDonagh's *Hangmen* (2015), and systemic gender inequality in both Cordelia Lynn's *Lela & Co.* and Penelope Skinner's *Linda* (2016) respectively, these defamiliarized objects symbolize forms of violence that might initially appear innocuous: the harm of bodies that comes from the enforcement of the law (*Hangmen*); the entrapment of women in severely oppressive social dynamics (*Lela & Co.*); and the damage that neoliberalism does to domestic relations and personal well-being through commodification, corporatism and coerced societal roles (*Linda*). The distinctly unappetizing cup of tea, like all these images, indicated how plays at the Court looked to express questions of what violence was, and what were its links to the otherwise innocuous and unseen.

Brad Evans and Henry A. Giroux's *Disposable Futures* (2015) focuses on violence's normalization by prevailing political and media discourses. They note that: 'Nearly a century ago Walter Benjamin responded to the tyranny of his times by writing his famous "Critique of Violence" [1921]. Ours is a different age. And yet the need for a critique adequate to our times is as pressing as ever' (10). As Benjamin writes, the critique of violence for his time required sustained philosophical interrogation on 'expounding its relation to law and justice' (2004: 236), demonstrating how atrocities and oppressions were made permissible by the dictates of a ruling hegemony. Evans and Giroux state why the violence of their times requires a novel response: 'Our claim is both that the violence we are exposed to is heavily mediated, and that as such we are witness to various spectacles that serve a distinct political function [...] Moving beyond the spectacle by making visible the reality of violence in all of its modes is both necessary and politically important' (2015: 11–12). Their call to 'move beyond the spectacle' to 'make visible the reality of violence' vindicates the contention made in the Introduction, that 2010s British theatre generally represented violence with less explicit spectacle than preceding decades to better consider its relationship to spectatorship, politics, ethics and affect.

Indeed, Evans and Giroux identify that an important method of critique for their contemporary time is in 'modes of artistic imagination' (10). With their claim that much violence is hidden from plain sight, normalized and permutating through political machinations and mediated spectacles, it is fitting that artistic imagination, with its ability to spotlight divergent perspectives or present new perceptions, is their suggested mode of critique. Still, Benjamin's work remained influential and relevant in the 2010s, and even informs this perspective. In response to an identified state-sanctioned 'lawmaking violence', Benjamin articulates 'divine violence', that is 'law-destroying', disrupts boundaries, expiates, and 'is lethal without spilling blood' (2004: 249–50). Though bound up to a certain degree in socio-political power structures, theatre can certainly interrogate violence without recourse to violent actions. It may not strictly adhere to Benjamin's divine violence, but to paraphrase Augusto Boal, theatre could be a rehearsal for it. This chapter evaluates how 2010s British theatre may offer a general critique of violence that reflects socio-political dialogue around violence and offers perspectives valuable for studies of violence more widely. In addition to Evans and Giroux, the chapter explores several other relevant theorists' conceptions of violence alongside theatre scholarship: their inclusion here being based on their influence, their explicit mention by 2010s British theatre and its studies, and their similar engagements with violence comparatively to the plays addressed in this study. These theoretical conceptions are analysed alongside and illustrated through the case study of Churchill's *Escaped Alone*, which was not only one of the most critically praised plays of the 2010s by arguably the decade's most influential living British playwright, but itself engages with several different forms of violence in various ways.

The Critique of Violence and *Escaped Alone*

Caryl Churchill has been creating theatre since the 1950s and possesses one of the most extensive and identifiable bodies of work in British theatre. With her sharply anti-capitalist tendencies tempered through work such as *Owners* and *Light Shining in Buckinghamshire* (Traverse, 1976) which became more pronounced through the years of Thatcher's government in plays like *Top Girls*, *Fen* (University of Essex, 1983), and *Serious Money* (RC, 1987), the 2010s saw many revivals of these politicized works, as well as Churchill's more dystopian plays like *Far Away* (RC, 2000) and *A Number* (RC, 2002). Her new writing, too, was prolific through the decade: debuting twelve new plays including *Love and Information* (RC, 2012) and the quartet *Glass. Kill. Bluebeard. Imp.* (RC, 2019). These drew on many of Churchill's established concerns: experimentation with narrative form, the influencing of perception and the normalization of violence. Indeed, Siân Adiseshiah writes that Churchill's twenty-first-century theatre engages in 'open dialogue with the political world', but 'simultaneously recognizes that staging critiques of the system is limited in its political potential' (2012: 119). This is supported by Elaine Aston (2013: 145), who argues in Anja Hartl's words that 'the Brechtian mode' of her 1960s–1990s plays 'have become increasingly compromised at the turn of the millennium by profound social and political transformations' (2021), becoming more 'Beckettian' (Angelaki 2017: 52). If this is also true of *Escaped Alone*, then the play rails against its limitations, being explosive in form and content: peeling back layers of society and exposing conditioned modes of perception to show audiences the violence that lies within the metaphorical teacup.

Directed by Churchill's frequent collaborator James Macdonald in January 2016 – being the first play performed for the Court's 'Sixty Years New' birthday celebrations – *Escaped Alone* opens with Mrs Jarrett, or simply Mrs J (played here by Linda Bassett), innocuously stating: 'I'm walking down the street and there's a door in the fence open and inside are three women I've seen before' (2019: 143). She is invited in, and the four women, '*all at least seventy*', chat over the course of several summer afternoons, '*but the action is continuous*' (142). They speak about topics ranging from family members, to where the local shops used to be, to mathematics, television and parallel universes. Their dialogue is scattered and fragmentary, like phrases have disappeared from their conversations, and it can sometimes appear as if they are pursuing their own trains of thought rather than speaking to one another. The audience learn that Sally (Deborah Findlay) has an obsessive phobia of cats, Lena (Kika Markham) has nihilistic tendencies and may suffer from depression, and Vi (June Watson) accidentally killed her abusive husband – though whether this was done in self-defence is debated by Sally. They discuss these aspects of their lives through an extended monologue each, none of which are immediately commented on by the other women. Macdonald's production casts a solitary spotlight for each character's monologue to infer these are a collection of internal thoughts, though in the text these could easily be temporally displaced – spoken at a different time to the action happening around them – or simply ignored by the others due to 'British politeness'.

At the conclusion of each of the play's first seven scenes, Mrs J describes an apocalyptic vision. These are perhaps hypothetical, prophetic, recounted, happen contemporaneously, or, as inferred by the women's conversations, exist in parallel universes. The situations she depicts are full of extreme imagery, which can be farcical ('lilos, rubber ducks and pumice stone floated on the stock market'; 150), eerily grounded in reality ('[g]as masks were available on the NHS with a three month waiting time and privately in a range of colours'; 155), or a mixture of the two ('[c]ommuters watched breakfast on iPlayer on their way to work'; 160). In Macdonald's production, designed by Miriam Buether, Linda Bassett's Mrs J would walk towards the audience at the end of each scene: leaving the picturesque idyll of Sally's summertime garden in pitch black to tell these reports while illuminated by a rectangle in the shape of a rough frame. Macdonald then, in these 'framed monologues', creates distinct spaces between Mrs J's speeches and the dialogue while implicitly connecting them through, predominantly, Bassett's matter-of-fact performance (which remains relatively similar in both spaces). In the eighth and final scene, Mrs J ruptures the conversation with what Bonnie Marranca calls a 'virtual sound poem of existential fury, shouting "terrible rage" twenty-five times' (2017: 4) which, like the other monologues, is not commented on. As this final speech from Mrs J is not 'separated' from the action, Churchill and Macdonald suggest that the crises described in the catastrophic intermissions are not distinct at all – they are somehow connected to the women's dialogue. The play concludes with the same simplicity with which it began, as Mrs J states: 'And then I said thanks for the tea and I went home' (179).

Escaped Alone, then, can be considered a critique of violence in Evans and Giroux's conception: the production looks to move beyond the spectacle, makes visible the reality of violence, and uses new modes of artistic imagination. To backtrack a little, though, it should be asked what exactly is being critiqued: to assess the scope of this critique requires an understanding of what violence *is*. A very direct adjective given by Lucy Nevitt is that 'it is, in its actual forms in the world, bad' (2013: 6). This is a simple but seemingly obvious judgement: violence certainly appears 'bad' because most human experience would qualify it as abhorrent and oppressive. The issue with the equation of violence as bad becomes more nuanced when we consider by whose standards 'bad' is being judged. How many people do or do not have to believe something is sufficiently bad for it to be considered violent, for instance? Bad can also describe behaviour that goes against authority, which may itself be bad: is revolutionary violence against an oppressive state or self-defence against assault *bad*?

Escaped Alone depicts visions of a world in which abuses of power and catastrophes run amok. The four women are aware of the violence in their contemporary world but lack the perspective to fully grasp it. Sally, for example, appears to have transferred her general fears to something as specific as ailurophobia: 'I know I've no reason I know it's just cats cats themselves are the horror' (163). Maybe the failure of humanity to agree on what is and is not bad for its overall well-being – or in Sally's case, the misidentification of what is bad – leads to the scenarios described by Mrs J. Perhaps, then, the totality of violence depicted in *Escaped Alone* is directly linked to the difficulty of locating and defining it. There are many different categorizations, concepts and contexts of violence – too many to fully address here – but are there any characteristics that link some, if not all of them?

Among the most seminal thinkers on violence is Hannah Arendt, who claims it is distinguished from other, often mistakenly interchangeable terms like power and strength by 'its instrumental character' (1970: 46). Therefore, it is a tool that can be used for 'good': what can be called a deontological understanding of violence that judges the morality of its action. The 1968 student protests in France were Arendt's impetus for writing *On Violence*, and this example of civil dissent adheres to her position that 'under certain circumstances violence – acting without argument or speech and without counting the consequences – is the only way to set the scales of justice right again' (64). As per Benjamin's writing, justice has its own issues of power structures and subjectivity, but a consequentialist view of violence shows that even if an act of violence could be performed for a beneficial, just purpose it may still result in – as Arendt herself even admits here – unforeseen consequences. The phenomenological inability to fully understand an act of violence's overall consequences troubles any essential labelling of it as ever being justifiable. So, if violence is a tool, it is not a particularly precise one. Even its most focused uses may, eventually, divert significantly from its wielder's original intentions, whether 'good' or 'bad'. To trouble this further, Arendt also explores the potential for 'ordinary' citizens to commit 'bad violence' due to 'circumstances that make it well-nigh impossible to know or feel that [they are] doing wrong' (1963: 276); reflected in Bond's treatise 'On Violence', for example. This is due to factors such as an unquestioning adherence to authority, the framing of circumstances by those in positions of power, and a lack of critical distance. In such cases, violence is still instrumental, but not necessarily in the service of its user.

Escaped Alone certainly troubles the morality of violence, and that which does not appear as 'bad'. At one point, the four women reflect on what was once considered normative: 'MRS J "no blacks no dogs no Irish" / SALLY I remember that / VI and we weren't even that shocked' (157).[1] Mrs J's reminiscence of such notices given outside pubs or against property listings reveals how considerations of violence are shaped by perception. With the critical distance afforded by retrospection, the women can better comprehend signs of derogation and oppression. The discussion also potentially invites the audience to wonder what contemporary activities might be seen as violent by better-informed perspectives – especially with Mrs J's proclamations of potential future catastrophes. Indeed, Macdonald's production moves from summertime chats to apocalyptic descriptions to bridge the conceptual link between the everyday and the catastrophic; any innocuous-seeming topic might plunge the stage into darkness and trigger Mrs J's next soothsaying. The women's conversation also raises a consideration of whether the definition of violence should be thought of as essentialist and permanent that becomes 'revealed' over time, or a classification that changes as socio-cultural attitudes shift.

An answer to this may lie in a consideration of violence's relation to power – as noted, a main concern of Arendt's. Though the above discussion in *Escaped Alone* shows that normalized violence is better comprehended once individuals are distanced from the power structures that enable it, the revealed oppression evidences a strategy by the powerful to keep others relatively powerless. Therefore, despite not being widely seen as such at the time, these are violent tactics. Arendt's theories demonstrate that the women of *Escaped Alone* were in positions where they were unable to comprehend this violence and were, likely, unknowingly complicit in it. So, though violence may be a tool, it is certainly not a clear-cut piece of equipment, with various operational factors including the inability to foresee its full consequences and how power structures may influence its use and perception. This is not to claim that necessary violence does not exist as Arendt and Benjamin both support, but that fighting violence with violence means compromising the ability to contain the effects of the counter-violence. Defensible as Vi's strike back at her abusive husband was, for example, she was unaware of the knife in her hand that dramatically changed the outcome of her action and was unable to predict her imprisonment – a continuation of the gendered oppression she received from her husband – or her resulting trauma: 'I can't breathe properly it all comes back in the night' (178).[2] *Escaped Alone* then warns of the inability of violence to ever be fully justified: 'Fires were lit to stop the fires' (174), or, 'just' acts of violence simply exacerbate it.

Whereas Arendt looks to define violence by its application and intentions, another prominent thinker on the subject, Susan Sontag, considers the affect it has on witnesses; particularly, on those who witness a mediated image of violence. For most living in 2010s Britain, a considerable number, if not the vast majority, of their experiences of explicit acts of violence will have been made up of simulated images and second-hand accounts. Sontag states that this procession of images threatens to blur fantasy and reality for individuals: 'a catastrophe that is experienced will often seem eerily like its representation [...] described as "unreal", "surreal", "like a movie"' (2004: 19). The scenarios of Mrs J's monologues appear to play on this blurring as they evoke real events and popular fictions simultaneously. For example, one of her monologues describes a London-like city beset by a cancerous virus caused by 'chemicals [that] leaked through cracks in the money' (155). This bizarre, anti-capitalist image is supplemented by depictions of miscarriages and birth deformities reminiscent of the 1986 Chernobyl disaster, an emptied London as in Danny Boyle's *28 Days Later* (2002), and a survivors' camp established in Canada echoing those of the Mediterranean refugee crisis.[3]

The combination of these elements may initially appear to perform what Sontag warns against – the confusion and provincialism of reality – yet there is an important distinction here. As emphasized in Macdonald's production, where she literally steps out of the narrative to directly deliver them to the audience, Mrs J's monologues are not spectacular images of violence but seek to find alternate representational modes that look to deny audiences the opportunity to become what Sontag calls 'bored, cynical, apathetic' (2004: 91). As Hartl writes, the performance incites 'spectators to re-establish connections between the fictional dystopian worlds on stage and their own lived experience' – rather than filmic spectacle, the dystopia of *Escaped Alone* 'fulfils eminent Brechtian functions of fostering analysis and critique' (2021). The fact that Mrs J gives verbal descriptions of violence rather than visual representations does not necessarily make what she describes any less violent for the audience (as argued in the second section of the Introduction) though, like *Mr Incredible*, *Escaped Alone*'s dramaturgy circumvents the impassivity of the spectacular image. This is in part due to Churchill's own specific dramaturgy of depicting imaginative and absurd situations that are sufficiently grounded to have socio-political concern, and Macdonald's direction, which slowly teases out the violent contexts the women and their society exist in, rather than making them immediately and spectacularly obvious. These techniques arguably seek to create a more considered, affective response to the violence, rather than bored, cynical apathy. The 'stories' Mrs

J tells her listeners are imaginative enough to invite individual interpretation that nevertheless present extreme visions – evoking familiarity and absurdity to simultaneously connect audiences to her tales while defamiliarizing them to be imaginatively judged.

Mrs J's veraciously repeated 'terrible rage terrible rage terrible rage' (179) performed by Linda Bassett seemingly out of nowhere, mid-conversation with the other women, is crucial to the affect of *Escaped Alone*. This 'sound poem of existential fury', as Marranca calls it, is described by Rebellato as 'an apocalyptic breakdown of linguistic invention that sears anguish and fury into the flesh of the play' (2017: 57). Whereas the other three women's monologues focus on themselves, Angelaki notes that 'Mrs Jarrett does not indulge in the narrative of the self, but vocalizes the narrative of society [...] While we spend time rehearsing our individualisms [...] Churchill suggests that the crisis has caught up with us' (2017: 25). These critical responses demonstrate how the vocalization of 'terrible rage' in the production cuts through the individualism, catastrophic visions and the intellectualization of violence. As Marranca continues, it employs 'the truth of poetry as more primal than fact' (2017: 5). Mrs J's 'mantra' simply and vehemently reminds the audience that 'bad' things occur around our contemporary lives, things we seem to implicitly know are wrong. Bassett's delivery affirmed this, and went through responsive stages including surprise, anger, exhaustion and determination. As Susannah Clapp's review surmises, '[t]he effect is revolutionary' (2016; quoted in Angelaki 2017: 25). While certainly not arguing that violence is uncomplex or easily reducible, *Escaped Alone*'s climactic 'sound poem' affectively asserts an understanding of violence's pernicious existence in the world, and that in our recognition of it as bad – especially in its more innocuous and often-overlooked forms – we should be angry about it, alert to it and critically combat it.

Making Invisible Violence Visible

Though the various modes of violence mean that it evades a single and unifying definition, there were nevertheless distinct 'violences' that proved to be of particular concern in the 2010s. As already noted, the comprehension of violence as a concept that extends beyond the directly visible became more widely understood and scrutinized in this decade. Such 'invisible' violence is particularly dangerous as its long-term effects are deleterious to society and individuals' well-being, but its solutions are not grounded in established juridical processes in the manner that obvious acts like physical assaults or illegal warfare are – even if many examples of these types of violence evade jurisdiction. As Evans and Giroux state: 'Violence is easily condemned when it appears exceptional [...] Normalized violence, by contrast, represents a more formidable challenge, requiring a more sophisticated and learned response' (2015: 7). In the 2010s, as mentioned in the Introduction, movements such as #MeToo and BLM gained widespread support to investigate and protest such normalized violence. As they were often spurred by blatant, identifiable acts that were consequences of more ingrained issues, they show that differentiated modes of violence exist in relationship to one another.

Escaped Alone's Mrs Jarrett is herself something of a 'whistle-blower' figure – likely informed by several real and fictional individuals – who steps out of her relatively everyday conversations to inform or alert the audience to nightmarish visions of violence. Linda Bassett's performance of the character and matter-of-fact mentions of ecological breakdown draw comparison to the climate scientist Chris Rapley, who too 'performed' at the Royal Court in Katie Mitchell and Duncan Macmillan's dramatized lecture *2071* (2014). Marranca writes that Mrs J 'seems like an older version of Joan from Churchill's *Far Away*' (2007: 4), who in the first scene of that play describes acts of violence committed by her uncle only to be 'gaslighted' and told otherwise by her aunt. Mrs J is also directly informed by the source of the play's title, included in the playtext's epigraph: '*I only am escaped alone to tell thee*' (2019: 141). In the Old Testament, these words are spoken by servants who separately inform Job of several disasters; in Herman Melville's *Moby Dick* (1851), they are quoted by the narrator Ishmael after he is left the sole survivor in the battle with the titular white whale. Mrs J joins the tradition of such 'cursed witnesses' like Dante Alighieri, and Samuel Taylor Coleridge's Ancient Mariner; connected to these other sources by her urgency to reveal situations of violence which no one else has seen or seemingly can see.

As mentioned, *Escaped Alone* does not recourse to more demonstrable representations of violence. There is, however, a distinction between the monologues and the dialogues: the violence of the former is catastrophic, while far more subtle and often identified in the everyday in the latter, as emphasized in the stark darkness / sunny idyll dichotomy of Macdonald's staging, with the 'transitions between the two spaces' accompanied by 'alarming noises, such as sirens' (Hartl 2021). Three terms that categorize these different modes here are presented by Slavoj Žižek; illustrating their relationship to one another to further reason why some kinds of violence are more perceivable than others. These are subjective violence, 'the most visible portion of [the] triumvirate'; symbolic violence, 'embodied in language and its forms'; and systemic violence, 'the often catastrophic consequences of the smooth functioning of our economic and political systems' (2008: 1). The last two types are termed 'objective' violence:

> subjective and objective violence cannot be perceived from the same standpoint: subjective violence is experienced as such against the background of a non-violent zero level. It is seen as a perturbation of the 'normal', peaceful state of things. However, objective violence is precisely the violence inherent to this 'normal' state of things. Objective violence is invisible since it sustains the very zero-level standard against which we perceive something as subjectively violent.
>
> (2)

Žižek's triumvirate then is something like an iceberg: subjective violence is that part that sits above water, while the systemic and symbolic inform and support it from below.[4]

Subjective violence fittingly refers to those acts of violence explicitly concerned with subjects (someone assaulting someone else, for example), and is more easily identified by subjects – not to say that it cannot be normalized, as Arendt's work argues. It can be 'spectacularized' by dissemination in the media, which is a focus in the work of Sontag. Though the audience does not see simulations of subjective violence in *Escaped Alone*, they are told of instances like Vi's murder of her husband, and the catastrophic scenes related by Mrs J; indeed, the scarcity of explicit images of subjective violence is generally characteristic of 2010s British theatre. Of Žižek's objective forms, symbolic violence is oppression constructed through modes of communication, such as slurs against specific groups which may be tacit (for example, microaggressions)[5] or more explicit, such as racist language; though these distinctions change over time, as Sally comments: 'they keep having to change what you can say' (156). Finally, systemic violence is woven into the fabric of society and culture, effecting different levels of everyday harm on individuals. Evans and Giroux's normalized violence certainly includes the systemic, as well as any forms of subjective and symbolic violence that have been made 'normal'. The systemic can be located, for instance, in the ways that a neoliberal society is designed to create commodifiable or disposable lives. This can normalize the persecution of certain groups and therefore can lead to acts of subjective violence, examples of which frequently appear in Mrs J's visions of a world in which human life has been trivialized and cheapened.

Systemic violence is very difficult to eliminate, if it can even be eliminated at all, and would likely require considerable long-term critical effort from nearly all members of a society. One of the main factors why systemic violence is so difficult to combat is its 'invisibility', with Žižek describing it as 'something like the notorious "dark matter" of physics' (2). As it arguably sustains much violence in the world, it is also the most pertinent to address. Perceiving similar distinctions of violence, Evans and Giroux write that: 'Representations of hyper-violence and human tragedy [...] structure social relations through the exposure to violence', but 'attempt to remove from sight the systemic nature of such violence by relegating it to a personal and individualized experience' (2015: 142). In other words, spectacles of subjective violence are a distractive sleight-of-hand that shields objective violence from being fully addressed. This means that systemic concerns such as a lack of social mobility or a rise in mental health issues become internalized in the context of 'larger problems' deceptively suggested by spectacular violence. Sally's phobia of cats illustrates this transmissive link: as Marranca notes, 'in the same section of the play there is talk of drone bombings and a long passage by Sally about cats that masks her fear of the outside world' (2017: 5). Her fear of their invasiveness – 'cat behind the books on the shelf behind the dvds a cat could be in the teapot' (Churchill 2019: 164) – matches the totality of violence and is implied to be a transferred dread of the spectacular and subjective violence she and her friends casually discuss.

Evans and Giroux continue that in the exposure to the spectacular, which normalizes and creates a 'zero level' of other forms of violence, 'we are taught to accept that things are fundamentally insecure, and thus we have no reason to struggle to identify the source of our suffering, let alone transform our conditions for the better' (2015: 142). Though Sally requires greater solidarity and support, stating in her monologue that she 'need[s] someone to say there's no cats' (164), she has no expressed desire to locate the source of her phobia and, underlined by Deborah Pearson's irascible performance, her friends must tread cautiously around the subject or risk upsetting her. As expressed through Kika Markham's more reserved characterization, Lena too has her own private anxieties which could perhaps be eased through open discussion, but she also seems paralysed against inspecting them more closely. Lena literally has an aversion to speaking which appears rooted in a form of depression, shown in her monologue: 'Why talk about that? Why move your mouth and do talking? Why see anyone? Why know about anyone?' (170). When the women discuss their preferred superpowers earlier in the play, she repeats that she'd 'rather be invisible' (165); likely having internalized her own feelings of powerlessness. Though the source of Sally and Lena's anxieties are not disclosed, their inability to meaningfully engage with them can be described as a symptom of systemic violence in that their isolating silence around their mental health has been normalized, neutering any cooperative solidarity.

This is just one example of systemic violence in *Escaped Alone*, as the four women by turns or simultaneously appear to be, or have been, variously afflicted by domestic violence, gender inequality and associated trauma. As Arendt writes of often-unknowing citizens and violence, the women also appear complicit in sustaining systemic issues including racism and resource exploitation. Indeed, the private issues disclosed in Sally, Lena and Vi's monologues – what Marranca calls 'sharp turns away from their casual banter to reveal disquieting inner turmoil' (2017: 2) – may find a rejoinder in Mrs J's speeches, as if to illustrate where personal alienation and diffusion of the public can eventually lead to. As the new member of their group, Mrs J herself occasionally pushes the others to speak more freely about what they would otherwise leave unsaid: for example, saying 'let's hear it' (154) when Vi and Sally argue about the latter's fear of cats, and 'lied in the witness box did you?' (172) when Sally insinuates the murder of Vi's husband was not accidental. Her role in the play appears to be that of a guide who illuminates the audience to secret or hidden acts and forms of violence, as per her real and literary sources. In addition to the references listed above, Churchill herself might be auto-fictiously added to the composition of Mrs J's character. This is because Mrs J's presence, both within the dialogue between the other women and in her monologues, looks to make the audience aware of objective modes of violence. She unearths the subjective violence Vi is invariably traumatized by; surmises the symbolic violence behind the women's speech with her jolting repetition of 'terrible rage'; and in the contemporaneous dystopia of neoliberalism and climate crisis – with the attendant prejudices, exploitations and innocuous behaviours the characters (and indeed the audience) are likely complicit in – creates absurd and cataclysmic stories out of this otherwise invisible violence, with mentions of corporate destructions of settlements, toxic currency, privatization and starvation.

So, the dramaturgy of *Escaped Alone* makes invisible violence visible, so to speak. Kim Solga's exploration of the presence/absence of gender-based violence on the Renaissance stage (referred to in the Introduction) speaks to Churchill and Macdonald's staging here: 'The in/visible act is the performance of violence against women as critical forgetting; it charges its witnesses to come to terms with what we've missed but also with *how* we've missed – with how we have failed to see the suffering before us, hidden in plain sight' (2009: 17; emphasis in original). Although gender-based violence was certainly more 'visible' in 2010s society than the Early Modern period, Solga's writing relates to both the gendered trauma variously felt by *Escaped Alone*'s characters and the exhuming of the otherwise-innocuous violence highlighted across the production. Solga draws on the works of Peggy Phelan (1993), Diana Taylor (1997), and Rebecca Schneider (2001) who, like Sontag and Žižek, variously contend that in/visibility and (re)appearance are essential components of performance. In day-to-day life, these elements are mobilized by hegemonic structures to train citizens 'to "overlook" what lies in plain sight' (Taylor 1997: 121; quoted in Solga 2009: 15), but on the stage they can be contested and defamiliarized. Jill Dolan's theories of 'performance-as-witness' (2005) are also influential for Solga and relevant for the representation of systemic violence, citing 'performance's power to stage an encounter with what has gone missing in public culture, and to make space for audience members to imagine their relationship to that culture and its acts of disappearance anew' (2009: 13). Again, this can be applied to theatre's efficacy in staging systemic violence: asking audiences to consider what is not visible as violence, and how invisible forms of violence operate.

Like Solga's contentions – and using the same metaphor as Žižek – Andrew Sofer uses the titular phrase *Dark Matter* (2013) to describe 'the invisible dimension of theater that escapes visual detection, even though its effects are felt everywhere in performance' (3).[6] He examines how such felt absences are created through devices like offstage events, masks and unseen characters. Sofer does not mention systemic violence, but he does assess Churchill's work through the more general term of trauma: '*Far Away* dramatizes a state of war that is always elsewhere, unrepresentable, and absent, and yet at the same time present, internalized, and inescapable [...] By play's end trauma is less an individual psychological event than the very air the characters breathe' (134). This palpable but unseen violence is constructed through making visible systemic violence through costumes – the garish hats crafted by Joan being worn in a parade of citizens who are to be executed by the state – and dialogue, as Joan and her family become increasingly confused about whom they are supposed to be fighting. In the production of *Escaped Alone*, though there is again an atmosphere or 'Pinteresque' menace of violence, it does not 'appear' onstage: Churchill almost solely uses characters' speech to create this felt absence. The sometimes hard-to-understand nature of the dialogue is indicative of the difficulty of normatively discussing or imagining the scale of the issues alluded to throughout the production; and Macdonald literally frames Mrs J's monologues as if to spotlight how Bassett's speech is 'standing in' for representations that are often depicted in spectacular modes. *Escaped Alone* then, like many other works of 2010s British theatre, looks to make such invisible violence visible without recourse to 'spectacularization' and its pitfalls.

Violence and 'Truth'

One of the foundational philosophical parables for ideas of spectatorship, perception and 'truth' is that of Plato's *The Cave*. Here, spectators are affixed within a cave; unable to move their heads, they look forwards at a wall on which are cast shadows from a fire behind them. It is, as Alan Read writes, 'a theatre in which the prisoners see a highly organised, staged spectacle' (2013: 5). Plato conceives of the philosopher as one who has seen the sun beyond the cave, though the other spectators cannot fully understand this because they know of no other reality. For the philosopher, the sun beyond the cave is dazzling and near-blinding; yet, much like the cursed witnesses of Ishmael, Dante or Mrs J, it is their fate to attempt to convey what they have seen. Read continues that, 'what is unsettling here is that Plato's protagonists are [...] *riveted* to their places. They are prisoners unaware of their imprisonment' (6; emphasis in original). For the spectators, the philosopher's tale must surely sound harrowing and violent, but in the hearing of it they can become aware of the violence of their own situation. Read notes that Plato's separating of performance from reality, despite the necessity for a 'shadowy group of stagehands' that prove the spectacle 'cannot be a free of an *outside*', makes a 'derogatory founding myth for drama' (ibid.; emphasis in original). Indeed, as Solga, Phelan, Taylor, Schneider and Dolan demonstrate above, the querying of the not-normally-visible, or the onstage reappearance of the made-invisible, shows that theatre reframes 'the outside' rather than separates from it, and in doing so reveals otherwise-shrouded aspects of the real.

Theatre like Churchill and Macdonald's *Escaped Alone* not only self-reflectively makes its audience aware of the production's own illusions, but the violence the audience is under that enforces them to perceive the particular 'illusions' of their reality. In the first of Mrs J's monologues, 'senior executives' bury settlements with paid-for landslides (2019: 146) in what could be seen as a retelling of Plato's *Cave*:

> Villages were buried and new communities of survivors underground developed skills of feeding off the dead where possible and communicating with taps and groans. Instant celebrities rose up on ropes to the light of flashes [...] Babies were born and quickly became blind [...] Stories of those above ground were told and retold till there were myths [...] Survivors were now solitary and went insane at various rates.
>
> (ibid.)

Here, the stagehands Read envisions in Plato's *Cave* are replaced by executives who force the cavernous space on those literally below them. Rather than the reality above being explained to Churchill's 'underground people' by a philosopher, those above are glorified rather than made accountable. The violence forced on them has altered the way they perceive the world to the extent that they literally cannot see.

The way in which the perception of violence is mediated and how violence mediates perception is a key concern of Judith Butler's, who asks how some images of suffering are more bearable than others: 'A hierarchy of grief could no doubt be enumerated [...] [W]e seldom, if ever, hear the names of the thousands of Palestinians who have died [...] or any number of Afghan people, children and adults. Do they have names and faces[?]' (2006: 32). Butler contends such lives are scarcely made 'grievable' as they are recounted through the spectacle of news media, so not only are these victims dehumanized for the spectator (often becoming, for example, no more than a statistic) but the spectator is dehumanized in being robbed of their ability to mourn or enact any change that might halt such violence. The monologue referenced above from *Escaped Alone* literalizes how casualties of violence can become unseen; buried by the powerful forces of ideology and corporatism. Rather than the editorial frames that Butler argues as keeping certain lives 'ungrievable', Churchill lifts these to be expansive enough to consider how a contemporary failure of perception might violently affect lives in the future.

Of the systemic violence made visible in *Escaped Alone*, that of ecological disaster is most apparent. Mrs J envisions great fires, floods and famines directly attributable to human activity, such as the executives crushing villages with rocks, and 'wind developed by property developers [that] started as breezes on cheeks and soon turned heads inside out' (166). Such absurd violence relates to its status as a 'misused tool' and emphasizes the systematic exploitation of the ecosystem which is so ingrained as to be normal and systemic. As further explored in Chapter 4, Churchill defamiliarizes this relationship by merging human–natural distinctions and presenting exploitative practices as supernatural:

Vi   People always want to fly

Lena   fly like a bird [...]

Sally   but we do fly now

Mrs J   planes isn't the same [...]

Vi   like starlings, that would be good [...]

Sally no we wouldn't have that sense of each other, we'd keep bumping

Vi but what people want is fly by yourself.

(161-2)

Mentions of anthropomorphism and dehumanization frequently appear throughout *Escaped Alone*, querying the norm of human superiority. Sally's note that flying humans would 'bump' into one another also poses that the conditions generated by resource exploitation and neoliberalism have resulted in individuals who can 'fly' yet are, ultimately, isolated from one another: interdependence has been eroded and the perception of the other is dimmed.

Sontag is an important touchstone for Butler's theorization of violence, as they elsewhere inspect the editorial techniques through which images of it are framed: the 'how' of showing violent images, which 'not only organizes the image, but works to organize our perception and thinking as well' (2009: 71). If images of violence affect the perception of violence, then the choices made in their presentation are crucial to this. Emphasized by Miriam Buether's set – which literally presents a rectangular frame for Mrs J's monologues – *Escaped Alone* does not so much reframe an image of violence as reframe an otherwise innocent and everyday situation to consider its potential connections to violence. The women's summertime conversations in Sally's garden are surrounded by a frame of catastrophic violence; a structure which Macdonald uses to link these otherwise disparate elements for the audience. The 'framing' monologues also further stress the mentions of violence within their dialogue, such as the murder of Vi's husband, drone strikes, and implicitly present a reason behind Sally's phobia. Whereas Butler explores how images of violence are packaged to alter perception, Jean-Luc Nancy contends violence is necessitated on perception – that it 'always completes itself in an image' (2005: 20) because it is something that, essentially, leaves marks:

> Violence can be defined *a minima* as the application of a force that remains foreign to the dynamic or energetic system into which it intervenes. Let us take an anodyne example [...] feeling the need to extract a recalcitrant screw by pulling it out with pliers, instead of loosening it with a screwdriver. Whoever does this no longer follows the logic of the screw's thread, nor that of the material.
>
> (16; emphasis in original)

Applying foreign force to a system would suppose that the physical make-up of the universe itself is violent: as Nancy contends, violence 'defines, in all its problematic character, the *habitus* if not the very *ethos* of our world' (20; emphasis in original).

Although to consider violence in Nancy's way is conceptually and ethically troubling (if everything is essentially violent, why not live violently?), this is like Žižek's conception of systemic violence: the 'base level' of violence on which societies operate. Moreover, with such an expanded view of violence, Nancy relates it to truth as it too 'shows or demonstrates itself [...] Violence and truth have in common a self-showing act' (21). From this relationship he devises a distinct 'truth of violence' and a 'violence of truth'. The former relates to how an act of violence can be used to assert one's own truth, echoing Arendt's understanding of violence as an instrument ('might makes right') while the violence of truth relates to how truth itself behaves by Nancy's definition of violence: it 'cannot irrupt without tearing apart an established order, like how truth forces Plato's prisoner to leave the cave, only to dazzle him with its sun' (17–18). Though this is somewhat unhelpful when practically defining violence, it does relate to the affect that images of violence like those staged by Churchill have: which look to open audiences' perceptions to think about otherwise unseen violence. This awakening may be discomforting, but like exiting Plato's cave it can offer a new truth. This definition of violence then allows an understanding that the way in which we view the world is a 'frame of truth' that has been *forced*: like pliers pulling out a screw.

In its instrumentality, the enaction of the 'truth of violence' looks to establish, effect or reaffirm: to make 'truths' like power, wealth, or racial and gendered superiority. The 'violence of truth', however, is a perceptual jolt that allows an understanding of these fabrications. Nancy calls the violence of truth – similarly to Benjamin's 'divine violence' – a '[v]iolence without violence' (26), though admits that he still refers to it through the description of 'violence' because he is unable to ascertain '[w]here does violation begin, and where does the penetration of the true end?' (19). In other words, where is the division between the violence of truth's ability to reveal something different or new, and the truth of violence's ability to forcefully make a new truth – can the editorial processes Butler critiques be seriously considered as acts of violence? They are certainly not an egregious form of it; but as Nancy poses, it is not *not* an act of violence. Finburgh Delijani applies Nancy's theories of violence to theatre, summarizing his contention that the truth of violence can be found within simulated images: 'At the same time as representing violence, symbols, icons and images can perform violence, by narrowing to the point of seeming disappearance the gap between the object, being or event that is represented, and the constructed means with which it is represented' (2019: 268–9). This adheres to concerns on spectacularized violence: if the gap between simulation and its reality is too narrow, the simulation may itself perform something like violence.

Theatre, then, is arguably the best-suited medium to portray 'violence without violence' because it 'is able consciously to show the audience that its fictions are grounded in nothing more than the bodies, voices, objects, sounds and lights on stage' (ibid.: 275). Though, of course, much theatre attempts to create a more realistic simulation, Finburgh Delijani argues that plays since the turn of the millennium are increasingly self-conscious of 'their own "distinct" theatricality – their groundless artifice – […] open[s] a breach that exposes and contest[s] the regulating violence of the spectacle' (ibid.). Focusing on a specific monologue from *Escaped Alone* in which there is a famine of food but a surplus of technology – '[s]martphones were distributed by charities when rice ran out, so the dying could watch cooking' (160) – she writes that Churchill 'draws an analogy between the consumption of screen images, and of food […] virtualized into nothing more than a flattened, pixelated, odourless, tasteless image on a screen' (166). This image effectively encapsulates the violence of truth of *Escaped Alone*: to ask its audience to view the distinction between the food and the smartphone, the fire of the cave and its shadows on the wall.

Churchill and Macdonald invite their audience to consider how what might be understood as 'true' may in fact be a simulation, established to become innocuous even if it is violent against, for example, the ecosystem, the poor or certain genders. Macdonald tacitly constructs this vision of a simulation through the staging of Mrs J's monologues which appear, within the lit frame, almost as if on a screen; casting questions on whether the garden towards the back of the stage could, perhaps, be a fabricated reality. On the other hand, the production presents new visions of truth where humans are inseparable from their environment, and everyday actions are comprehended through their potentially violent implications in the future. *Escaped Alone* then suggests that violence alters perception, using the 'framing' device of Mrs J's monologues to reveal these future possibilities that have been shaped by the matrices of power discernible in the women's conversations; and, indeed, how the women's identities have themselves been informed by violence. This is achieved while circumventing the spectacle of violence, what Finburgh Delijani calls a drawing-attention to its 'distinct theatricality', with monologues which distinguish the violence within the play while making its representation theatrical; as opposed to the dialogues which reveal glimmers of the structural violence running under its surface. If the narrative were framed a different way, *Escaped Alone* might have been an unassuming play about four women talking together with some undertones of past traumas. Instead, the images of summertime garden chats are reframed to be snapshots of human catastrophe: making visible the tar inside a cup that otherwise appears as tea.

Conclusion

As a concept, violence is slippery, expansive, and has different facets and levels: there are actions which many could easily label as being violent, those which only a few would see as such, and perhaps other phenomena which do not appear violent to any yet may eventually be proved otherwise. Defining violence, especially as ratified by existing power structures, runs the risk of excluding other forms of suffering and silencing those that the power behind the definition would seek to oppress. In lieu of a unified definition, we might generalize an 'essence' of violence, which is what is perceived when one comprehends 'badness' in the world as per Nevitt's writing: injustices of power, assaults, attacks, violations, oppressions, forcefulness. It is, then, a concept closely related to perception, phenomenology and the human experience of being in the world. Žižek's three main classifications of violence therefore reflect this: the subjective, the symbolic and the systemic. Additionally, Evans and Giroux write of two modes by which violence can be disseminated: the spectacular and the normalized. Characteristics of violence are identified by Arendt, who sees it as instrumental, and Nancy, who expounds on the truth of violence: the ability of violence to assert and change perception; and its reverse, the violence of truth, that presents perception as formulated by such constructed 'truths'. These terms do not bring us closer to a concise definition of violence; rather, they enable the ability to comprehend and challenge its many forms.

Evans and Giroux hope for a critique of violence alike to Benjamin's for their contemporary times, but since 1921 the scope of what violence is and how we understand it has widened to the point where no one critique is enough. Instead, there must be multiple critiques of violence to respond to its contemporary multifariousness. British 2010s theatre is exemplary of this position: it possesses the resources to 'move beyond the spectacle'; fulfils Sontag's criteria of countering the spectacle of the image by the 'length of time one is obliged to look, to feel' (2004: 110); possesses similarities to Benjamin's 'divine violence' and Nancy's 'violence without violence'; and like violence is tied to concerns of perception. This last point especially means that theatre can untangle and understand violence's relation to performativity, which is the focus of the next chapter. Though Adiseshiah contends that Churchill's twenty-first-century work is aware of its limited political potential, *Escaped Alone* offers much in the way of recognizing violence and itself, I contend, can be considered as a critique of violence. It presents how violence changes our perception and looks to counter it by changing our perception against violence, makes visible hidden forms of violence in a way that does not sensationalize the content but allows critical distance and interpretation, and asks the audience to have a better consideration of the consequences of actions, and to question when we have power and what innocuous actions are affecting others. Moreover, it is a critique that does not preclude the human. As Žižek contends, 'the overpowering horror of violent acts and empathy with the victims inexorably function as a lure which prevents us from thinking […] Yet there is a sense in which a cold analysis of violence somehow reproduces and participates in its horror' (2008: 3).

Escaped Alone finds a 'Goldilocks' position between these two stances; for example, Mrs J's monologues theatrically reveal the artifice of the play and expand our perceptual view, but Churchill balances such catastrophic visions with glimpses of the contentment and sometime joy her characters feel in the very act of being in shared company. This is best seen when the four women sing together, '*for themselves in the garden, not performing to the audience*' (2019: 166). Macdonald's production had them harmonizing The Crystals' 'Da Doo Ron Ron' (1963) which – like Churchill's own dramaturgy – strips language down to only the essential. *Escaped Alone*, then, is arguably more political than the ostensible limitations Adiseshiah discerns in Churchill's later work might suggest. Despite the perceived Beckettian turn in her post-millennial writing, Aston revaluates this in the face of *Escaped Alone*'s 'breaking of the fourth (garden) wall' and its 'reprise of Brechtian estrangement' (2018: 308). As a critique of violence it better informs its audience to perceive violence in its many forms: like all the theorists explored here, the production asks us to reconsider assumptions about violence, and comprehend it from non-normative perspectives. Additionally, the production offers images of a world without violence, however momentarily, such as four older women – rarely represented in such a capacity on the British stage – sitting in the garden together, forgetting the structural violence that has framed their lives and may yet frame their futures.

2

Performativity

'In a world of globalization and greed, of zero-hour contracts and *The Big Bang Theory* [2007–19], violence worms its way into every aspect of our lives.' This assertion is taken from the playtext back matter and advertising of Lulu Raczka and Barrel Organ theatre company's *Some People Talk About Violence* (2015). It articulates the landscape of systemic violence in 2010s Britain and demonstrates an urge shared with other theatre-makers during this decade to stage it. Still, we might wonder, how is a popular sitcom like *The Big Bang Theory* emblematic of violence being present in every aspect of our lives? The play's title too hints that violence might come about through talking – that certain speech might bring about violence. To better inspect how systemic violence 'worms its way into every aspect of our lives', and to query how theatre might represent this, an understanding of performativity is arguably essential. This term was coined in the 1950s by the philosopher J. L. Austin to contend that language is not simply descriptive or constative (a declarative statement being either true or false) as was generally accepted by linguists and philosophers, but that '[w]e very often also use utterances in ways beyond the scope of traditional grammar' (1962: 3). He called these utterances 'performatives', identified as: 'A. they do not "describe" or "report" or constate anything at all, are not "true or false"; and B. the uttering of the sentence is, or is a part of, the doing of an action, which again would not *normally* be described as saying something' (5; emphasis in original). Put simply, Austin contended that language could not only interpret reality; it actively participated in it.

As the last chapter displayed, the enactment of violence and the mediation of its definition can serve to alter perception and construct truths. This is a characteristic shared with performativity, which creates and reinforces 'the way things are'. Furthermore, performativity since Austin has been theorized as an effect latent in all forms of communication, including symbols, gestures and images. It has been argued to not only shape the way in which reality is perceived but also its very physicality, moulding bodies, societies and even the Earth itself through the performative actions of environmentally exploitative societies. With this potential to 'mark', can performativity be called violent? And, in the way that violence can construct truth, is violence essentially performative? This second chapter explores performativity's potential violence through communication as well as how different forms of violence are performative of one another and establish themselves as societal rituals. These positions are illustrated through *Some People Talk About Violence*, which focuses on mental health, (social) rituals, and language and violence; and Martin McDonagh's *A Very Very Very Dark Matter* (2018), an irreverent yet damning play on cultural narratives and the legacy of colonialism. The first section here inspects the theoretical connections between the concepts of performativity and violence, as well as their relevance in the analysis of staging systemic violence.

Violence and Performativity

Though examining the relationship between violence and performativity is not novel in theatre and performance studies, it rarely receives sustained critical attention. Nevitt offers an introductory intersection between them, relating to how theatrical depictions of violence can be thought through with performativity: 'performance tends to be treated as descriptive rather than performative [...] But what can be gained by considering simulated violence from the perspective of what the representation (the act of showing) *does*?' (2013: 30-1; emphasis in original). The enactment, perpetuation and spectacle of violence have the capacity to *do* something to the viewer and, more generally, to society. Indeed, performativity here is enhanced by theatricality. The nature of the relationship between these two terms is explored by Teemu Paavolainen, who generally defines them as being 'between *seeing* [theatre] and *doing* [performativity]', though admits 'the conceptual positioning of the two terms is radically contextual and utterly flexible' (2017: 174-5; emphasis in original). Paavolainen theorizes the terms as 'textures', which connote performativity's 'iterative process of its weaving' and theatricality's 'very substance or as the mere surface of something' (175). These textures are respectively that of a 'meshwork', something consistently 'wrapped up in'; and a 'network' which – like a stage – allows a wider perception of connections between elements like characters, space and audience (178-9). His argument is that performativity, at least in its normative use, creates a 'zooming in' effect where 'both body and performance recede from consciousness' (181). Put otherwise, most performative actions are performed unwittingly of what standardized modes of behaviour or power structures they are advancing. I contend that the way in which different modes of violence inform one another is through performativity.

Étienne Balibar argues that ultra-subjective (generally, what Žižek calls subjective violence) and ultra-objective (the symbolic and systemic forms) seek to dehumanize individuals, the former through 'a fantasy of animality' which 'blurs the limits of the human' (2016: 70) and the latter 'proceeds by way of an inversion of the utility principle and the transformation of human beings into not useful commodities but disposable waste' (61). Therefore, both kinds of violence are 'at once distinct and inseparable, of which one is something like the other's underside' (72). Balibar – through a series of sketched models – sees the relationship between his two classifications of violence as like a Möbius strip, connected and consistently informing the other side (74). This relationship is arguably performative: 'reiterated' subjective acts of violence continue their 'rituals' and so inform systemic violence; and systemic violence is the ritual through which many acts of subjective violence are performed. This Möbius strip of violence can be described overall as 'structural violence' – as a symbol through which to understand that violence persists through a structure consisting of different forms of violence stretching over institutions, ideologies, language, acts and behaviours. I use this phrase, somewhat interpretatively, from Johan Galtung – who articulated intangible, less visible forms of violence in the influential 'Violence, Peace, and Peace Research' (1969). My use of Galtung's term 'structural violence' here relates to his own investigations into the '*structure* of structural violence' (190; emphasis in original), which he poses as constituted by different social ranks and elements (176) and that the existence of personal and structural violence 'presupposes the latent presence of the other' (177). Though the interconnection of forms of violence was advanced and pronounced by Balibar, Galtung's earlier work gestures towards this structural Möbius strip.

Although structural violence seems to 'lock us in' to a revolving situation of violence – advanced by the performative interconnection between (ultra) subjective and (ultra)objective forms – the use of theatricality can allow a wider view of what might be otherwise innocuously established and advanced by performative actions. Paavolainen continues that it is 'in theatrical acts of "zooming out" – or stepping aside – that the entangled lines of such performative meshworks gain the optical quality of *objecthood* prerequisite for acts of attentive manipulation, and also perhaps for a Brechtian sense of estrangement' (2017: 181; emphasis in original). This can be seen, for example, in how *Escaped Alone* poses tea, isolation and certain acts of violence as constructing a catastrophic future; with Brecht's influence here analysed by Hartl (2021). So, theatre offers a way of articulating performativity to track its effects in the world. As Paavolainen writes, 'if the performative names a dramaturgy of becoming (of identity, species, climate), then the theatrical provides an optic for its analysis' (185). Yet, performativity in the theatre is also actual, in that the audience is both impacted by the performance and, with their very presence, impact the efficacy of the performance. Therefore, an engagement with it in theatre allows an understanding of performativity's effect as enabled by performance-like strategies: that is, showing, reiteration, and 'ritualized' legitimacy through plural spectators/provisional participants. It follows then that many examples of 2010s British theatre employ this interplay between theatricality and performativity – of 'zooming-in' and 'zooming-out' – to make visible those forms of violence that are often performatively established and establish one another unnoticed.

Counter to its understanding in philosophy and cultural theory, a colloquial use of 'performative' emerged in the 2010s which came to denote an empty or hollow action. This was especially notable in social media activism and corporate gestures towards movements such as BLM, with the phrases 'performative activism' or 'slacktivism' being regarded as a pejorative to indicate one's (online) activism as primarily motivated by increasing their own cultural capital. This falls under the term 'performative wokeness', the accusation that progressive attitudes are performed disingenuously which, on one hand, is a judge of 'authenticity' and on the other, is a way of demeaning left-wing social activism (Grech 2020).[1] Unfortunately, this colloquial use of performativity has superseded the useful ways in which this term can locate and deconstruct social and embodied power operations. Therefore, alongside my contention that 2010s British theatre reflected a growth in public awareness of structural and systemic violence, I argue that performativity is necessary to my analysis because of its articulation of the ways in which normative practices are spread, asserted and (re)enacted.

The Violence of Performativity and *Some People Talk About Violence*

The last chapter introduced Žižek's classification of symbolic violence: a term through which to identify how images, language and other means of cultural communication might be violent. An explicit example would be hate speech, which looks to directly 'attack' an individual through words and so is comparable to a physical assault. This phenomenon is examined by Butler in *Excitable Speech* (1997), where they ask: 'What does it mean for a word not only to name, but also in some sense to perform and, in particular, to perform what it names?' (43). In the manner that Austin theorizes performatives of 'doing something', hate speech is performative of violence as it exacerbates forms of oppression in society, effects pain receptors,[2] and is a potential prelude to more egregious assault as it opens a path to, and makes possible or 'permissible', physical violence. It is, to relate to the Möbius strip of structural violence, performative of other forms of violence. Though this is an example of how a performative could be understood as violent, there is a contention that the entirety of human communication may be somewhat violent. As Pierre Bourdieu – the coiner of symbolic violence – writes: 'relations of communication are always, inseparably, power relations which […] help to ensure that one class dominates another (symbolic violence) by bringing their own distinctive power to bear on the relations of power which underlie them' (1991: 167). If communication implicitly constitutes tacit background power relations between humans, can it be said that all communication is symbolic violence? In applying these positions to *Some People Talk About Violence*, this section explores the potentiality of performativity itself being 'violent'.

Bourdieu's argument is predicated on all communication being, to an extent, performative. Austin certainly entertains the notion that language exists on a spectrum of performativity, and that his initial distinction between constatives and performatives is blurred. He gives an example of a sentence such as 'I warn you that the bull is about to charge' (1962: 55), which can be construed as a constative statement that performs the action of warning, or a performative statement that may either be true or false. Austin is best aware of the collusion between performatives and constatives in this footnote: 'That the giving of straightforward information produces, almost always, consequential effects upon action, is no more surprising than the converse, that the doing of any action (including the uttering of a performative) has regularly the consequence of making ourselves and others aware of facts' (110). As well as hinting at the idea of actions being performative here,

Austin admits that constative statements can produce performative effects and performative statements can contain constative information: just as all language is in some way constative, all language is somewhat performative. Butler develops this position, influenced by Bourdieu's conception that communication is a structure of coercive power relations, and Louis Althusser's understanding of interpellation: the process by which ideologies 'recruit' individuals as linguistic subjects.[3] As Butler queries: 'Could language injure us if we were not, in some sense, linguistic beings, beings who require language in order to be? Is our vulnerability to language a consequence of our being constituted within its terms?' (1997: 1–2). Communication is a mode through which the subject is shaped and negotiates their way through the world; just as it is inaugurative and a source of navigation, it is also a source of vulnerability.

Though the potentiality of the performative effects of communication being themselves violent may initially seem excessive or overstated, it is particularly pertinent to the 2010s as concerns over communication's possible harmfulness were widely considered. For example, many institutions looked to establish inclusive environments that tackled offensive language and behaviour; popularizing emergent and sometimes ridiculed phrases such as 'safe space'. Debates in this area centred on the appropriateness of platforming controversial speakers on university and college campuses (Turner 2017; 2018), with the other side of the argument criticizing the permissiveness of free speech. For instance, the philosopher Brian Leiter claims that it 'hardly warrants [...] the damage to truth and to the well-being of the victims of bad speech' (2016: 435). Leiter identifies such damage in an example as extensive as the Iraq War: a conflict influenced by the mobilization of dubious facts and discourse (418). With a perceived rise in the 2010s of 'post-truth' politicians who appeared to increasingly disavow fact-checking and (inter)national law, further victims of 'bad speech' were found, for example, among those marginalized by the xenophobic tendencies of populist movements.

In the context of such concerns circulating in the public sphere through the 2010s, it could be said that *Some People Talk About Violence* has a particularly apt title. Directed by Ali Pidsley, it debuted in August 2015 at Summerhall during the Edinburgh Fringe before a run at Camden People's Theatre (CPT) and an autumn 2016 national tour. Its narrative centres on an unnamed character, called only 'The Girl' or 'Her', who is unemployed and struggles with severe apathy and isolation that likely stem from a form of depression. *Some People* follows Raczka and Barrel Organ's debut, *Nothing* (Warwick Arts Centre, 2013), which also dealt with issues of alienation through a series of monologues assigned at each performance's start. *Some People* similarly had characters allocated with each show, with audience members presenting the four performers with an envelope containing their allotted character's name and, in early performances, their script. Such devices are a staple of Barrel Organ's theatre as Euan Kitson, one of its members, states, '[w]e didn't want sets or costumes or naturalism or puppetry or anything other than playful, honest performance' (Barrel Organ 2015). In Raczka's revisions of classic drama and original writing, which includes *Grey Man* (New Diorama, London, 2016) and *Clytemnestra* (Gate, 2016), she has consistently experimented with theatrical form to complement the concerns of the text. In terms of making systemic violence visible, *A Girl in School Uniform (Walks into a Bar)* (West Yorkshire Playhouse, 2016), for example, has periods of extended blackouts that literalize the invisibility of gender-based violence.

The experimentation of *Some People* could be said to complement the text by challenging it. Emergent from ideas to create a show 'around the notion of violence in which nothing traditionally "violent" happens', according to its sound designer Kieran Lucas (Barrel Organ 2015), various 'interjections' are scattered throughout the performances in which the company 'slip more into their performer selves' (Raczka and Barrel Organ 2015: 55). These playfully performed activities and games changed with each performance, but some listed in the playtext include:

SLAPSIES

[…] For Slapsies you stand opposite your opponent, attempting to slap their hands, while dodging their attempts to do the same.

While doing this, the performers recited selected lines from the text.

[…]

IN YESTERDAY'S SHOW

Another game. The performers line up, and in turn walk to the middle of the stage, and state an invented occurrence that happened 'In Yesterday's Show'. These were supposed to be shockingly violent – increasing in violence through out the game – but weren't allowed to be inflammatory or obvious […]

If performers broke a rule, or didn't appear to out-do the previous person, they were out of the game.

(55–6)

These interjections tease and test the conventions of theatre in their slips between characters and performers, which like the blackouts of *A Girl in School Uniform* extend the concerns of the performance beyond the stage by playing on the 'reality' of the audience and the 'performer selves'. The use of competitive games within the drama creates a sense of inter-performer conflict and 'non-traditional violence', such as the above examples' pairing of physical hits with dialogue and play on the audience's ability to imagine shocking violence – converging violence and communication.

Some People presents the constraints and coercions of communication through its characters, narrative and the play's very form. Butler contends that communication is never truly possessed by the one who communicates, 'is never fully one's own' (1997: 140), with identity markers such as gender and social categories being constitutive of power matrices which performatively shape individuals. Communication, which establishes these categories, also has a codifying affect: 'The "constructive" power of the tacit performative is precisely its ability to establish a practical sense for the body, not only a sense of what the body is, but how it can or cannot negotiate space, its "location" in terms of prevailing cultural coordinates' (159–60). The performativity of communication then is like Paavolainen's 'meshwork': it can be forced or pushed against to change its shape, yet it remains enmeshed around the individual. Take the opening of *Some People*: 'We're looking at a girl. / A girl. / Maybe not a girl. / Maybe a woman. / But she is definitely someone that is called "Girl". / She's just been arrested' (9). Although playing on how the performers are allotted their characters with each show, these lines codify the character through the somewhat belittling term 'girl' (for the performance I attended at CPT in December 2015, Ellice Stevens became 'the girl' we were looking at). The note of her being 'arrested' can apply to how she has been incarcerated by language: as 'a girl', she carries certain connotations such as dependency and immaturity that would not necessarily exist if she were titled as 'a woman'. Her 'practical sense for the body', as Butler puts it, has been allotted the cultural coordinates set by others.

Furthermore, The Girl expresses a distaste at going to see her friends as 'they'll talk about their lives - / And I'll say nothing - / And they'll talk about their jobs -/And I'll say nothing' (23). Such conversation, too, restricts her ability to engage because of her mental health and unemployment. Additionally, language appears to rob her of her autonomy; unable to linguistically articulate her state of mind a '*visual/physical representation*' of her screaming is offered which, in the performance I attended, was a frenetic dance to techno (38). The performativity of language evidenced in descriptions such as 'girl' indicates how power works through communication. As Bourdieu writes, such labelling 'is the condition for the effectiveness of all kinds of symbolic power that will subsequently be able to operate on a habitus predisposed to respond to them' (1991: 24). His definition of habitus – as explained by Butler – refers to 'those embodied rituals of everydayness by which a given culture produces and sustains belief in its own "obviousness"' (1997: 152). It is the aspect of the self that culture is embodied in for the ideologization of the subject and exacerbation of that culture. In the case of The Girl, she is not so much 'predisposed' to operate by the dictates of the symbolic power forced upon her by language but is nevertheless oppressed by it. Language entraps her, proliferates her depression and shapes her identity with its performative meshwork.

Her general awareness of the symbolic violence enclosing her is expressed through a morbid obsession with *The Big Bang Theory*. Although seemingly benign, this sitcom has been critiqued for its broad and often prejudicial humour: 'it propagates the worst of society's tropes – for a regular audience of 20 million' (Manavis 2018). The Girl states that:

> I talk to people and I say I hate The Big Bang Theory.
> And they say then why do you watch it?
> And it's –
> Cause –
> The thing is.
> And I don't wanna say it –
> Cause no one wants to say it –
> And the fact that they ask means they don't get it and that's the whole problem.
>
> (17)

Though unwilling to vocalize her simultaneous critique and fascination of the show, it is perhaps due to its propagation of symbolic violence, with its reinforcements of normalcy, reiterations of prejudices and the innocuousness by which these things are packaged. The Girl's distaste for popular entertainment (with a specific target here) seems due to its symbolic reinforcement of violence in society and a willed ignorance towards this.

Raczka and Barrel Organ also make use of the role of The Narrator to literalize the coercive and threatening aspect of language. This character (played by Joe Boylan in the performance I attended) comes from a theatrical convention of an onstage, commentative role such as a Greek Chorus. Rather than being simply descriptive of the action, The Narrator attempts to steer and interpret it to their own dictates – as the character notes read, '[t]hey are aggressive [...] They want to tell the story, even though it's not theirs to tell' (7). He casts judgement on the other characters, introducing The Girl's Brother as 'shitty' (13), and teases out prejudicial impulses, encouraging The Girl's Mother to view her daughter as a 'thing that sits on the sofa all day' (21). His antagonistic presence throughout the performance appears to highlight the physicality of speech. Butler writes that '[i]mplicit in the notion of a threat is that what is spoken in language may prefigure what the body might do', so The Narrator's presence onstage could be seen as an implicit threat if he does not get to tell the story he wants to tell; yet Butler argues that 'this view fails to take into account that *speaking itself is a bodily act*' (1997: 10; emphasis in original). This is illustrated in one of the Interjections, the 'Cracker Challenge', in which the performers 'ate crackers' and 'would try and recite lines from the text' (55). This resulted in the words attaining a 'physicality' as cracker detritus were phonetically spat out, propelled by the literal force of the words.

With the corporeal nature of communication, *Some People* argues it possesses a performative and potentially violent effect on the body. Apparently influenced by the symbolic violence that The Girl is oppressed by, she makes a concerted decision to similarly affect others. She watches a late-night poker game and begins to desire the way that the players manipulate one another: 'could I make someone else look that shit scared? / Could I get them sweating? / Hyperventilating?' (44). Her motivation is then shaped by wanting 'to become a Monster' (42), which haunts her Brother as he travels to retrieve her from jail: 'he thinks about that word she said on the phone from the police station' (16). To this end, she breaks into a couple's house (resulting in her being arrested) and self-harms herself in their bathroom, or at least narrates herself doing so:

> A guillotine-sized razor is slicing through my arm
> Slicing through my arm as it lies on the rim of the bath just beneath
>   my elbow
> And off it goes
> And that feels so much better because it was just getting too heavy.
>
> (49)

With the questionable 'reality' of this act of violence, its narrated enaction underlines the deleterious performativity that communication has generally had on The Girl. Being, as Butler puts it, a 'linguistic being' constituted by language, this excessive description reveals the vulnerability of subjects to communication. Furthermore, with The Girl's ontological status made explicit by the play's form, with Barrel Organ assigning performers their characters, the fact that she, like all characters in theatre, is, literally, largely constructed by communication (through Raczka's lines, the varied performers' gestures, etc.) dissolves any physical and symbolic lines between the constitution of subjects. The symbolic violence of communication here performatively maims The Girl.

The final scene of *Some People* takes a formal turn away from its preceding action, being a letter sent to The Brother, as he retrieves his sister from prison, by his estranged Boyfriend. Read by the same performer playing The Narrator, the impassioned letter continues themes of communication's creation of subjects, declaring that 'I don't believe in "The Self" as some solid centre' (52); and self-referentially noting how The Boyfriend and his feelings are being evoked onstage: 'I decided to write a letter – because I thought it was suitably dramatic' (51). It also records how The Boyfriend has managed to evoke The Brother through a performative re-ascribing of a 'terrible song [...] It's awful and I listened to it 22 times in a row' (ibid.). The letter/performance ends with: 'Please come back. I love you I miss you come back to me' (54). This shows similar ideas of subject-formation through communication, but language here is not violent in the same manner as earlier in *Some People*. It could be said to be symbolic violence by Bourdieu's definition, as The Boyfriend may be deploying coercive emotionalism as a power-play to force The Brother to return to him. Yet its distinctly impassioned wording and delivery moved some audience members, at least at the performance I attended, to tears. Interestingly then, *Some People* concludes a performance hitherto concerned with the violence of words (as its title suggests) with an example of the ability of words to convey heartfelt, genuine interpersonal connection; if not between fictional characters, then between theatre-makers and audiences.

So, does the association between violence and communication presented in *Some People* illustrate that performativity is in fact violent? To return to the 'essence' of violence as established in the last chapter – that violence is a notification of misuses between power and powerlessness – the answer is *sometimes*. Though Bourdieu contends that all human communication is a negotiation of power relations, it does not follow that all such negotiations are violent, as illustrated in The Boyfriend's letter. Still, the consideration of communication as a matrix of power that is forced upon its users means that language and utterances exist on a spectrum that at one end can be termed violent, as hate speech reveals. *Some People*, like *Escaped Alone*, looks to affectively open a wider perception of violence for its audiences, with the assistant director Jack Perkins stating that it 'interrogates the inherent violence that we not only ignore but never recognize as violent [...] re-fram[ing] what is violent collaboratively [...] [with] the audience' (Barrel Organ 2015).

As for The Girl, communication is not the main cause of violence in her life: rather, it appears to proliferate it. What the performance particularly highlights is how the force behind words and other symbols can affect individuals into violence: whether that is the choice of a Girl to become a Monster, or the language of a society ascribing an individual as a Girl. Adhering to Butler's position that (re)citations are mediations between their contexts and their meanings, the character's labelling as The Girl, for instance, carries a wider societal oppression against women – especially those with mental health concerns – and a context of being belittled by The Narrator and the other characters. Both context and meaning align to performatively oppress her with, and through, communication. Performativity, while not being essentially violent, may be utilized through symbolic violence to verbally attack others (subjective violence) and continue normative power structures that can oppress certain groups and retain unjust hierarchies (systemic violence).

The Performativity of Violence and *A Very Very Very Dark Matter*

If performativity is the process of shaping reality through reiterated adherence to certain rituals or norms – and through establishing new or altered rituals and norms, as Butler argues – then many acts of violence could certainly be classified as performative. Subjective and symbolic acts of violence may be performative of systemic racism and gender inequality, for example. Connections between rituals and violence are contended by René Girard; stating that ideological or state violence 'protects man from his own violence by taking it out of his hands, transforming it into a transcendent and ever-present danger to be kept in check by the appropriate rites appropriately observed and by a modest and prudent demeanour' (2013: 152). In such contexts, the act of violence is ostensibly removed from the agency of the subject and performatively conferred to a pre-established system of law and power: perpetuating the Möbius strip of structural violence. So, how does violence contribute to such pre-established rituals; or, in other words, what makes violence performative? To answer this question, Martin McDonagh's *A Very Very Very Dark Matter* is illustratively read through with a continued utilization of the work of theorists such as Butler, Bourdieu and Paavolainen, as well as that of Girard and Balibar.

A British-Irish writer raised in London, McDonagh's Irish heritage has been thoroughly mined in his early plays such as *The Beauty Queen of Leenane* (Town Hall, Galway, 1996), *A Skull in Connemara* (Town Hall, 1997), and later in *The Lieutenant of Inishmore* (RSC, 2001).[4] His concerns with UK-Irish relations, narrative and violence are tinged by influences including J. M. Synge, Franz Kafka and Quentin Tarantino. Directed by Matthew Dunster, *Dark Matter* debuted at the Bridge Theatre in October 2018, being McDonagh's subsequent project after his Oscar-winning film *Three Billboards Outside Ebbing, Missouri* (2017). Critics were ambivalent on *Dark Matter*, often simultaneously entertained, outraged, impressed and confused. Andrzej Lukowski captures much of this attitude, writing that 'the play is indulgent, opaque and messy, and risks coming across as more offensive than it probably is simply because its intent isn't all that clear' (2018). The play offers a (hopefully) fictionalized narrative of the author Hans Christian Anderson played by Jim Broadbent, whose stories are secretly written by the imprisoned Mbute (Johnetta Eula'Mae Ackles). Much like The Girl of *Some People*, she is referred to as 'Marjory' by Hans and, tellingly, 'interpellatively' by the script.

In Dunster's production, the action opens in Hans's Copenhagen house, with Marjory trapped in a small, mahogany box which swung pendulum-like in a dark attic full of peculiar marionettes. A disembodied Narrator (voiced by Tom Waits) informs the audience of her situation:

> **Narrator** […] You've only got one foot left […] You're one of the most iconic writers of your generation, in fact, aside from your sister. But you're a pygmy, and you're a woman, and you were born in the Congo in 1869, the worst time for anybody to be born anywhere ever, let alone a black dwarf.
>
> (McDonagh 2018: 4)

It is revealed that Marjory and her sister Ogechi (Kundai Kanyama) transported back in time during the Belgian occupation of the Congo, following the death of the rest of their family at the hands of the colonizers Dirk and Barry (Ryan Pope and Graeme Hawley). Aping the plot of *The Terminator* (1984), Dirk and Barry have also travelled back in time, literally covered in blood, to kill Marjory before she can kill them in the future, while she intends to stop the Congo's colonization from ever occurring. Meanwhile, Hans, despite his poor level of English, travels to London to stay with Charles Dickens (Phil Daniels) – whom he continually mistakes for Charles Darwin – and learns that Ogechi was also used as a captive writer by Dickens until her death. When Dirk and Barry find Marjory, she pulls a submachine gun from an accordion gifted through a ghostly visitation from her sister and kills them. She and Hans then have their own stand-off before he relents, and Marjory leaves to attempt to save the Congo.

As can be guessed from this synopsis, *Dark Matter* irreverently hops between different tones and levels of incredulity, blending gallows humour alongside fantastical devices and historical figures and events. It also, unlike the other plays closely analysed here, represents violence explicitly as per McDonagh's established dramaturgy. Other recurring features of his in the text include concerns with the tension between fiction versus illusion, and reality versus fact. Visually conveying this theme is Anna Fleischle's production design of dozens of uncanny puppets hanging in Hans's loft. The puppets, like the characters of the play, are a blend of garishly fake and 'realist' depictions, a mishmash of recognizability and creative liberty. The characters, also somewhat 'bound by strings', find themselves conjoined through an implicative network that extends to the audience through the play's meta-theatricality. As Michael Billington discerns, 'McDonagh suggests that writers appropriate other people's narratives in a way that echoes the infinitely larger crime of colonialism' (2018). *Dark Matter* suggests that certain everyday performances and perceptions may contribute to the acceptance of atrocious, global violence. This adheres to how reiterated acts (of violence) performatively 'make meaning', specifically of structural violence. Such violent acts in the production include Hans's imprisonment and renaming of Marjory, their joint murder of an investigative journalist, and her gunning down of Dirk and Barry. The context and meaning of these acts performatively establish the larger issues the play looks to address: the suppression of voice, and the legacies of colonialism.

As per Balibar's Möbius strip of violence, these subjective acts of violence inform wider systemic issues and vice versa – it is perhaps telling that there is an open time-travel loop in the narrative of the play. Marjory's imprisonment, for example, perpetuates European imperialism through colonialist oppression, while being motivated by this performative ritual of constructed racial superiority. *Dark Matter* attempts to present this performative constitution and reiteration of violence through somewhat distancing the audience from the action. This is exemplified in a scene where the resurrected, time-travelling Belgian brothers Dirk and Barry recount the atrocities they have committed in the Congo. Drawing on accounts of colonizers' actions mostly garnered by McDonagh from the historian Jan Vansina (2010), they attest to going to settlements to 'lop a few hands off', leaving 'villages massacred, willy-nilly' (McDonagh 2018: 21); with this information revealed in Dunster's production through the performers reciting their lines like a music hall double-act. This performance initially eases the audience into being irreverently entertained due to the 'ritual' they are performatively citing, before causing bouts of discomfort: '**Dirk** Ten million people! / **Barry** That's a lot of fucking people! / **Dirk** If you think about it' (21). The conflation of the music hall two-hander, something of a traditionally 'British' medium of performance, with statistics of colonial atrocities serves to suggest that the relationship of violence to European culture is not so much a series of isolated phenomena, but intrinsic to its constitution. European colonialism can be examined by Girard's conception of the cultural ritualization of violence: 'The function of ritual is to "purify" violence; that is, to "trick" violence into spending itself on victims whose death will provoke no reprisals' (2013: 39). Because of the context they deem to be partaking their actions in, the deaths and dismemberments caused by colonizers alike to Dirk and Barry become more than isolated violent and reprehensible actions – they are performative of a ritualized European superiority that annexes the guilt and barbarity of these actions.

Though European neo-colonialism was still very much in effect during the 2010s, it was no longer enacted with forms of 'hard power' comparable to, for example, the Belgian massacres of Congolese people. Yet, these legacies remained in the continued ritual of European superiority attributable to structural racism, which is related to by the production's 'distancing' of the audience seen, for example, in Dirk and Barry's double-act. McDonagh's ironic distance has been prevalent in earlier works such as *The Cripple of Inishmaan* (NT, 1996), where the audience is meta-theatrically made aware of the ontological status of the work – critically placing them to reflect on their own culpability in the issues at play. *Dark Matter*'s conclusion has the appropriative Hans describing its tone – '*Upbeat!* More or less' (59; emphasis in original) – and sees Marjory leaving in the manner of a lone-ranger figure not dissimilar to Tarantino's *Django Unchained* (2012). As the Narrator puts it, 'she lit a cigar. And she holstered her guns, and she strode out of the puppet attic, to go and save the Congo' (58). The tongue-in-cheek conclusion is citational of Westerns and revenge narratives and is as subversive as it is problematic because of its meshing of fiction and history. Her exit to 'save the Congo' – despite the audience's knowledge that its colonization historically occurred – relates to contemporary culpability in that it queries how performative actions can continue, or make reparation for, the legacies of colonialism: 'The story isn't over yet. Is it? / *She winks at us*' (59). To apply Paavolainen's conceptions here, such devices in *Dark Matter* are not so much meta-theatrical but *particularly* theatrical, 'zooming-out' from an otherwise irreverent period piece to encompass both the atrocious events that follow in the Congo some decades after, as well as the contemporary context from which the audience watch the production. The implicative network of structural violence that reaches across time periods is stretched by this theatricality, while specific actions are highlighted as being performative of the racism which led to the occupation of the Congo and still plays out in contemporary society.

The violence of colonialism – as a series of subjective acts and as contributing to systemic racism – is performative through its embodiment. *Dark Matter* explicitly shows this with Marjory's mutilation, her lost leg being an obvious site where the performativity of violence has effaced reality. However, violence's performativity through embodiment may take less visible forms, such as Bourdieu's conception of habitus. As Butler writes:

> [Bourdieu] understands social conventions as animating the bodies which, in turn, reproduce and ritualize those conventions as practices. In this sense, the *habitus* is formed, but it is also *formative*: it is in this sense that the bodily *habitus* constitutes a tacit form of performativity, a citational chain lived and believed at the level of the body.
> (1997: 155; emphasis in original)

So, the habitus is not only created by performative practices but also is itself performative. Bourdieu perceives subjects as formed through language; a coercive practice he regards as symbolic violence. But other kinds of violence may shape the habitus, such as specific ways that cultures with legacies of colonialism may have impacted certain social conventions. *Dark Matter* demonstrates how examples of cultural capital and symbols are themselves marks of violence's performativity, with McDonagh employing tropes of revenge narratives and popular action movies as well as Dirk and Barry citing how 'Joseph Conrad's *Heart of Darkness* [1899] was inspired by the Belgian Congo. [...] So you can't say the Congo didn't get anything out of it' (21). Such cultural inscription is perhaps a reference to one of McDonagh's influences: Kafka and his short story 'In the Penal Colony' (1919), in which a machine literally inscribes the bodies of colonial subjects. Indeed, as Fintan O'Toole writes in the production's programme, '[s]tories take on their own lives. They generate and regenerate, multiply and proliferate, as if they are outside of our control, as if it is not we who tell them but they who tell us' (2018). Like legacies of colonialism then, cultural narratives of violence become inscribed on, and through, the body/habitus.

If Bourdieu's habitus allows us to perceive the body as a site performatively affected by culture while being generative of that culture, perhaps it can also be viewed as a site affected by violence (Bourdieu even asserts that the habitus is coercively shaped by symbolic violence) while also propagating that violence. In other words, is the habitus – or, more generally, the body – the locus of Balibar's Möbius strip of violence; where ultra-objective violence becomes ultra-subjective, and vice versa? Marjory appears to suggest that this may be so. Just as The Girl in *Some People* makes subjective the symbolic violence of her society by breaking and entering and, perhaps, slicing off her own limb, Marjory's body is a site that displays an act of subjective violence (also subject to a lost limb), as well as being literally imprisoned by an author (symbolic violence) because of his fantasy of superiority (systemic violence). In turn, she becomes a perpetrator of subjective violence but, crucially, offers an 'open ending' where the occupation of the Congo may not have occurred, or at least, its legacy may be performatively altered in the present day. If violence is performative, it may well be because of its exacerbation by the body, and therefore prevented by the actions of the body.

To conclude, although *Dark Matter* perhaps looks to make sense of the Congo's occupation through Marjory's character, the ironical tone prevalent in much of McDonagh's work means that the scale of the tragedy cannot fully affect the audience. Critical distance is a useful approach when addressing violence, and theatricality is a valuable optic for this task, but compared to the position between criticality and investment in *Escaped Alone*, for example, *too much* theatricality results in emotional detachment from the issues. As Lukowski argues, *Dark Matter* is too 'messy' in its tone, plot and themes to give a concise analysis of its concerns. Still, there are strong indications here that violence is contended as being performative through the locus of the body, exacerbating systemic violence through culture's connection to the habitus and being the 'bridge' on the Möbius strip between Balibar's ultra-objective and ultra-subjective violence. Ultimately, the 'mess' of *Dark Matter* is due in no small part to its representations of explicit violence.[5] Though this undoubtedly suggests the wider systemic violence of the legacies of colonialism, this dramaturgy places the play in a difficult bind where it seems to suggest how violence is performative through bodies and their transmission of cultural capital, while aping examples of cultural capital in doing so.

Conclusion

The application of performativity allows a more thorough understanding of how violence operates on a socio-cultural level. As Nevitt writes, '[v]iolence tells us things about the culture that produced it: the kinds of power relationship on which it is built, the attitudes and values that it takes for granted' (2013: 29). Navigating this contention through performativity enables better insight into how and why violence is connected to culture: whether through its varying effects on and in communication; its ritualization and performance to enforce the superiority of that culture (colonialism); or in its marking on the very body or habitus of the cultural subject. More generally, thinking of violence with performativity challenges the standard ways through which violence is understood and highlights its more enduring effects. As for the 'essence' of violence proposed in the last chapter (in lieu of a definition) – that violence is an alert to the misuse of power and 'what is wrong in the world' – it could be said that performativity can reframe this 'essence' to be that violence is *performative* of injustices and misuses of power. For critiques of violence then, performativity allows focus on violence's socio-cultural elements; and it is in this regard that it is arguably necessary for exploring the representation and conceptualization of violence in 2010s British theatre. Scholars such as Butler, Evans, Giroux and Žižek (among others) have suggested that an exploration of such violence requires comprehension of how innocuous acts, repetitive practices, and reiteration of norms help to establish systemic violence and perhaps even construct it. These requirements are evident in the dialogue of *Escaped Alone*, the coercive language of *Some People Talk About Violence*, and the silencing of disenfranchised voices and perpetuation of colonialist legacies in *A Very Very Very Dark Matter*. In short, these theatrical critiques of violence are predicated on performativity; and through a consideration of it, systemic violence can be made visible and recognizable.

3

Protest

Perhaps more than any other aspect, the decade of the 2010s shows clear signs of being remembered and historicized in Britain – and arguably globally – for its numerous protests. As Lara Shalson cites, even as early as 2011 their newfound significance was being recognized in popular media with *Time* magazine's awarding of 'the Protester' with its 'Person of the Year' accolade (2017: 73–4), which claimed that '["m]assive and effective street protest" was a global oxymoron until – suddenly, shockingly – starting exactly a year ago, it became the defining trope of our times' (Anderson 2011). The global use and volume of protest was tracked by several surveys and databases dedicated to monitoring social unrest, which reported a worldwide intensification in mass demonstrations particularly between 2011–12 and 2015–16.[1] Although it is difficult to quantify whether there were more or less protests in the 2010s than in any other decade, their organization and proliferation through social media platforms generally increased their international exposure and in many cases their interconnectivity (Gray-Hawkins 2018; Richardson 2020). With protest being framed throughout the 2010s as a vital if contentious technique of public debate and civil dissent, contemporaneous British theatre engaged with it through staging those socio-political issues being raised and – like other modes of cultural commentary during the decade – even queried protests' methods and effectiveness.

Another cover story, written by Gary Younge for *The Guardian*, titled the 2010s 'the decade of protest' even as he questioned the success of such events: 'It is in the nature of protests that, for the most part, they highlight problems they are not equipped to resolve', with 'some of the largest and most widespread leftwing protests in history' being witnessed, yet 'we end the decade with the most rightwing governments in living memory' (2019). Though the latter fact arguably explains the former, Younge's reservations speak to the frustrations of those who attempted to counter, for example, right-wing politics through demonstration. It was notably felt by many in the decade before, as Shalson records that '[t]he failure of the largest protest event in history, the anti-war protest of 15 February 2003 in which up to

30 million people around the globe participated, to prevent the invasion of Iraq was seen by many as a sign that protest could no longer effect change' (2017: 69). The question of what protests can *do* – and how certain forms of protest can influence this outcome – was certainly not novel to the 2010s, but their perceived newfound relevance made it a fundamental one to ask, and one that theatre-makers were arguably well positioned to respond to.

Protest, Theatre and (Non)Violence

As Judith Butler's work came to focus on protest in the mid-2010s, they argued that protests can indeed *do* because they are plurally performative: 'These forms of embodied and plural performativity are important components of any understanding of "the people" even as they are necessarily partial' (2015: 8). As with the contention in the last chapter on the authorizing power of gatherings, Butler states that assembled individuals in their very plurality legitimize and construct a (re)definition of what the public is, who the people are and what they want. If protests are socio-politically valid in that they can construct notions of personal and public identity, Younge's suspicion of their efficacy remains valid because, as the 2010s made evident, this does not automatically result in marked socio-political change. This criticism can similarly be directed at theatre; a criticism articulated by Shalson as influenced by 'a common belief that theatre in its more institutionalized forms is hopelessly removed from real political action' (2017: 18). Despite being apparently 'removed', many protests adopt certain theatrical flourishes. This can be overt, as in the symbolic 'props' and 'costumes' of Hong Kong's Umbrella Movement (2014) and the 'Gilets Jaunes' of France (2018); or less explicitly, as the cultural sociologist Jeffrey Alexander writes of the Black Lives Matter movement: 'Racial injustice creates enormous frustration and anger, but organized protests must be scripted, acted, directed, and performed vis-à-vis skeptical audiences if justice is to be won' (2017: 7).

Citing how the 1960s Civil Rights movement in the USA elicited sympathy particularly from white citizens of the northern states (24–5), Alexander notes that, to be socio-politically successful, protests are predicated on the effect its enactors garner on spectators – utilized particularly on social media by BLM with 'evocative, highly condensed slogans and visual symbols' and on the street 'producing choreographed demonstrations that contrasted black innocence with police brutality' (27). Such factors support Shalson's contention that theatre and protest 'work so well together' because 'protest is *itself* a form of performance [...] which make[s] use of a wide array of expressive techniques to make [its] claims' (2017: 15; emphasis in original). One such technique is the practice of non-violent protest, which is effective in creating spectatorial sympathy and looks to curb any potential 'inherent' violence in protests. Nonviolence became a chief concern of Butler's in the 2010s, possessing a 'strong view' that protests 'can succeed only if they subscribe to principles of nonviolence' (2015: 187). A pertinent reason for this is that spectatorial sympathy can generally be better gained by behaviour that appears less destructive or unruly; for example, mass media coverage and public opinion became largely critical of the 2011 England riots because of widespread reports of looting, despite initially being a demonstration against police brutality (Bassel 2013).

As Alexander mentions with BLM, nonviolence provides a 'dramaturgical' tactic of presenting the civility of the protesters in response to the violence of the state. Perhaps then, with the apparent authorization that it creates, nonviolence can enhance the performative ability of a protest – its ability to affect the public sphere. However, Younge's criticism remains, and the sociopolitical effect of (even non-violent) protest remains questionable. Another perspective holds that violence – specifically, revolutionary violence – is the only sure way to achieve the ends of protest, despite its unpredictability. This is mentioned by Butler: 'One of the strongest arguments for the use of violence on the left is that it is tactically necessary in order to defeat structural or systemic violence, or to dismantle a violent regime' (2020: 12–13). Such perspectives themselves find a rejoinder in reservations of violence's instrumentality as expressed in Chapter 1; as Butler writes, they depend 'quite crucially on being able to show that violence can be restricted to the status of a tool, a means, without becoming an end itself' (13). As far as meeting the demands of protest, especially those that rely on spectatorial sympathy, violence too is a questionable 'dramaturgy'.

British theatre's engagement with protest through the 2010s – and, arguably, its engagement with societal issues of violence and politics more generally – was somewhat shadowed by debates over its relevancy and legitimacy in doing so. As Shalson mentions above, the ability for theatre to broadly effect society and politics has been suspected of being worryingly minimal. This is a chief concern of Christopher Balme's, who explores how theatre's 'state of enclosure, which pertains equally to the black box of artistic absorption as well as good-night-out amusement, threatens to relegate theatre to political irrelevance' (2014: 14). Many examples of 2010s British theatre used concerns, or sometimes even the practices, of protest in their dramaturgy to reinforce or critique protests' tactics and efficacy. Yet, these were done so in a medium that itself has seen its socio-political influence called into question. Central here are the concepts of performativity and violence: the former being contended by Butler as how assemblies can affect society and politics; and the latter because of a historical suspicion of protests and crowds as being violent – a potential characteristic that can result in their delegitimization, whether in the street or in the theatre.

The ability of a citizenry to enact socio-political change is conceptualized as occurring through the public sphere, a term coined by the philosopher Jürgen Habermas to generally describe 'private people gathered together as a public and articulating the needs of society with the state' (1991: 176).

Habermas believed that most contemporary societies had transformed from possessing 'representative' public spheres, where political action occurred in secrecy but included public displays and ceremonies to represent politics to the people, towards 'bourgeois' public spheres, which aspired to debate public issues through reasoned discourse, have equal status granted to participants and allow near-universal access. Though these conceptions have been critiqued and expanded on, with the bourgeois mode, for example, retaining certain exclusions despite its ostensible openness (Fraser 1990), the term 'public sphere' has been used to refer to spaces and events in which the public and politics were exposed to one another, and debate could occur. Examples include news media, public arts and the internet, though such public spheres are constricted by specific limitations such as commodification. One major appeal of protest may be its offer of a public sphere unhindered by private elements; however, as they are necessarily bound with their own restrictions of accessibility, the appeals of protest must often be filtered through other mediums to reach larger portions of the public. Therefore, to speak to a broader public sphere, protests must be self-conscious of documentation, reporting and the disruption of its objectives by the private or political elements that may exist in other mediums. In other words, the efficacy of a protest is in no small part dependent on how it is performed.

British theatre in the 2010s also had limitations in the public sphere. Moreso than protest, theatre of this time continued to struggle with its own structural inability to (in most cases) reach a larger audience. Though theatre possesses elements of Habermas's ideal bourgeois public sphere, with private people gathered in a space where certain issues can be performed, contemplated and potentially debated, the theatre space of the 2010s was often perceived and administered as more private than public. As Balme claims:

> The very artistic achievements of the past century that have successfully transformed the theatre from a rowdy, potentially explosive gathering into a place of concentrated aesthetic absorption have been obtained at the cost of theatre's very publicness. The darkened auditorium has become to all intents and purposes a private sphere.
>
> (2014: 3)

If theatre once offered a medium for alternative and potentially subversive ideas to be explored in the public sphere to large and diverse parts of the citizenry, Balme perceives it as having become more insular. Shalson too notes that 'modern theatre, as it developed as an institution of art and moved away from "popular" nineteenth-century forms such as melodrama, became increasingly a bourgeois enterprise' rather than a 'form of political action' (2017: 22). Instead of a bourgeois public sphere, then, theatre of the 2010s appeared to offer a private sphere largely attended by the bourgeoisie, though this lingering cultural bias was in many cases unwelcome.[2]

Still, 2010s British theatre could certainly not be branded as devoid of relevancy to the public sphere. As Balme offers towards his conclusion: 'theatrical performances should be seen as just one component of a wider public discussion and deliberation. Theatre productions can be regarded as agents in such processes, as nodes in a network rather than self-contained, originary works of art' (2014: 201). However minor then, 2010s British theatre can at the very least be regarded as a tributary towards a broader public sphere – and the lack of a quantifiable method for discerning the socio-political impact of theatre audiences more widely means that defining theatre's effectiveness in this regard remains elusive. Certainly, discussion over theatre programming in 2010s Britain was significant enough to suggest it held importance in the national consciousness. Examples include the contentious termination of the National Youth Theatre's *Homegrown* (2015) because of its subject matter (the radicalization of British schoolchildren) and the Royal Court's reprogramming of both Abhishek Majumdar's *Pah-La* (2019) and Out of Joint's production of Andrea Dunbar's *Rita, Sue and Bob Too* (1987; 2018). Of the latter, initially cancelled because of the allegations towards the company's director, Max Stafford-Clark, Vicky Featherstone stated of being 'rocked to the core by accusations of censorship and the banning of a working class female voice' and the decision to re-programme was 'a result of this helpful public debate' (2019).

Homegrown and *Pah-La* demonstrate some of the difficulties 2010s British theatre faced in relation to the public sphere. With *Homegrown* axed due to political pressure and *Pah-La*, which focuses on the Chinese oppression of Tibet, deferred following advice from the British Council as it coincided 'with "significant political meetings" in China' (Quinn 2018), the public and private funding through which many 2010s British theatres acquired large amounts of their revenue meant that external agendas effectively 'censored' many programmes despite theatre censorship officially ending in the UK in 1968. As Effie Samara states, 'theatre, despite its much celebrated revolutionary potential, is also an institution often funded and supported by the official state' (2021: 53). The representation and discussion of the contentious issues in these curbed productions may have been of merit to the wider public sphere. For example, Andrej Mirčev – who describes how an Oliver Frljić production in Split, Croatia, was disrupted by singing protesters only for the audience to 'sing a *counter* song' – contends that such interventions make 'visible the antagonistic formation of the public sphere' and societal 'unresolved tension' (2018; emphasis in original).³ Indeed, *Homegrown*'s director Nadia Latif remarked that the 'show was about having an intelligent conversation around an issue that has hysteria attached [...] Instead, voices have been silenced' (Ellis-Peterson 2015). Perhaps such censoring in 2010s British theatre can be tracked by the relative absence of protests against it.

As Helen Freshwater writes, theatre protests and riots 'suggest a bygone age when theatre was a venue for genuine public debate and dialogue where audiences could express themselves without inhibition and effect social change' (2009: 26). With precedents such as the 1809 Covent Garden Old Price Riots, Mary Whitehouse's 1982 campaign and protests organized by Sikh community leaders against Gurpreet Kaur Bhatti's *Behzti* (Birmingham Repertory, 2004), 2010s British theatre perhaps appears, relatively, uncontested and detached. Even if British theatre productions themselves incurred little protest in the 2010s, protests more widely surely traced important concerns in the public sphere. The 'node' of theatre reflected protests in this regard, with the issues of the Arab Spring finding rejoinders in the 'One Day in Spring' festival (2012) at Glasgow's Òran Mór and Edinburgh's Traverse, and London's July 2018 'Together Against Trump' rally was preceded by Theatre503's 'Top Trumps' festival (London, 2017). Though British theatre representing contemporary socio-political issues is certainly not a distinct phenomenon of the 2010s, demonstrations on climate crisis, neoliberalism and racial and gender inequalities were certainly echoed in the concerns of many 2010s British plays.

Some protests themselves even came to be represented onstage. These included LUNG Productions' verbatim piece *E15* (BAC, 2018), which documented how a women's refuge fought against eviction from Newham council in 2013 through a campaign of public awareness and occupations. Additionally, the 2011 England riots were dramatized through verbatim theatre by Gillian Slovo's *The Riots* (Tricycle, London, 2011) and Alecky Blythe's *Little Revolution* (Almeida, 2014). Counter to news reports of the events, which framed dehumanized, violent thugs ransacking stores and a law-abiding community arriving with brooms to clear up the debris in the aftermath,⁴ Nadine Holdsworth writes that Slovo, through interviewing various police officers, locals, rioters and politicians, 'presents an alternative vision of a community rallying to defend itself' (2014: 93). Taking a more specific focus, Blythe centres on a Hackney corner shop 'completely trashed in the riots' that she describes in interview with Chris Megson as 'sat on a road between two extremes of London living: the wealthy, gentrified, beautiful townhouses on one side and then estates and a much more impoverished community on the other' (2018b: 228). Despite *Little Revolution*'s documentation of locals working together to raise money to rebuild the shop,

Blythe notes major 'tensions in terms of class: it threw up a lot of stuff that was, I think, uncomfortable for people to talk about' (ibid.). Both plays then present alternative narratives to the more dominant depictions of 'riot clean-up' coverage.

Žižek states of the various global protests of 2011 that '[t]he media killed the radical emancipatory potential of the events or obfuscated their threat to democracy, and then grew flowers over the buried corpse' (2012: 1). Holdsworth cites this in her analysis of how riots were treated in contemporaneous British plays, holding that 'theatre has been used as a way of pulling up the flowers and revealing the corpse' (2014: 78). Much like the alternative perceptions offered by *Escaped Alone* on neoliberal life, both *The Riots* and *Little Revolution* reveal the wider contexts, unheard perspectives and nuances behind the riots that neither the mainstream press nor the flat condemnation of the coalition government generally afforded them.[5] Still, as the recordings from Mohamed Hammoudan in *The Riots* attest (whose house burned down in the large Tottenham fire), the vilification of the riots was enabled by acts of violence and destruction. Such acts had a 'spectacularising' effect: as one of Blythe's witnesses mentions, 'it was almost like a media event' (2014: 24). The images that launched the riots widely into the public sphere and branded them in the public imagination were the very images that served to undermine and delegitimize them: they were 'framed' to become the dominant political narrative of the riots. In this context, it is interesting that both *The Riots* and *Little Revolution* are verbatim theatre: the form's curation of interviewed voices lending it a perceived documentarian legitimacy. It could be said that Slovo and Blythe attempt to mediate the perceived illegitimacy of the riots through a form that generally looks to 'get beyond' such violent, mediated images through testimony and transcription.

With certain political and media agents ready to frame protests as violent in the public sphere, it is unsurprising that nonviolence has been touted as the most effective way to enact protest and so mediate this common criticism, with Alexander exploring the 2011 Egyptian protests as a successful example that became 'coded as civil, and eminently worthy of identification and respect' (2017: 83).[6] Nonviolence can be typified as a refusal to normatively reiterate the conditions of violence: as Butler writes, it 'comes into play with the threat of violence' (2015: 190). In other words, it exists as a practice against violence, whether reactive, as surrogate for, or against the systemic violence that makes vulnerable the 'precarious character of living beings' (191). Just as 2010s British theatre was contextually engaged with protest, so too did examples explore nonviolence onstage. These include Majumdar's *Pah-La* – which eventually opened in 2019 – with its plot focusing on a young Tibetan nun's resistance against Chinese authorities through self-immolation, questioning and blurring distinctions between violence and nonviolence. Rather than explicitly seeing the representation of this act, the audience instead views the stage lit up in an alarming amount of flame: enough to feel the heat and smell the smoke, making her protest spectacularly visible. Still, this troubles whether nonviolence should itself be spectacularized – does its image, especially out of context, exacerbate forms of violence? Questions of nonviolence and its image are also raised in Lucy Kirkwood's *Chimerica* (Almeida, 2013; later adapted for a 2019 Channel 4 mini-series), which charts a world shaped by economic and political antagonisms between China and the USA, with an American photographer who captured the 'Tank Man' of the 1989 Tiananmen Square massacre attempting to seek out his identity.

Kirkwood looks to defamiliarize an iconic image of nonviolence, influenced by Susan Sontag's position that '[p]hotographs objectify: they turn an event or a person into something that can be possessed' (2004: 72), 'making subject' the objectified Tank Man image by fictitiously investigating his motives and personality. Interestingly, Chris Thorpe's *There Has Possibly Been An Incident*, directed by Sam Pritchard and opening at the Edinburgh Fringe in 2013, also adapts this famous occurrence of nonviolence. The narrative takes the form of three intertwined monologues told from the perspectives of a survivor of a plane crash, a politician who muses on her current, authoritarian actions in comparison to her revolutionary past and a witness of the Tank Man. Additionally, there is an intermittent dialogue between an interviewer and an Anders Breivik-like figure 'spoken by any of the performers' (2013: 15), as well as a final speech from the perspective of a survivor of this figure's attack, spoken *'in unison by all the performers'* (58).[7] All the narratives are framed around an act of incidental or authoritative violence experienced by an assembled group. Each narrator reacts in a specific way on a spectrum between violence and nonviolence, and in their description of the events, seems to ask the audience what they would think, feel and do in similar circumstances. Like *Chimerica* and the staged documentation of *Little Revolution* and *The Riots*, Thorpe looks to 'get inside' the image of a violent situation, but does so by denying any visual representation of these events beyond the reserved physicality of the performers, the space they are in, and the present audience.

The dramaturgy of *There Has Possibly Been An Incident* downplayed traditional theatrical conventions through a skeletal mise-en-scène, with performers directly addressing the audience, reading from held scripts, remaining seated for the performance's duration and speaking through microphones.[8] These techniques – which as Simon Stephens writes, make the theatre space 'unapologetically shared' (2014) – allow Thorpe to draw attention to the status of the audience as a gathered assembly. Like Crouch's

The Author, Thorpe also positions them to better experience the orated occurrences over, for example, visual representation. As Lulu Raczka writes in her review, it 'constructs a sense of the unseen' (2013) and does not reproduce images of the violence. Additionally, in downplaying the virtuosity of the performers and heightening the congregation within the theatre space, Thorpe accentuates nonviolence's mindful abandonment of egoism. This is matched in the narrative's depiction of the Breivik-like figure, as his violent reaction against 'the creeping Islamification of Europe' (2013: 35) resembles Nancy's conception of violence as wilful stupidity and self-assertion; a performative creation of his own (European) identity through concerted violence. Though the play seems to speak to the worth of individual action, it argues that success is often predicated on solidarity as seen in the final lines, spoken from the perspective of the person who incapacitates the gunman: 'I did that. I stopped it. Not on my own' (62).

The play's dramaturgy also actively seems to contest the gunman's ideology: it does not place emphasis on the individuality of its characters, gives the task of visualization to the audience, and queries acts of violence in a 'tribunal-like' setting while not 'reproducing' its effects. In these ways then, *There Has Possibly Been An Incident* could be said to have a 'nonviolent dramaturgy', shared in some measure by the 'unspectacular' *Mr Incredible*, *Escaped Alone* and *Some People Talk About Violence* (Raczka's review suggests that her own work was perhaps inspired by Thorpe) – which speaks to how 2010s British theatre represented violence overall. Furthermore, the performance invites the audience to reflect on their status as a gathered assembly, even if this is not for the direct purpose of starting a demonstration; as Raczka states, this 'gives the audience a sense of power' (6). Indeed, those assembled can potentially imagine and consider themselves as part of an interdependent, considerate and powerful collective: an actualizing public sphere. David Greig's *The Events* (Traverse, 2013) also offers a theatrical response to Breivik's attacks and has a comparable dramaturgy: the action includes a choir which, in the initial production, were local to each of the communities toured to – emphasizing the necessity for shared grief and solidarity. Though neither *The Events* nor *There Has Possibly Been An Incident* explicitly advocate nonviolence as always viable, or even successful, they present and puzzle it as a behaviour that can be used in a plurally performative way to begin to formulate and reiterate a less violent world, incorporating its considerations on dramaturgical, representational levels.

So, potential criticisms of irrelevancy or illegitimacy towards theatre and protest in affecting the public sphere can be countered by the two mediums utilizing one another's tactics and concerns. The 'black box absorption' of theatre noted by Balme may be broken by connecting to socio-political issues of interest, making such performances a partial node in the public sphere. Additionally, the representation of certain protests in theatre as in *E15*, *The Riots* or *Little Revolution* may grant them an awareness or alternate perspective not otherwise afforded in more mainstream mediums of the public sphere. Tactics of protest evidenced in Thorpe's dramaturgy – and indeed theatre that incurs protest – also affords plays a greater urgency in relevance to public debate. The connection to or the use of protest in theatre can enhance the performativity of performances as socio-politically relevant; just as the use of theatrical strategies in protest increase the performativity of protests as socio-politically legitimate.

Witnessing Black Witnessing in *ear for eye*

If *There Has Possibly Been An Incident* is exemplary of what could be called a non-violent dramaturgy, that of debbie tucker green's *ear for eye* pushes and pulls at the validity of violence and nonviolence through three distinct styles; specifically in relation to structural racism. This sprawling play not only contextualizes itself within the many traumas inflicted on Black people in the UK and the USA through the 2010s, but also peels back the layers of the systemic, racist violence represented to reveal its roots in legacies of slavery and segregation. *ear for eye* is also highly concerned with assembly: responding to the civil demonstrations organized by anti-racist organizations such as BLM and referring to its own status as a work embodied by a collection of (all but one) Black performers being themselves witnessed by an audience in the affluent, predominantly white metropolitan area of Chelsea. In many ways, *ear for eye* asks its audience to be witnesses to what Alissa V. Richardson calls 'Black witnessing'. Through an application of performativity alongside her work, *ear for eye* illustrates how Black witnessing – like nonviolence – looks to radically alter the performative effects caused by violence.

debbie tucker green is undoubtedly one of the most distinct and critically acclaimed British playwrights of the twenty-first century. Siân Adiseshiah and Jacqueline Bolton state that her 'ability to penetrate the socio-political textures of now in such dramaturgically invigorating and distinctive ways positions her as one of the most significant playwrights in contemporary times' (2020a: 17), cemented through *stoning mary* (2005) and *random* (2008). These both debuted at the Royal Court, which tucker green wrote prolifically for over the 2010s with other pieces including *truth and reconciliation* (2011) and *hang* (2015), which like *ear for eye* focus on the failings and limits of the justice system, particularly regarding the treatment of Black citizens. Indeed, Lynette Goddard poses that *random* and *hang* are informed by the Stephen Lawrence case, which 'highlighted the difficulties for Black people when relying on the state to execute justice' (2020a: 123). tucker green has also increasingly directed her own plays ensuring that, as Adiseshiah and Bolton note, her 'theatre intervenes in discourses of race and gender not only at the level of representation but also within the sphere of production' (2020a: 3). tucker green's interventions at the Court create a space where 'majority-white audiences are brought into frequently uncomfortable, typically compelling, encounters with black rage' (ibid.); a fact that at once emphasizes and challenges the specific limitations and accessibilities of 2010s British theatre as a site of the public sphere.

Though several critics and academics have compared tucker green against a milieu of white British playwrights such as Caryl Churchill, Sarah Kane and Harold Pinter (myself included: see Watson 2021a), she asserted in interview that 'I just don't see it [...] I think it says more about critics' reference points than my work' (Gardner 2005). As Goddard identifies, tucker green's 'style of using repetition and poetic word-play are [...] influenced by Black women's theatre, music, poetry, and spoken word' including work by Louise Bennett, Lauryn Hill and Ntozake Shange (2020a: 111). Similarly, the influence of tucker green can be seen, for example, in plays by Black women analysed later in this study: Jasmine Lee-Jones's explorations of fractured Black identity in *seven methods of killing kylie jenner*, and in the depiction of white liberal racism in Somalia Nonyé Seaton's *Rise of the Foot Soldier, Fall of the Kingdom*. Furthermore, Goddard argues that '[w]hile it is not unusual for theatre critics to compare plays with others that are thought to be similar in style or content', the tendency to compare work by Black British playwrights such as tucker green exclusively against established, white playwrights endorses 'ideas of white authors as the canonical norm against which all plays are measured while limiting the comparisons of Black plays on their own aesthetic terms' (2020a: 110). Though this study certainly looks to make connections and identify overarching concerns between 2010s British theatre-makers, Goddard's position informs an exploration of tucker green's dramaturgy (and, indeed, all Black writers that feature here) as distinctly existing in the British playwriting canon independently from what might troublingly be perceived as the 'necessary' influences of white theatre-makers.

ear for eye itself, which debuted at the Court in October 2018 before becoming a BBC film in 2021, opens on a stage image which exemplifies Goddard's concerns of judgement against a 'white norm' surely linked to wider socio-cultural biases. As Sally Hales's review describes, '[t]rapped inside an obscured glass box, people drift eerily in and out of view [...] A low primordial hum of white noise creates the feel of a thriller set in a dystopian future [...] The box rises, and the cast spills out' (2018). As the large glass cube hangs over the action, the performers are illuminated by a clinical, white glow that seeps through the smoke around them as a literalized toxic whiteness; even Hales's use of 'white noise' draws attention to the innocuous way whiteness is recognized as normality. *ear for eye*'s narrative is split into three distinct but connected parts, the first of which features scenes of Black British and African American characters in situations including two different families tutoring their sons in how to react to a police encounter; as well as individuals who have been wrongly incarcerated and subjected to police brutality; a conversation between two men on how to respond to societal racism; and protesters attending pro-Black rights marches. As Hales continues, the characters (and, indeed, the theatre-makers involved) 'circle their subject, slowly painting a verbal picture of their condition' (2018), that is, the experiences of Black people within fundamentally racist systems.

In a context of such socio-cultural inequalities Alissa V. Richardson, who specializes in Black experiences with the media, contends that the way Black identities view and are affected by the signs of structural racism can be classed as markedly distinct from other modes of spectating. Whereas media scholars have posed that 'distant witnessing is just as effective as firsthand viewing', these perspectives 'do not help us understand why black people are more likely to engage in either frontline or distant witnessing of police brutality than other ethnic groups' or why, for example, 'the thousands of international Black Lives Matter protesters who were not present to view Michael Brown's death firsthand [...] took up picket signs' (2020: 6).[9] Therefore, she formulates 'Black witnessing' to describe the specific experience of Black identities experiencing or perceiving systemic racism: which, in its capacity to urge action – or, 'take up picket signs' – is performative. Indeed, Richardson contends that Black witnessing makes individuals 'want to *do* something with what they just saw. And they want to link it to narratives they may have seen before' (5; emphasis in original). With her further definition of the term through three elements – an 'investigative editorial stance' to advocate for Black civil rights, a co-opting of 'racialized online spaces to serve as its ad-hoc news distribution service', and a reliance 'on interlocking black public spheres [...] to engage diverse audiences' (7) – Black witnessing is a process that performs a socio-cultural connecting of various instances of systemic racism and urges debate and demonstration against this structural violence.

An example of the performative 'desire to do' that is urged by Black witnessing is explored in *ear for eye* through two demonstrators of different generations. The elder (played by Angela Wynter) contrasts the pro-Black rights struggles of their youth with the contemporaneous fight of a young woman (Kayla Meikle). The presence of Wynter's character is indicative that, as Alexander notes, '[t]he iterative performances of the mid-century civil rights movement left behind a deeply ingrained culture structure, an intensely redolent set of background representations upon which later black protests felt compelled to draw' (2017: 25–6). So, groups like BLM were performative of a history of pro-Black rights movements, a (re)iteration that tucker green dramatizes in *ear for eye* as not only performative of the struggle against continuing socio-cultural racist violence, but thereby becoming a target for racist and state attacks to demonstrate their dominance and so performatively perpetuate structural racism. For example, the older character recounts 'when protest was a risk / when lynching was sport' (tucker green 2018: 13) and though the Black rights demonstrations of the 2010s generally posed fewer risks for their attendees than those in the 1960s, the monologue later delivered by the Young Woman troubles the comparison of contemporaneous violence against other periods and expresses how (specifically Black) protesters face serious risks.

The Young Woman played by Meikle narrates the experience of being in a demonstration attacked by police 'flashbang[s]' and 'tear gas', with 'crowds of us scattering vomiting crying panicking [...] aimed at/fired at' (65-8). The scene depicted evokes the demonstrations of the 2010s in which overwhelmingly non-violent Black rights protesters suffered violent encounters both from law enforcement and counter-political groups. Her description of the 'casual-white-cloud' (67) of the tear gas relates to the white haze that surrounds the performers at the play's opening: to be Black against a frame of whiteness in the UK and USA still carries a toxic threat of violence. Richardson writes how Black witnessing can have the effect of causing harm: whether through lingering trauma and resulting mental health issues, oppressive surveillance, social restrictions and punitive measures from the state, or indeed from the violence encountered at demonstrations. Though protests often organize under the threat of violence – with Butler even identifying them as 'mobilizing precarity, and even sometimes quite deliberately mobilizing the public exposure of the body' (2015: 150-1) – some demonstrations appear to 'invite' extreme subjective violence due to the performative identities of the attendees. One of Richardson's interviewees, the activist Brittany Ferrell, attests to this in comparison to the media framing of the 2017 Women's March at Washington, DC: 'our demonstrations were also peaceful, but [...] white women are not going to be met with the same type of aggression from police officers as a community of traumatized, torn black people' (2020: 69). tucker green shows that characters who experience and mobilize Black witnessing become targets: their performative identities, highlighted when on public demonstration, are bound with a reiterated, racist violence compulsively performed by the state.

The recounted march depicted by *ear for eye*'s Young Woman, along with the accounts of characters wrongly suspected, imprisoned or abused, also identifies the limits of nonviolence particularly when utilized by Black identities. Just as the son in scene one puts his 'hands up' in a near-universal sign of peaceful non-resistance against a hypothetical police officer, only to be told by his mother that this would be construed as 'a threat, threatening' (4; mirrored later by a UK family; 52), nonviolence appears to be of limited help for identities culturally ascribed as themselves violent and disposable. As Butler queries, '[d]oes the police officer who strengthens the hold to the point of death imagine that the person about to die is actually about to attack [...]? Or is it simply that this life is one that can be snuffed out because it is not considered a life[?]' (2020: 177). Though commentators such as Alexander have praised the performance of nonviolence in pro-Black rights protests in both the 1960s and 2010s, tucker green characterizes a counter perspective of frustration at the tactic's apparently slow efficacy. This is best seen in the four scenes between a young adult activist (Tosin Cole) and his older mentor (Nicholas Pinnock) set in the USA. As with Wynter's experienced demonstrator, the elder here is an avatar of the mid-century civil rights movements – which the younger student simultaneously praises and criticizes: 'I respect y'shit thatchu did [...] butchu need to respect and accept the fact that it failed' (51).

In what could be considered the central question of *ear for eye*, the Young Adult poses the non-violent tactics historically utilized by pro-Black rights movements (or 'progress') against urgent revolution ('change'): 'Progress is a slow bitch with a wandering mind that drags her bare feet / but / change kicks ass [...] Change is somethin thass *done* – gets shit done "progress" meanders' (49; emphasis in original). Against the advice for consideration and thoughtfulness posed by his mentor, the Young Adult responds to the violence around him with clarity of its presence rather than accepting its innocuousness:

Adult   ... (It) would lead to a bloodbath

Young Adult   this is a bloodbath.

Adult   Would lead to a war

Young Adult   this is a war

Adult   you couldn't survive the –

Young Adult   barely surviving now.

Adult   ... It won't help.

Young Adult   You don't know.

(30)

ear for eye does not appear to significantly lean towards the ideology of either of the debaters: though the Young Adult's dialogue is rousing, it borrows the problematically naive 'with us or against us' language of post-9/11 US politics as well as Nancy's 'anti-rationalization' view of violence ('change kicks ass'), while the degrading feminization of 'progress' speaks to the heterosexual, male-dominated direction of pro-Black rights movements.[10] Like the young boys of scenes one and eight who are both faced with the impossible question of how to respond to a police officer, the dialectics of the Adult and the Young Adult seem to face Black witnesses with another difficult question of how to respond to structural, racist violence.

Such dialogues occur frequently over part one of *ear for eye*. As Hales describes, the performers 'stand and sit around and on the kind of spartan chairs beloved of community and civic buildings. It's a public meeting, or a therapy group, or neither, or both' (2018). With experiences shared and parallels drawn between the experiences of the UK and US characters, tucker green is arguably visualizing a Black public sphere onstage. Richardson notes that in response to the generally Eurocentric, male-oriented and white bourgeois public sphere coined by Habermas, African American scholars developed an alternate perspective which 'draws energy from the vernacular practices of street talk and new musics, radio shows and church voices, entrepreneurship and circulation' (B. P. S. Collective 1995, 3; quoted in 2020: 18). Richardson adds that social media such as Twitter can be attributed here also, which were instrumental in disseminating information and organizing various pro-Black rights demonstrations through the 2010s. tucker green appears to address this as one of two friends at a demonstration 'WhatsApped [...] some shaky footage shot from far'; though the limits of witnessing without motivating action are also questioned here as the other, less mindful friend actively gets involved 'at the front' (37–9).

Alongside the doubt that theatre occupies space in the public sphere, fostering a specifically Black public sphere at the Court faces significant challenges – in no small part due to its situation in a square named after Hans Sloane, who gained significant wealth from his wife's inherited Jamaican slave holdings ('Fulke Rose' 2021).[11] The journalist Afua Hirsch has contended that theatre, and the Court as a specific case study, remains predominantly white and middle-class despite exploring issues of race and class 'in an environment that remains inaccessible to the vast majority of people most affected by those issues' (2010). Samara, too, writes that 'theatre remains a site of privilege, an imagining of what the colonized, the subjugated, and the oppressed *might* be thinking, or, worse still, what they *ought* to be thinking' (2021: 53; emphasis in original). Though the last criticism does not specifically apply to tucker green, and both statements perhaps inadvertently assert the 'whiteness' of theatre even as they condemn it, the Court nevertheless remained through the 2010s a questionable site for a Black public sphere. tucker green has arguably used these factors as a productive part of all her Court plays. For example, Mireia Aragay and Enric Monforte argue that *random* 'makes spectators racially self-conscious and asks them to step out of any rigidly defined identity category' (2013: 110). They believe tucker green uses such tactics to ultimately create empathy between the audience and her characters, also held to an extent by Marissia Fragkou and Goddard (2013).

Though part one of *ear for eye* illustrates several different communal dynamics that audience members could potentially sympathize with, the specificity of racial oppression as central to these dynamics elicits a 'racial self-consciousness' that presents Black experience in the USA and UK as an identity category that cannot be easily 'stepped into'. tucker green's common feature of nameless characters, which recurs in *ear for eye*, might suggest them as avatars for general identification – but, again, they reassert rigid identity categories such as 'US African American adult male' or 'UK Black British mum' (2). Racial self-consciousness becomes particularly pronounced in part three, in which a series of pre-filmed USA and UK '*Caucasian non-actors/actors*' (3) recite '*some Jim Crow laws*' (123) and '*excerpts from slave codes, British (Jamaican) codes and a few French codes. To be spoken direct to camera*' (129). By specifically having white non-actors/actors read the extracts, tucker green confronts the audience with a lineage of white oppressing rather than presenting victims of oppression. Though Aragay and Monforte identify tucker green's ability to make audiences racially self-conscious, specificity of identity with attendant historical and systemic violence means that 'stepping out' of identity categories is problematic and the limits of inter-racial empathy in this regard are made apparent.

The characterization of oppressed individuals who do not perform along traditional lines of victimhood is another motif of tucker green's. This is asserted by Adiseshiah and Bolton who, counter to Aragay and Monforte, contend that she withholds characters' 'assimilation into a liberal ethics of care […] [to] produce an aggressive but energizing demand for a different form of relationality' (2020b: 86). The situations represented in part one certainly demonstrate that the issues on display cannot be solved by established conventions of care due to the implicative network of systemic violence dramatized in part three. The recorded speakers appear almost as *deus ex machina* figures projected over the action, marking them as somewhat omnipotent and positions them similarly to what Hales calls 'the prison cell-like box' that has hung above the action 'as a threat' (2018). As Adiseshiah and Bolton continue: 'tucker green's plays work to produce non-normative performative acts, performative and politically enabling because through their repetition the possibility of de-authorising normative scripts of subjectivity emerges' (2020b: 72). Though guilt and remorse are certainly detectable in the speakers and the script names them familiarly such as 'Girl

Child' and 'Her Dad' (130), the performative repetition of the racist laws 'de-authorises normative scripts of subjectivity'. In other words, the speakers are repositioned as an interdependent matrix of systemic oppression, a matrix that, in the shared racial identities between them and much of the audience, implicates them together in the toxic fog of normative whiteness.

Adiseshiah and Bolton's analysis of tucker green's work parallels Paavolainen's conceptions of theatricality and performativity – an expansive view of systemic racism is mapped out even as performative actions are emphasized – as well as Balibar's Möbius strip of violence, with the ultra-subjective acts of part one of the play linked to the ultra-objective roots of part three. Furthermore, Richardson's concept of Black witnessing as 'linking narratives' and 'investigatory' could be understood as an embodied, perceptual stance that implicitly recognizes the overall connections of structural violence. This is best articulated in part two of *ear for eye*, which is an extended dialogue between a younger African American female and an older white American male (who tucker green's writing and directing suggests are a university student and her sociology tutor) as they debate a school shooting by two white gunmen.[12] Reflecting the tendencies of the media and political responses to these tragedies to compartmentalize the perpetrators as disconnected anomalies – often with 'mental health issues' – the tutor contends the murderers are 'Lone-Wolves, mentalists' (121), whereas the student understands them as part of an interconnected structural phenomenon proliferated by 'white supremacist white male' tendencies (119) summarized as: 'Bullets, bombs, burnings, hangings, lynchings, mutilations, shootings, destructions, defacing, torture, intimidations, abominations, perversions, organised, militarised, uniformed, hierarchical, vitriolic, ritualistic, political-death-cult-European-Protestant-immigrant-psychopathic white-sheet-wearing cross-burning motherfuckers [...] Terrorists' (120–1). Her diatribe, which begins with various terms of violent attacks, seems to linguistically 'peel back' these actions to reveal their interconnected 'ritualistic' nature and then pin them on a legacy of racially motivated violence.

The student's labelling of the gunmen as 'ritualistic' also evokes the theories of Girard, that violence can be 'spent' on those whose deaths will provoke no reprisal. It also speaks to shootings as being part of a performative history, 'a form of violence articulated through U.S. empire, antiblackness, and the spatial and political economy of late modern racial capitalism' (Mirpuri 2016: 76). Ironically, however, the violence of the two gunmen is framed as indivisible from the West's most infamous post-millennial nemeses: 'terrorists' – an affective word that can alert the truth of the structural horror that informs such violence. In moving from various situations of contemporaneous racism in part one, to a focused event thoroughly analysed in part two, and then to the filmed readings of part three, tucker green guides the audience through an investigative historical examination of racist violence: clearly and unflinchingly demonstrating that systemic racism has been sewn into the very make-up of UK and US law.

ear for eye is exemplary of what Adiseshiah and Bolton characterize as tucker green's 'refusal to disaggregate personal experiences of violence and abuse from broader political oppressions and histories' (2020b: 86). I contend that her implication of the (white members of the) audience within an interdependent matrix of performatively enacted systemic violence is not for the purposes of heightening a feeling of 'white guilt' – but to reframe the audience's perception to understand the position of the Black witness, even if the experiences of this position are beyond the full and empathetic understanding of white audience members. This 'energizing demand for a different form of relationality' (ibid.) can assist a fuller awareness of that which those who experience Black witnessing know: the connection between subjective acts of 'lone' gunmen with 'mental health issues', and structural racism. Following the historical traumas made plain in part three – and the audience's witnessing of Black witnessing earlier in the production – an epilogue has the young female demonstrator and the young male activist asking a question to the older mentor that has echoed through the play: 'Gimme one reason to not' (21; 135); or, why not enact revolutionary violence against an oppressive system? From their perspective, nonviolence appears to have failed as a useful 'dramaturgy' because of the slowness of its 'progress'. As *ear for eye* shows, Black lives are repeatedly proved to not matter against a background of whiteness; and until they are performatively ascribed as mattering – as grievable – nonviolence recourses to a too-slow progress. Even as protest is shown by tucker green to be worthy up to a point, the witnessing of Black witnessing by the audience poses whether the current methods for tackling structural racism will ever be sufficient.

Conclusion

This chapter's exploration of 2010s British theatre and protest evidences an ongoing anxiety about both mediums' socio-political efficacy and relevance to the public sphere. Somewhat paradoxically, the very awareness of theatre's potential entrapment within 'the black box of artistic absorption' rallied theatre-makers to contest this to varying degrees. *There Has Possibly Been An Incident* and *ear for eye* both demonstrate how an awareness of these limitations can productively attempt to utilize the assembled audience as part of the dramaturgy and even implement them as a rudimentary public sphere. This is created by making the spectators aware of their assembled status, stripping the onstage action of conventional theatricality and provoking them into a self-conscious reflection of their assembled identities. These effects utilize the plural performativity of the audience – the authorizing power of their assembly – and can grant a powerful sense of an interconnected, influential assembly or question how the matrix of systemic racism can be disentangled from such interconnections. As in Butler's definition of plural performativity, that assemblies can authorize and construct elements of their identity as a collective, these plays then borrow from protest to invite their audiences as a node of the public to reflect on who they are, what they want and what they can do.

As for the plays' explorations of nonviolence as a dramaturgical application to both protest and theatre, *ear for eye* seems far more wary of the strategy, framed as it is by the context of Black witnessing. It recognizes and emphasizes what Paavolainen calls the 'meshwork' of performativity but regards any alteration of it as 'slow progress' that does not react quickly enough to the violence that such progress seeks to combat. Still, tucker green's dramaturgy here does suggest that nonviolence may remain the most valid response: like *There Has Possibly Been An Incident*, interconnected and performative actions are foregrounded in *ear for eye* over character individuality; the narrative is orated rather than visualized; and violence is queried in a shared space. Facets of nonviolence then – particularly those pertaining to the alerting of violence without reproducing its effects and the reframing of normative subjectivity – are woven into the dramaturgy of these plays. As I argue in the next chapter, similar questions were a crucial part of 'climate crisis theatre', with the primacy of human subjectivity brought into doubt. Climate crisis representation in 2010s British theatre, as with all the other major socio-political issues explored in this work, affirms the contention evidenced here that theatre-makers diligently cultivated their 'node' of the public sphere, and that the tactics and concerns of protest found their way onto the stage as much as theatrical considerations found their way into the demonstrations beyond the walls of the theatre.

4

Climate Crisis

In the previous chapter, I contended that the 2010s will be remembered in Britain (if not globally) as a decade of protest. It may also become historicized as the decade when the adverse impact of human activity on the environment began to be seriously considered in the public sphere. In February 2010, it was reported that only 31 per cent of British adults believed it to be a reality (Jowit 2010); by October 2021, 75 per cent stated that they were worried by its impacts (ONS 2021). Towards the end of the 2010s, the phrase 'climate change' began to be replaced with terminology that better expressed a necessary urgency: climate *crisis* and *emergency*;[1] as well as the highlighting of the extent of our damage to the planet through the naming of a new geological epoch, 'Anthropocene' (Carrington 2016) or, 'Capitalocene', which more fairly places the onus of this damage on the Global North and capitalist structures (Moore 2017). Furthermore, research over the decade showed that art is a better motivator and engager on climate crisis issues than scientific discourse (Jasanoff 2011; Kluwick 2011; Hoffman 2015): as Catherine Love summarizes, 'educating the public about climate change will only go so far' (2020: 232). Fortunately, adhering to Balme's contention that theatre is a partial yet responsive node in the public sphere, just as the British public further engaged with climate crisis in the 2010s, so did theatre. With an understanding of climate crisis as informed by violence and performativity, this chapter explores 2010s British theatre concerned with ecological issues.[2]

The Violent Performativity of Resource Exploitation in *Oil*

As touched on in Chapter 1, violence has traditionally been theorized anthropologically. The philosopher Newton Garver, for example, states that violence is grounded specifically in the human and cannot occur in nature: 'a violent blizzard is nothing but a blizzard with very great force. The same is true of a violent sea and other bits of violence in nature. It is simply some aspect of nature manifested to us with especially great force' (2009: 171). Garver's position assumes an essential human/nonhuman distinction which was increasingly challenged through the 2010s: not least by posthumanist theory, which is described by its advocate Cary Wolfe as seeking to 'throw out the distinction between "human" and "animal" – and indeed throw out the desire to think that we can index our treatment of various beings, human or not, to some biological, taxonomic designation' (2018: 125). Wolfe believes this taxonomic designation to be key to an assumed human superiority that authorizes exploitation. Furthermore, the advancements of climate science demonstrate that such human activity escalates a 'feedback loop' which returns as catastrophe against the ecosystem – humanity included. The environmental philosopher Adrian Parr articulates this as '[b]ecause human activities cause this environmental damage, our species is culpable for a crime we are committing against ourselves' (2018: 58–9). The effects of climate crisis, then, could be termed a 'posthumanist violence'; human activity is implicated in Garver's 'bits of violence in nature' and so, even by a humanist definition of violence, the environmental catastrophes of the Capitalocene are violent rather than being an 'especially great force'.

The violence of climate crisis is not always as discernible as catastrophic occurrences such as 'a violent blizzard', just as it is not as easily reducible to each (British) person placing 'ten thousand tonnes of CO_2' into the atmosphere; or 'the weight of the Eiffel Tower' as described in Duncan Macmillan's *Lungs* (Studio Theatre, Washington, 2011; 2016: 170) – which is credited as among the first British plays to make an 'urgent, knowing statement' on the climate crisis (Angelaki 2017: 113). Instead, the Capitalocene has resulted from, and effects, what Rob Nixon calls 'slow violence': the 'long dyings' that imperceptibly take place beyond normative human understanding – particularly from the more secure perspective of the Global North (2011: 2). Comparable to systemic violence (of which it could be categorized as a form of), slow violence gradually increases the plight of climate crisis and constructs conditions that damage ecosystems and displace populations. It again highlights the problem of perception: as Nixon asks, 'how do we both make slow violence visible yet also challenge the privilege of the visible[?]' (15). Relating to Paavolainen, slow violence invites a performative understanding of climate crisis: it does not emerge from extravagant acts, but rather from a meshwork of small, often imperceptible actions and behaviours that 'add up'. For example, the philosopher Timothy Morton writes that '[e]very time I start my car or steam engine I don't mean to harm Earth, let alone cause the Sixth Mass Extinction Event [...] Furthermore, I'm not harming Earth! My key turning is statistically meaningless' (2018: 8). Though Morton's key turning is not strictly violent, the reiteration of this activity is performative of wider, slow violence – as well as being performative (meaning-making and, indeed, condition-making) of the social, political and economic identity of the privileged Global North.

To perceive the Möbius strip of Morton's ecological activity loops, as well as trace the effects of slow violence across the generations following their genesis, the normative ways in which humans understand time, effect and action must be unsettled or supplemented with alternate imaginations. Inherent in representations of climate crisis, as Ella Hickson states, is a 'formal challenge of how we tell the size of the stories we need to tell' (Solnick 2020). Her own, theatrical response is *Oil*, which debuted at London's Almeida Theatre in October 2016 with direction from Carrie Cracknell. Preceding her experimental works *The Writer* (also at the Almeida, 2018) and *Anna* (NT, 2019), *Oil* marked Hickson's move to more grandiose theatre after the nightclub-set, site-based *Hot Mess* (Fringe, 2010), and the university common room drama of *Boys* (HighTide, Halesworth, 2012). *Oil*'s narrative follows May, played by Anne-Marie Duff, as she forgoes her life on a pre-industrial farm, becoming enraptured by the 'magic' of a kerosene lamp. Seeking a better life for her daughter Amy (Yolanda Kettle), May spends the next 150 years – the 'Age of Oil' – in pursuit of the fleeting resource. The expansive story, as Matt Trueman's review describes, 'lets us time travel, giving us a gods-eye view of our own little lives' (2016a). The slow ageing of May and Amy is a trope of magic realism that comes from, for example, *Orlando* (1928); but rather than the sexed metamorphosis of Virginia Woolf's hero/ine, May's change is from part of a rural, familial group into an individualist capitalist engendered by the power of oil.

Oil's magic realism seems apt for the eponymous subject. As Alireza Fakhrkonandeh writes in his own analysis of the play, it is 'the most vital, valuable, ubiquitous and yet, paradoxically, invisible commodity of modern and contemporary global economics and history' (2022: 1776). Nixon quotes of the journalist Ryszard Kapuściński that 'oil creates the illusion of a completely changed life, life without work, life for free [...] in this sense it is a fairy tale and like all fairy tales a bit of a lie' (Kapuściński 1965: 36; quoted in

2011: 72). Nixon surveys how oil's semi-fantastical aspect has been seized on in fiction, citing Jennifer Wenzel's discernment of a 'petro-magic-realist' genre in Nigerian literature (2006), with writers articulating how 'the undifferentiated oil blessing becomes institutionalized as class distinction and racial segregation: nature's unbounded bounty becomes incrementally bounded, privatized, partitioned' (Nixon 2011: 83; see also Fakhrkonandeh 2022). Hickson also realizes the twin aspect of oil as magic and exploitative through May. Her gradual transformation from exploited to exploiter is signalled explicitly by a costume change with each period, which takes place front-and-centre stage as Lucy Carter's lighting and Luke Hall's videography project historical scenes on and around her. May's behaviour, too, becomes more authoritative – the performativity of which appears predicated on the exploitation of others, particularly the peoples of Iran, Libya and Iraq. So, the 'magic' of oil that effects May's transformation is her increasing ability to bound, privatize and partition it for personal gain. As May states of herself: 'There's still blood on my hands from hauling myself up' (2016: 77). Furthermore, Hickson's magic realism is informed by the work of Caryl Churchill: specifically, the neoliberal-hijacked feminism of *Top Girls*; the collision of corporate exploitation with the rural and mythical in *Fen*; and the time-hopping of *Cloud Nine* (Dartington College, 1979) which, as Marco De Ambrogi's review of *Oil* compares, also 'reflects on the emancipation of women and the change in the power balance between colonial empires' (2016: 13).

Oil's specific interrogation of female contribution to climate crisis is made clear in the centrality of its mother and daughter relationship. As Angelaki writes, Hickson pays 'specific attention to female lineage. As women, through childbearing, create the future of humanity, so too are they the agent for its destruction' (2019: 16). This touches on how criticisms of women who have and raise children as potential ecosystem destroyers are problematic in their gendered blame (as I have explored elsewhere; see Watson 2023). However, the fear this derives from connects to the population growth that has been achievable because of fossil fuels – and potential overpopulation and fight for resources once they are depleted. Birth and destruction, then, are seen in the narrative's charting of the Age of Oil as well as being physicalized by May and Amy. It is also evident in the narrative cycle that ends where it began, with its characters living in scarcity and Amy now entranced by a new, 'magical' energy source (cold fusion) that undermines the illusion of capitalism's exponential growth and offers, as Angelaki continues, a caustic take on 'past-future and ignorance-knowledge binaries' (2019: 19). These features espouse a dramaturgical move away from the linearity of 'patriarchal realism' to reflect the 'cycle' of the ecosystem. As Morton writes, 'human interference has a loop form, because ecological and biological systems are loops' (2018: 6), which Patrick Lonergan believes is echoed by Hickson, whose 'use of theatrical form registers the sense of "weirdness" that arises from ecological awareness' (2020: 38). Feminist, anti-capitalist and ecological concerns, then, tie together in *Oil*'s 'weird' and 'looped' dramaturgy.

The cycles that *Oil* represents, particularly that of the relationship between humans and the ecosystem, can be described as performative in their operation: 'certain phenomena only exist in the doing of them – [...] they have to be continually performed to exist at all' (Szerszynski, Waterton, and Heim 2003: 2–3). That is, human activity alters the reality of the nonhuman, which can then return to effect humanity – sometimes, as Parr writes, violently. Illustratively, though *Oil*'s narrative is cyclical, its end is similar but different to its beginning because of the resource manipulation May has helped to propagate, ultimately causing violence and new forms of scarcity. Influenced by Morton, Katie Schaag also writes on the performative cycle of human activity through the case study of plastics – the use and disposal of which performatively affect the materiality of the ecosystem through the process of human behaviour and action. This then returns to our biological materiality through micro- and nano-plastic consumption: 'a function of the continuous performativity of plastic molecules within the interconnected "mesh" of the body [...] dissolv[ing] boundaries between self and other, biological and chemical, living and inert' (Schaag 2020: 19). Though *Oil* does not specifically dramatize the ways in which fossil fuels literally enter human biological systems, it does more generally demonstrate how the processes through which oil is used materially affect us.

These performative processes often take generations before their effects are fully understood. For example, though microplastics were identified in the environment in the 1970s (Buchanan 1971), it has taken around half a century to discern their ability to reduce human fertility (Swan and Colino 2021) – somewhat ironically, given overpopulation fears. Such slow violence became increasingly recognized in fossil fuels over the 2010s: with the high energy use of the Global North powering its nations and their citizens' performative identities while encroaching violence elsewhere in the world, spatially and temporally. To view this, Hickson theatrically 'zooms-out' to demonstrate how performative actions, such as May's fight for Libyan oil reserves to preserve British lives (and her and her daughter's lives specifically) that benefit from food, cars and commodities (2016: 59; 77) create violent situations later with May, now an MP, mobilizing a 'second Iraq War' (93) to secure more oil in a theoretical 2021. As Fakhrkonandeh deduces, 'the historical structure and vision of the play is reminiscent of Benjamin's "angel of history"' (2022: 1799): collapsing the 'distinction between temporal dimensions (of past and future) into a perpetual and irredeemable moment of catastrophic Now' (1801). Underlining how much Britain depends on oil, and how long this dependency has lasted, Hickson suggests that it has seeped into all corners of society, culture and human relations; particularly highlighting those advancements that have assisted in improved conditions for women, such as contraception (59) and higher status occupations (67). May's improving positions are regarded by Kimberly Skye Richards as a move 'away from clichés about male oil executives as cutout villains of fossil capitalism to spotlight the journey of a single mother determined to better the situation of her child' (2017: 582); but, like *Top Girls*, this particularity is troubled in relationship to feminism since May is certainly not actively improving women's lives: especially seen in her utilization of the Iraqi woman Aminah (Lara Sawalha) to retrieve her daughter, even after May has declared war on her country (94).

Indeed, *Oil* poses that the comforts of consumer culture, pro-environmental liberal values and even the connections between individuals under capitalism are powered by the eponymous fuel. The production's dramaturgy aligns with Parr's argument that fossil fuel use is densely intertwined with capitalism and consumerism, 'which combine to produce a terribly exploitative, oppressive and violent structure that has come to infuse all aspects of everyday life' (2018: 59). If oil has powered the actualities of life, the performativity of this behaviour has also allowed the symbolic 'death' of fossilized resources to seep into interpersonal relations: best seen in the juxtaposition of businesswoman May being confronted with the ghost of her rural husband, Joss (Tom Mothersdale): 'I bought it, I worked for it [...] there's no life in it – no blood' (81). Hickson poses that the performative actions generated by oil, allowing humans to exploit and sever themselves from the nonhuman, appear to symbolically return in ecological processes by siphoning human vitality, corroding interdependency and making humans vulnerable to capitalist violence. The slow violence demonstrated in *Oil*, then, is located in exploitation against the planet, which returns to enable inter-human violence due to resource dependence: not only through the explicit, subjective violence of international wars and colonial oppression but also in the systemic and symbolic violence of performative relations. There is a further 'weird loop', then, in the Möbius strip of such interrelated, posthumanist violence.

Though Lonergan discerns that the play spoke to its immediate context, debuting 'only four months after the Brexit referendum had demonstrated that nostalgia for Empire remained a damagingly potent force' while taking an 'unambiguously negative perspective on its imperial past', he states that *Oil* 'transcends those particulars, sweeping across continents and historical epochs [...] seeking to enhance the audience's capacity to think on "more than one scale at once" themselves' (2020: 38). The production's affect in this regard is evident in the reviews and responses of De Ambrogi, Skye Richards and Trueman – among others. The sense of scale created by Luke Hall's videographical projections, Hickson's narrative and Cracknell's theatricality is nevertheless grounded by specific relations between characters. These are focused on in various places and time periods, while the narrative itself breaks down the past–future binary to examine a broader conceptualization of the scale of slow violence. Central to this are May and Amy. The connection and tension between the ecological scale of *Oil* and the mother–daughter relationship is the core dramaturgical conflict of the production: illustrated in May's interaction with her mother (Ellie Haddington) before she abandons the farm: 'MAY. Mother does best for her babby. [*sic*] / MA SINGER. Mother does best for the whole house' (25). In actions done out of love for her daughter, May performatively causes emotional isolation, war, and climate crisis. Consumed by desire to do the 'best for her babby', she forgets 'the whole house'. Rather than simply blaming climate crisis on a lack of altruism, Hickson troublingly poses that the primal urge to do better for oneself and one's children – familial love – is destroying the planet. Or, at least, the version of this love mutated by human dependency on oil is destroying the planet, a dependency predicated on the performative consumerism and exploitation of the Global North, which violently alters ecological processes such as, in another 'weird loop', familial love.

The narrative and production of *Oil* are centred on perspective, particularly, that of exploitation and violence. It understands violence as 'posthumanist', as more expansive than the humanism espoused by Garver – merged in the relationship of humans and their ecosystem as the work of Parr, Wolfe and Nixon show. Reflecting Morton's ecological loops, as Lonergan argues, *Oil* reveals the process of how resource exploitation – which fuels the performative actions and behaviour of British citizens – return violently on (and in) humans. Hickson's dramaturgy, relatively untethered from time and space by (petro-)magic realism, depicts a world where fossil fuels are irrevocably intertwined with human actions, culture and relations. In its extraction, oil fosters values of dependency and materiality that are inevitably destructive. The performativity of Britain as a nation and on the individual level of its citizens as 'fuelled' by oil is therefore presented as causing slow violence. By imaginatively and affectively constructing multiple levels of scale through theatrically 'zooming-out' while 'zooming-in' to the interpersonal drama of May and Amy, *Oil* contends that it is the entrenched, cyclical actions of cultural behaviour that perpetuate self-destructive violence against the ecosystem and ourselves.

Performative Taxonomical Violence and *The Children*

Oil demonstrates that human relations are caught in the same ecological (performative) processes that govern the rest of the ecosystem. Another play that formally and thematically balances posthumanism and anthropocentrism in its dramaturgy is Lucy Kirkwood's *The Children*, directed by James Macdonald at the Royal Court – the production of which highlights this 'looped' situation of humanity in the ecosystem with humans as both 'parents' and 'children'. As theories of posthumanism explicate, understanding humanity as necessarily implicated in the environment (rather than as detached sovereigns over it) is vital not only for tackling the climate crisis but also for comprehending inter-human forms of violence; in other words, posthumanist theory can advance humanist objectives. Informed by the work of Cary Wolfe, this section takes an analysis of *The Children* to evidence the play's engagement with how the taxonomical, performative assertion of humans at the top of the ecosystem sanctions violence against those deemed 'lower down', whether they are resources, animals or other humans denoted as inferior.

What Wolfe calls the 'pernicious ethical hierarchy' of anthropocentric authority (2018: 125) – of rating different lives and beings based on their perceived ethical value or ontological importance – can be understood as performative. In other words, the assertion of humanity as dominant authorizes violence, oppression and engineering of the nonhuman, which in turn proves humanity as superior and justified in its dominance, as seen in *Oil*: a positive feedback loop of exploitation. The utterance, attitude or behaviour of taxonomic superiority is performative of climate crisis: everything 'below' the human is ours to do with as we will. In the Global North, such ideology has developed in part from humanism and human exceptionalism: evident, for example, in the Renaissance-era philosophy of Francis Bacon, whose *Novum Organum* (1620) conceives man as unable to attain knowledge or affluence without conquest over nature and is therefore pitted against it. Such anthropocentrism and assumed 'inheritance of the Earth' likely derives from the Judeo-Christian tradition. That said, as the theologian James Rimbach contends, '[o]nly by the most heavy-handed and insensitive treatment can the bible be used to support the view that the natural world is "at our disposal"' (1982: 206) which he traces to capitalism, as '[e]xploitation and compulsive manipulation were simply not possible on so vast a scale in pre-industrial, pre-technocratic societies' (Santmire 1970: 57; quoted in Rimbach 1982: 206). So, the deployment of hierarchical denotation as justification for conquest was exacerbated when industrialization and colonization were solidifying other taxonomies like class and race for additional forms of domination.

Morton, however, collectively understands these phenomena as driven by 'agrilogistics', a logic established by the development of agriculture that territorializes, utilizes and often harms the environment; and has in turn led to 'the contemporary concept of self', as well as 'patriarchy, the impoverishment of all but a very few, [and] a massive and rigid social hierarchy' (2018: 44). Agrilogistics, then, inform the taxonomical and portioning systems that govern contemporary life – and which have been historically engineered for modes of control and oppression. Though contemporary life is unimaginable without agrilogistics, structural violence is nevertheless woven into its advancements. It also feeds into Nixon's concept of slow violence: farming the land for (relatively) short-term gain, only for it to eventually become unusable. So, a humanist ethical hierarchy enables exploitative and violent attitudes: whether informed by Judeo-Christian tradition, capitalist assumptions, normative human perception of time, or an agrilogistical interrelation of these elements. Somewhat antithetical to these positions is posthumanism, which 'fundamentally decentres the human in relation to the world', described by Wolfe as giving a 'vocabulary that can describe the complex ways that human beings are intertwined with and shaped by the nonhuman world in which they live', that looks to get beyond 'the old humanist taxonomies' (2018: 118–19). Like Rimbach, Wolfe locates the emergence of a taxonomic ideology in the cultural advancements of the last four centuries, specifically 'the Enlightenment idea of the self' which 'everything in our culture encourages us to invest in' (123) – an advancement that has, as *Oil* illustrates, corroded human interdependence between one another and with our own ecosystem.

Fed by the material comforts of capitalism and growing disconnection from others, the egoistic categorization of 'the self' in the Global North especially has directly contributed to the furthering exploitation of the ecosystem and the hardening of taxonomic lines. Essentialist, autonomous ideas of 'selfhood' enables the theoretical separation of humans from nonhumans and divides humans themselves into hierarchical categories, with the civilized and civilizing white, ableist, heterosexual European cis-male at the head of the world order (Yusoff 2018). The nonhuman/human distinction, Wolfe argues, feeds directly into the taxonomies that regulate identity inequalities and justify inter-human violence: 'As long as you take it for granted that it's OK to commit violence against animals simply because of their biological designation, then that same logic will be available to you to commit violence against any other being, of whatever species, human or not, that you can characterize as a "lower" or more "primitive" form of life' (2018: 125).

The translatability of this oppression is evident in plays such as Churchill's *Far Away*, Dawn King's *Foxfinder* (Finborough, 2011) and Stef Smith's *Human Animals* (RC, 2016), where the persecution of nonhuman life enables and 'spills over' into inter-human violence. This demonstrates that the current cultural modes through which humans conceptualize their place in the environment, both temporally and as assumed sovereigns, may be root causes of exploitation. Moreover, such modes may even be a source of performatively authorizing further systemic violence on those who, as Wolfe writes, 'are assumed to be lower or lesser and who in that sense somehow "deserve it"' (ibid.). So, a humanist ethical hierarchy, and normative human perception (of time), can exonerate certain forms of violence as 'permissible'. Though *The Children* does not explore all the factors discussed here, it does – I contend – offer a posthumanist analysis of the cultural assumptions of 'the self', temporality and the taxonomic authorization of exploitation and violence. Furthermore, in combining posthuman elements with naturalistic 'anthropo-scenes', *The Children* arguably better demonstrates the mobility of taxonomic violence between the nonhuman and the human.

Playing on different connotations to 'children' in relation to the environment including responsibility and autonomy, Kirkwood productively dramatizes human agency in a context of climate crisis while collapsing distinctions between the human and nonhuman. It continues Kirkwood's highly successful and laudable playwriting career in the 2010s, following *NSFW* (RC, 2012) and *Chimerica*, and precedes *Mosquitoes* (2017) and *The Welkin* (2020), both for the National Theatre. *The Children* opened on the Jerwood Theatre Downstairs in November 2016 before transferring to Broadway in 2017 and followed Macdonald's production of *Escaped Alone* on the same stage at the Court earlier that year; Corrie Tan's review even poses that 'it inhabits that same universe of apocalypse and tea' (2016). The production enjoyed favourable reviews and the play has since been produced in Toronto, Melbourne, Sydney, Dublin, Chicago, Houston and Frankfurt between 2017 and 2019. The sometimes slow, methodical action of *The Children* is set on a '*small cottage on the east coast*'; picturesque, though on a slight, barely noticeable tilt as '[t]*he land beneath it is being eroded*' (4) Billington describes Miriam Beuther's set as 'meticulous in creating a world of precarious normality' (2016) and Tan notes how Peter Mumford's lighting design illustratively bathes it 'with a dying of the light – the warmth of a coastal sunset' (2016). These indicate the innocuous domesticity of disaster that climate crisis threatens, as well as the intertwinement of human elements (the cottage and characters) with the nonhuman (the sun, the coast), and the time-based, nostalgic end of 'the old' – in cataclysm, or through a change to a new mode of being.

The action that these scenographic elements frame centres on the visitation of Rose (played by Francesca Annis) to the seaside cottage home of her old friends and colleagues Hazel (Deborah Findlay) and Robin (Ron Cook). All three are retired nuclear scientists in their sixties who once worked at the nearby power station, which has since been damaged in a similar incident to Japan's 2011 Fukushima Daiichi disaster – noted in Tan's review (2016), as well as by Kirkwood herself (Morrison 2016). As Hazel recounts: 'I saw the road cracked down the middle [...] I saw the tide had gone out [...] and then I saw the wave' (2016: 11). Like, as Julia Hoydis mentions, the 'unexpected guest plays' of Harold Pinter (2020: 84), Rose has a disruptive, ulterior motive. She has returned on an ultimately fatal mission to repair the station and halt its radioactivity, while looking to recruit an older team to assist her in place of the currently assigned younger engineers – again, modelled after the 'Skilled Veteran Corps' clean-up team for Fukushima. As Rose challenges them: 'You have power, and you've both already had long and full lives' (53). Though initially met with hostility, wilful ignorance, and the 'scapegoat' of being around for their now-adult children, Rose's request is eventually accepted. Yet the audience is left with ambivalent symbols: Robin tidies a plumbing spill, Hazel practises yoga and Rose states she could 'hear the bells [...] [f]rom the church under the water' (79).[3] As the audience too hears them ring at the close of the production, these could be interpreted as a call to arms to combat ecological damage, or a melancholy reminder of the finitude of human civilization despite King Canute-like efforts to, as Rose comments, '[h]old back the tide' (15).

The merging of human and nonhuman elements in the image of the submerged bells is reflected through the rest of the play, often in the seemingly innocuous dialogue of its characters. For example, Robin, who suffers from radiation exposure, expresses: 'I feel eroded' (64), and Rose jokes that if she had a baby at her age '[i]t would have flippers' (59).[4] Even their names, as Hoydis notes, 'all reference (quintessentially British) nature' (2020: 85). The characters' relation to the nonhuman figures them as indelibly part of an ecological system which they are hesitant to altruistically preserve. Specifically, Hazel and Robin have permanently moved to their cottage as their home is in sight of the power plant – they have literally turned a blind eye to ecological disaster. As Hazel states, '[w]e'd earned the right, on this one occasion, just to say: at our time of life, we simply cannot deal with this' (21). They also seem to have chosen their own satisfaction over the environment on more than 'this one occasion', as Rose berates Robin: 'Name one thing, in your life, that you wanted and couldn't have' (61). Blood becomes a symbol of exploitation here: Robin jokes that Hazel 'drinks the blood of virgins' (43), and that their needy daughter is a '[v]ampire' (37). Hazel even defines 'blood' along with 'semen' as 'oil-based products' (5), connoting anthropocentric exploitation cemented by her action of startlingly punching Rose at the play's opening and causing a nosebleed – drawing her blood. Robin states 'we've decided that natural decay is unnatural' (70), espousing a self-betterment and preservation that Wolfe might call Enlightenment-influenced individualism. In *The Children*, such egoism is sacrificial, or ritualistic in Girard's sense: to live and grow, something or someone else – in the present or the future – must be exploited.

Additional symbols that appear in *The Children* are milk and eggs. The power station has a 'great white dome like a duck egg' (13); during the disaster Hazel is in her kitchen, and describes 'the eggs, they started shaking in the box and – this sounds stupid, but I thought they're hatching [...] a Gremlin' (10); she also notes the tsunami 'looked like the sea was boiling milk' (11); and Rose tells Hazel she can't have milk in her tea because it exacerbates her cancer: 'Dairy promotes cell production [...] That's why we give milk to babies' (72). The connection milk and eggs have to infancy, fertility and growth is highlighted while grounding them in the human and in potential disaster. As culinary items that are, crucially, not on a vegan diet, they inform Rose's belief that humans should be '[l]earning to live with less' (30). They are also further examples of ambivalent images in *The Children* alike to Morton's 'looping logic': of both life and decay, the inseparability of the human and nonhuman, and small actions in multiplication being performative of crises. Hazel offers Rose milk, a boiling-milk wave causes widespread disaster; Robin boils eggs to eat, the duck-egg dome sits atop a reactor that may begin 'spilling into the sea' (51). They hint at wasted potential – of things not born and infants not fed by their parents – engineered as consumer choices that performatively affect the ecosystem.

The symbols of blood, eggs and milk point to forms of sacrificial exploitation, which connects to the ethical hierarchy identified by Wolfe and its justification of violence inflicted on those taxonomically 'lower down'. Like Macdonald's earlier production, *Escaped Alone*, the cast and characters are all over sixty (Deborah Findlay, notably, stars in both). This is a significant dramaturgical factor in the discourse around climate crisis in 2010s Britain. Individuals around this age – 'those infantilised as "baby boomers"' as Jen Harvie writes (2018: 332) – represented (for some) a generation that had an abundance of wealth, opportunity, and social infrastructure that squandered the world's resources and 'pulled up the ladder' against those that came after (Nuccitelli 2016). For example, as Evans and Giroux state, bearing comparison to Kirkwood's symbol of eggs, '[y]outh have become a marker for a mode of disposability in which their fate is defined largely through the registers of a society that readily discards resources, goods, and *people*' (2015: 58; emphasis in original). Hazel and Robin's initial response to the disaster, of 'we simply cannot deal with this', seems to vindicate these concerns – in this case, those born later or yet to be born – will pay the price for the older generation's comfort and apathy.

Hazel and Robin's performative identity construction of casting themselves as having earned ease and leisure 'at our time of life' in this sense 'kicks the can' of crisis down the road, where the slow violence of their local plant's radiation will only exacerbate. Valerie Barnes Lipscomb views 'all ages as performative' (2016: 3): as she elaborates on Butler, 'the repetition of an action over time creates reality', therefore 'the repeated performance of a particular age [...] creates the semblance of the reality of that age' (42). As *Oil* depicts, this performativity is bound up in consumerism, particularly in the Global North. The disposability of those taxonomically 'lower down' seems to extend to Rose who, suffering from terminal cancer, is dismissively told by Hazel to 'dig her own grave' in response to the call to repair the station (46). With Rose's pressing mortality, she deems herself as disposable, as '"killable but not murderable"' (Wolfe 2018: 125) – a self-understanding that she convinces Hazel and Robin to share as they have 'already had long and full lives' (53). Hoydis articulates that the play's 'underlying ethical question is about the hierarchy of values, of whether sacrifice and death for the greater good of the community should take priority over the (by comparison short-term) protection of one's own life' (2020: 92). Although deconstructive of the neoliberal and Enlightenment understanding of the self, this acknowledgement of the specifically older self as disposable is problematic. It too evidences violence by taxonomic registration: from this perspective, the older generation has little status in the humanist ethical hierarchy because of their increasingly apparent ontological finitude: if they are going to die soon (relative to others), why not sacrifice themselves?

Though Rose approaches the catastrophic situation with altruism, even if her motives seem partly driven by redemption and self-destruction, there is an element of ageism in her wilful disposability. The optics of Kirkwood – a writer, at the time, in her early thirties – having three older characters sacrifice themselves to amend past mistakes and preserve the young potentially hints at the 'hyped-up intergenerational "conflict"' Harvie identifies which 'work[s] against the best interests of almost everyone' (2018: 333), fuelled by the contexts of climate crisis, the fallout from the 2007–9 financial crisis, and the perceived generational divide of the Brexit vote which occurred a few months before *The Children*'s debut. That said, Kirkwood certainly does not depict a caricaturist, selfish cast of 'baby boomers'.[5] Instead, as Billington writes, the audience must debate who 'has the more active conscience' between Hazel and Rose (2016), though both stances seem to lead at least partly to a form of taxonomic-informed violence. Further comparison to *Escaped Alone* is warranted here, in that ageism in Churchill's play seems to simmer in the embodied, symbolic violence gleaned from the four women's dialogue, rather than posed as a dialectical tension as in *The Children* – likely in part due to Churchill and Kirkwood's respective ages. Harvie contends that *Escaped Alone* invites 'audiences to listen and pay attention to old women for their demonstrable self-reflexivity and accumulated knowledge' (2018: 343). Their singing of The Crystals shows they can still be 'youthful', however; as another ageing Churchill character queries in *Here We Go* (NT, 2015), '*are* you any wiser when you're older I feel sixteen all the time' (39; quoted in Harvie 2018: 343; emphasis in original).

The characters of *The Children* also demonstrate behaviour performative of youth: they dance, can be petty and are playful – Robin even enters on a salvaged children's bike (23). Much like the symbolic merging of the human and the nonhuman, age distinctions are collapsed somewhat through the characters' performative behaviour. This is not to say that 60-year-olds are never playful – in fact, audience members commented on the 'authenticity' of the characters (Morrison 2016) – rather that they demonstrate performative behaviours that are not normatively associated with their age. Like the twenty-first century US plays explored by Lipscomb, *Escaped Alone* and *The Children* subvert 'cultural norms about age through the employment of theatrical conventions' (2016: 117), and challenge 'age as [a] binary that privileges youth' (154). But both conflations here (of human/nonhuman and young/old) relate to Nixon's concept of slow violence; as he contends, [v]iolence, above all environmental violence, needs to be seen – and deeply considered – as a contest not only over space, or bodies, or labor, or resources, but also over time' (2011: 8). Slow violence then brings attention to nonhuman exploitation as justified by attitudes of human taxonomic supremacy in addition to the perceptual inability to fully comprehend the effects of such exploitation over time. To regard slow violence requires non-normative ways of perceiving time, which is perhaps why standardized age identities are troubled by the performativity of *The Children*'s characters.

Unlike the temporality of *Escaped Alone*, which is ruptured by the soothsaying of Mrs Jarrett, the action of *The Children* is more traditionally realist: linear and continuous to the point of being 'meticulous' (Tan 2016) and 'slow-burning' (Billington 2016). Running for nearly two hours with no interval, the audience witnesses Rose's measured disclosure of her visit's purpose and the eventual persuasion of Hazel and Robin in 'real time' (Kirkwood quoted in Morrison 2016). Sarah Hemming, interviewing James Macdonald, recognizes his productions as 'slow theatre' that 'redefine the scope of naturalism [...] dramatis[ing] a world apparently antithetical to drama, quietly enfolding the audience in the experience of the characters' (2018). She cites his direction of Churchill's *Here We Go*, Annie Baker's *John* (NT, 2018), and to which could be added his later collaboration with Kirkwood, *The Welkin*, Cordelia Lynn's *Sea Creatures* (Hampstead, 2023) which shares many thematic and tonal similarities with *The Children*, and, in some ways, *Escaped Alone* – even with dialogue that sounds 'sped up' rather than 'slowed'. Hemming's description bears similarity to Una Chaudhuri's 'anthropo-scenes', of the 'reckonings we must now make in our little rooms' common to the realist tradition which can 'reveal the "footprints of hyperobjects" all around us and within us' (2016: 320). The slow violence of environmental exploitation is one such hyperobject in *The Children*: it is not only 'within' the characters (Robin's radiation poisoning) but 'around us': for the characters in the offstage 'exclusion zone', and for the audience in their contemporary world. Quoting the literary ecocritic Pieter Vermeulen, Hoydis contends that this coming to terms with death – and the death humans are causing – is 'an affective, even therapeutic reckoning with species finitude' (2017: 877; quoted in 2020: 94). Indeed, Macdonald's slow theatre is, as *The Children*'s reviews, audience reactions, and the lighting and set suggest, affective in its highlighting of a slowly dying, ephemeral temporality.

Though limited to the restrictions of mainstream theatre, the 'slow theatre' of Kirkwood and Macdonald emphasizes the slow violence that occurs over time, while simultaneously using that duration to deconstruct the performative taxonomies that assert (older, white, middle-class, British) humans as superior to younger generations, the nonhuman and to the future. *The Children* takes from the influence of Churchill – both in Kirkwood's writing and through Macdonald's past productions of her work – to depict 'posthumanist violence', that is, an understanding of violence that goes beyond the normative human perceptions of time, self and taxonomy. The play locates the hubristic, taxonomic placement of (some) humans as assumptively, performatively superior as grounds for the structural exploitation of the nonhuman and those humans 'lower down'. Through symbolically merging human/nonhuman and age distinctions, *The Children* invites its audience to deconstruct such human exceptionalism and identity superiority through the 'teasing out' of Macdonald's slow theatre. This slow theatre, too, gives some consideration to Nixon's slow violence: the methodical duration of the action allows a better understanding of the eventual ravages of agrilogistical exploitation, seen in Robin's radiation poisoning, the scenographic 'dying of the light', and the symbolic ringing of the submerged bells.

Conclusion

The plays explored here illustrate how theories of violence and performativity are vital to fuller comprehensions of the climate crisis; and indeed, these theories are reflected in the plays' dramaturgies. Once again, perception is a key concern – the magic realism of *Oil* and the slow theatre of *The Children* both serve to provide a 'zoomed-out' perspective on human life in the ecosystem, utilizing affective theatrical devices to convey this over hard scientific fact, which research has shown can only go so far to mobilize action. Additionally, the plays explored here demonstrate the intersection climate crisis has with other major concerns of violence. *Oil*'s specific focus on women, for example, should not preclude research that shows them as more vulnerable to climate crisis (Balestrini 2020: 40), and indeed anti-natalist and population control arguments often verge into gendered blame (Watson 2023). As Chapter 6 further explores, the effects of climate crisis have informed xenophobic nationalism. Populations displaced by environmental issues – such as many of those who were part of the Mediterranean refugee crisis – sought shelter in the wealthy nations that most effect global ecological damage; yet were met with hostility and protectorate 'island-mentalities'. Perhaps most prominently, the materialist excesses that exacerbate climate crisis are tightly interlinked with neoliberalism: seen in the corrosive performativity depicted in *Oil* and the challenge to 'live with less' raised in *The Children*. The next chapter looks at how 2010s British theatre responded and represented the violence of neoliberalism, with specific attention given to its performative embodiment: a factor that 2010s British CCT has often highlighted to alert audiences to their own innocuous complicity in performatively maintaining violent conditions.

5

Neoliberalism

The consequences of the 2016 referendum for the UK to leave the European Union (EU) are perhaps the most prominent set of phenomena in both 2010s British politics and, to date, twenty-first-century British–European relations. The next two chapters take as their focus the 2010s British theatre that represented and responded to the prominent socio-political concerns that informed Brexit, such as considerations of Britishness and Europeanness within neoliberal societies; the various crises felt by Europe more widely through the 2010s; and the implication of British identity and culture in structural racism. Though head figures among the Brexit referendum's Leave campaign and Eurosceptics more generally have espoused a 'love' for Europe but a 'hatred' of the bureaucratic institutions of the EU (Glencross 2020), this was mobilized by a more general 'island-mentality' that effectively wished to halt the homogenization of the EU's single market and restrict free movement and immigration – certainly informed by a latent abjection of migrants exacerbated by the Mediterranean refugee crisis.

Still, Brexit is far from the clear-cut narrative about misinformed, provincial, working-class 'Little Englanders' looking to establish socio-cultural insularity (Obordo and Rahim 2016). For example, it is intertwined with anti-establishment concerns on increasing wealth disparity (Pettifor 2017; Rebellato 2018), even if such criticisms against the EU should have been levied just as strongly – if not more so – at the preceding thirty years or so of UK governmentality. The neoliberalism, racism and the toxic performativity of xenophobia-inflected national identity that all feed into Brexit are highly urgent and important areas of structural violence, particularly in 2010s Britain, and have been addressed in a variety of imaginative dramaturgies by theatre-makers over this decade. Whereas the next chapter will focus more on the structural racism evident in, and exacerbated by, Brexit, this one will chart considerations of neoliberalism and the structural violence that 2010s British theatre – and European theatre on British stages – have represented.[1]

Theatrical Visions of Neoliberal Dystopia and Apocalypse

Neoliberalism unequivocally remains the primary economic, political and social ideology of Europe, particularly in Britain. With three previous decades shaped by Thatcherism and New Labour's Third Way, the 2010s saw the continuation of neoliberal policies by a 'Cameronism' that favoured low taxes, particularly for corporations and the rich, alongside cuts to welfare and the social system (Fuchs 2016: 172). These conditions were continued under the Conservative Prime Ministers Theresa May, who declared free-market economics the 'greatest agent of collective human progress ever created' (2017); and Boris Johnson, whose long campaign for the UK's departure from EU – counter to the policies of Cameron – resulted in an exit deal at once nationalist and exclusionary in its objectives but ultimately assessed 'neoliberalism on steroids' (Choudhury 2019). Indeed, the economist Ann Pettifor contends that the Brexit vote was a reaction against the 'repressed wages, diminished public services, rising household costs and shortages, and insecure employment' dictated by neoliberal economic policy (2017: 130), yet Brexit has actively exacerbated these conditions.

Neoliberalism is, linguistically, 'new' or 'renewed' liberalism – this being a school of economic policy devised during the Enlightenment. One of liberalism's most noteworthy proponents was Adam Smith, who believed a more just society would be obtained through individuals and corporations gaining financial autonomy from the state. In 1947, a circle of like-minded thinkers called the Mont Pèlerin Society devised neoliberalism along a similar basis, seeking to promote a 'free market economy' and 'limit government to its basic functions' (Ther 2016: 16). Rather than effecting a more just society, its implementation has been summarized as 'reducing taxes, liberalizing exchange rate controls, reducing regulations, privatizing national industries, and drastically diminishing the power of labour unions' (Steger and Roy 2010: 39) – essentially, laissez-faire, free-market capitalism. The thorough indoctrination of neoliberal ideology into Western society and politics by the 2010s appeared to have caused an endemic cynicism and resigned malaise towards it: variously characterized, for example, as 'neoliberal affect' (Veldestra 2018); 'negative capitalism' eroding a social understanding of what it means to live well (Taylor 2013); and 'cruel optimism' normalizing the day-to-day struggles of neoliberalism's economic underclasses (Berlant 2011). British theatre-makers of the 2010s took these sentiments to dramaturgical extremes, presenting visions of a world made dystopian or apocalyptic by the ravages of neoliberalism.

Of course, rather than being conceived of by 2010s British theatre-makers as an issue only tied to Brexit, many productions explored in this work present neoliberalism as inseparable from many key socio-cultural issues, including mental health (*Some People Talk About Violence*), the climate crisis (*Oil*), and gender-based violence (*Bird*). The totalizing implication of neoliberalism as a global force of violence is articulated by Evans and Giroux: 'Neoliberalism is violence against the cultural conditions and civic agency that makes democracy possible. Its relentless mechanisms of privatization, commodification, deregulation, and militarization cannot acknowledge or tolerate a formative culture and social order in which non-market values [such] as solidarity, civic education, community building, and justice are prioritized' (2015: xiv–xv). With the condition of precarity proliferated by neoliberalism's corrosion of social responsibility, Evans and Giroux's statement of neoliberalism being violent can be taken as more than metaphorical in that it augments structural violence against certain individuals. Neoliberalism is tied up with the concerns addressed above in 2010s British plays because it forms the socio-political ground on which these issues persist. In the UK, which has seen neoliberal policy in effect since the 1980s, several cultural theorists have stated, for example, that neoliberal capitalism is 'taken for granted as a virtually natural state of being' (McGuigan 2009: xi), and that it 'seamlessly occupies the horizons of the thinkable' (Fisher 2009: 8). Mark Fisher calls this ideological blinker on perception and imagination 'capitalist realism', a grimly Thatcherite diagnosis that there is no conceivable socio-political alternative (ibid.).

Therefore, 2010s British plays that depicted and critiqued neoliberalism did so with dramaturgical modes that generally departed from the theatre of earlier decades. The 1980s, for example, saw uses of stark, disjointed realism as with Martin Crimp's *Dealing With Clair* (Orange Tree, 1988), or a blend of this with magic realism like Churchill's *Top Girls*. As mentioned earlier, much theatre of the 1990s presented audiences with visceral and explicitly violent images, illustrating the exploitative savagery of neoliberalism as seen in Mark Ravenhill's *Shopping and Fucking*, or its fracture of society and humanity depicted in Crimp's *Attempts on Her Life* (RC, 1997). The 2000s saw a trope of 'adult-children' characters in its new writing who, Angelaki writes, had been infantilized by a capitalist system 'which mimicked the protective features of a supportive system, only to be exposed as a vacuum' (2013: 70), seen in the plays of Mike Bartlett, Dennis Kelly and Polly Stenham. Additionally, the intertwined relationship between neoliberalism and neoconservative security in the post-9/11 world was satirized by Ravenhill's *Product* (Traverse, 2005), while Simon Stephens's *Pornography* (Schauspielhaus, Hamburg, 2007) depicted a society pervaded by conflict and commodities and Lucy Prebble's

Enron (Chichester Festival Theatre, 2009) articulated the 2007–9 global financial crash through excessive theatricality. After three decades of such productions offering various imaginative responses to neoliberal culture, what began to emerge in 2010s new British writing was a predilection for making visible the structural violence of neoliberalism through what Dan Rebellato defines as 'an apocalyptic tone [that] has recently been adopted in British theatre' (2017: 27) and Trish Reid calls a 'recent dystopian turn in playwriting' (2019: 86).

Terms like 'cataclysm', 'catastrophe', 'apocalypse' and 'dystopian' are widely used in the language of neoliberal criticism. For example, the documentarian Sut Jhally argues of advertising that it contributes, and is leading towards apocalypse (2017); and the cultural theorist David Hancock stresses '[w]e must continue to imagine ways to move beyond the logic of neoliberalism' as the alternative is to 'act in a way that is complicit with a system that we know to be bringing about a cataclysm' (2019: 2). These terms do, however, have differences – with apocalypse's linguistic roots, for example, relating to perception: 'disclosure, discovery, uncovering, unveiling, the veil lifted from about the thing' (Derrida 1984: 4); an occurrence that transcends normative human perception and structures. Dystopia, however, relates to place – literally meaning the 'bad' or 'hard' place. That said, as Reid notes, dystopia 'is not a simple mode', with there being no easy 'middle ground between tucker green's *hang* and [Rory] Mullarkey's *Wolf from the Door* [RC, 2014], for example' (2019: 76). The dystopian vision of *hang* is located in a judicial institution somewhere not dissimilar from 2010s Britain, whereas *Wolf from the Door* appears to open in contemporary Britain before moving into described scenes of near-farcical revolution. Apocalypse generally speaks to large-scale disaster, or a rupture that causes perception to be altered, whereas dystopia might be loosely defined as a society where a violent state of being has been imposed or is being effected.

The terms, then, are not interchangeable, but complementary – and not easily divisible in theatre. Some plays use apocalyptic forms to demonstrate how contemporary neoliberal society is dystopian; others show dystopian worlds (that are sometimes our own) to apocalyptically reveal an obscured truth to the audience. Arguably, though, they all attempt to provoke their audiences into an alternative way of seeing – often, a way of seeing that looks to shake the perceptual bonds of capitalist realism. It is telling, for example, that both Reid and Rebellato take *Escaped Alone* as a predominant example in their explorations of a dystopian turn and an apocalyptic tone, while Anja Hartl's analysis of the play sees her coin the term 'dystopian performatives'. Taken from Jill Dolan's concept of utopian performatives, which are 'small but profound moments' at the theatre that give 'a hopeful feeling of what the world might be like' (2005: 5), Hartl states dystopian performatives 'blur the boundaries between the familiar and the unfamiliar, the recognizable and the estranged', employed in *Escaped Alone* as a 'post-Brechtian *Verfremdung*' (2021). They are, in other words, used to make non-normative connections to open audiences' perceptions.

As mentioned in the last chapter, there have been criticisms of such apocalyptic-dystopian narratives, voiced for example by Ella Hickson's statement that they risk a 'weird voyeurism' for 'the white theatre-going audiences of London' (Solnick 2020). Indeed, those most oppressed by neoliberal policy in 2010s Britain were not the standard make-up of theatre audiences; like Fisher's assessment of viewing anti-establishment narratives in popular film, such theatre may perform 'our anti-capitalism for us, allowing us to continue to consume with impunity' (2009: 12). Commentators have criticized the scope of such narratives as they 'serve mostly to reconfirm well-established views of the present, failing to outline a persuasive alternative' (Heise 2015: 300). However, Rebellato and Reid have both identified such 2010s British theatre as strikingly imaginative. Citing plays like Bartlett's *13* (2010, NT), Smith's *Human Animals* and Churchill's *Escaped Alone*, Reid claims: 'the dystopian turn in new writing highlights the inadequacies of realism as a mode for staging neoliberal experience. Although mostly set in near-future worlds, the plays are typically peopled with characters disabled by the terrors of precarious living, neoliberal (in)versions of personal freedom, environmental disaster, and the demeaning effects of corporate capitalism' (2019: 73).

Additionally, Rebellato – who advances on Derrida's writing on the apocalyptic to explore work including *The Author*, *Pomona* and *Wolf from the Door* – writes:

> It is tempting to see this imagery as nihilistically apolitical, as a turning away from political engagement in favour of wilful destruction, even self-destruction (even as a theatrical version of Brexit!); to understand why this is not the case, it is important to recognize these images as a response - and a constructive response - to a key feature of contemporary neoliberal capitalism: its totalizing absorption of realism.
>
> (2017: 38)

If apocalyptic-dystopian narratives offer a limited vision of the future then, they often look to approach the issues of the present from a new angle, beyond the restrictions of realism's contemporaneous temporality rather than offering an apolitical distraction. Apocalyptic-dystopian plays arguably exist between two points of tension: on the one hand, they face the risk of 'performing anti-capitalism' on the behalf of voyeuristic liberals, and moreover are limited in that they cannot see beyond the end of neoliberal capitalism; and on the other, they use dystopian performatives to depart the confines of more recognizable realist modes and settings in attempts to 'zoom out' of capitalist realism and critique neoliberalism in a defamiliarized manner.

The many adaptations of classic texts focused on societal chaos and totalitarian control through the 2010s are interesting examples to apply between these two points of tension. These include Kelly's revision of Shakespeare's *King Lear* into a dystopian narrative of corporate war, *The Gods Weep* (Hampstead Theatre, 2010); Duncan Macmillan and Robert Icke's celebrated retelling of George Orwell's *1984* (1949; Nottingham Playhouse, 2013); and Dawn King's version of Aldous Huxley's *Brave New World* (1931; Royal & Dengate Northampton, 2015). Additionally, classic dystopian texts from Europe were also adapted: Nick Gill's production of Franz Kafka's *The Trial* (1914; YV, 2015) timely debuted before the bureaucratic processes of the Brexit withdrawal began; and Neil Bartlett's staging of Albert Camus's *The Plague* (1947; Arcola, 2018) saw crisis workers recount their struggles with a virulent outbreak – just a couple of years before the global spread of COVID-19. Though adapting pre-established works might seem to support Fisher's contention of capitalist realism cauterizing originality and imagination, the above productions arguably reiterated these plots not so much to annex audiences' guilt of their capitalist behaviours, but because the theatre-makers saw the contemporary relevance of their social critiques: to use the dystopian performativity of these works to encourage audiences into new modes of seeing. The close of Macmillan and Icke's *1984* even has a meta-theatrical, 'modern-day' book club apparently discussing the classic novel as a historical text, posing if the Big Brother-led ruling party still governs through a less visible, neoliberal-like system.

Indeed, reservations against apocalyptic-dystopian visions in theatre perhaps focus too much on their aesthetics and scenography – the fact that they appear to show a hopeless, inescapable 'end' of communitarian society because of capitalism – without enough credit on the performative potentiality of their dramaturgy: how they present their images, plots, themes and engender audience affect. A significant case in point is the US writer Anne Washburn's *Mr Burns, a Post-Electric Play* (2012), directed by Robert Icke at London's Almeida Theatre in 2014. With its post-apocalyptic narrative chronicling a theatre company cobbling together a 'late capitalist' palimpsest made up of half-remembered episodes of *The Simpsons* (1989–), it 'metatheatrically chronicles how stories shape listeners and their cultures' (Snyder 2020: 283), and advocates for theatre not to 'decline into "meaningless" entertainment advocating status, materialism, and human commodification'

(293). The dystopian performativity of *Mr Burns* reminds theatre-makers and audiences that it is the dramaturgical content of plays, more so than aesthetics, that can critique neoliberal attitudes and performatively alter reiterations of capitalist realism. Other examples of theatre that appear to lean more towards explicitly apocalyptic-dystopian scenarios offer similarly ambiguous readings: showing violent, disorienting or oppressive futures which are supposedly inevitable given contemporaneous, neoliberal trajectories, while posing to various extents the capacity for change, often through elusive communitarian values.

These include Mullarkey's *Pity* (RC, 2018), where absurd, destructive violence like that of *Wolf from the Door* occurs, but here appears to have no reconciliation – presumably because of a global lack of the titular feeling. Keiran Hurley's *Heads Up* (Summerhall, 2016) depicts disparate individuals coming together in the face of their city's destruction, while Tajinder Singh Hayer's *North Country* (Wild Woods, Bradford, 2016) sees post-apocalyptic communities form 'along religious and cultural lines' (Farnell 2019: 122). Rose Lewenstein's *Darknet* (Southwark Playhouse, London, 2016), EV Crowe's *The Sewing Group* (RC, 2016), Stef Smith's *Girl in the Machine* (Traverse, 2017), and Eve Leigh's *Midnight Movie* (RC, 2019) display future visions of virtual worlds encroached upon by neoliberal violence, while still acknowledging that their governing systems can be altered or reconstructed. Fraser Grace's *Always Orange* (RSC, 2016), which played in a double bill with Seaton's *Rise of the Kingdom, Fall of the Foot Soldier* (analysed in the next chapter), presents a version of a hyper-capitalist London where terrorist attacks are frequent, and a resignation with contemporary London is detectable in its opening preamble: 'Why tell how a city was lost when/ there is no longer a city to save?' (2016: 77). Yet, like *Mr Burns*, it offers hope through storytelling and interdependence, as Lyn Gardner's review states: 'when our culture is reduced to consumption [...] it is our ability to communicate with each other and have access to the same shared spaces that offers the only chance of making us recognise our shared humanity' (2016a).

If *Always Orange* offers a world where random violence has grown through the cracks of neoliberalism, other examples of apocalyptic-dystopian theatre demonstrate how violence constantly simmers beneath and maintains contemporary neoliberal society. These include Anders Lustgarten's *If You Don't Let Us Dream, We Won't Let You Sleep* (RC, 2013); the title even referencing the occupation of the imagination by capitalist realism. The play is almost an inverse of Crimp's *Attempts on Her Life* or Stephens's *Pornography* – though it similarly depicts a series of scenes making plain the everyday violence and oppression individuals face under neoliberalism, it concludes with disparate characters coming together to debate the injustice of the neoliberal system in an abandoned courtroom. In Stenham's *Hotel* (NT, 2014), the play, like her earlier work, begins with a focus on a dysfunctional upper-class British family, here on a retreat to a Kenyan island resort. In an echo of Kane's *Blasted* (also set in a hotel room), the second act dismantles the narrative when the family are suddenly taken hostage by their maid, Nala, whose parents have been killed by faulty British pesticides. As she states to them: 'It's the same old colonial shit, just dressed in the shiny drag of free-market capitalism' (2019: 354).

Mullarkey's *Cannibals* (RE, 2013) too highlights the dystopian nature of contemporary Britain, charting the journey of Lizaveta as a farmer in the USSR through to being sold to a 'husband' in London. As Sam Haddow writes, 'the inscription of a new identity follows or precipitates the violent destruction of the old' (2014: 276) as Lizaveta takes on multiple roles over the play charting the fall of the Soviet Union to the 'end of history' represented by neoliberalism. This teleological sentiment is challenged by *Cannibals*'s 'Kane-esque' dramaturgy, such as when a ghost enters and proceeds to eat his own corpse, interpreted by Haddow as signifying '[o]nce capitalism is implemented, in short, there is nowhere else to go, and the violence that has saturated the illustration of end-narratives in the play up to this point is directed inward; it becomes cannibalistic' (281). As with Lynn's *Lela & Co.*, Lizaveta's non-consensual trafficking to London, a situation from which she cannot escape, appears to signal this violent, imaginative entrapment as she is 'cannibalized' as a commodity. The commodification of citizens under neoliberalism recurs in Rose Lewenstein's *Cougar* (Orange Tree, 2019), which follows the successful executive Leila taking her younger lover John to a dizzying array of identical hotel rooms in cities around the world, again in an echo of *Blasted*, as she attends a series of conferences to push a 'Green Agenda' she is actively profiting from. As the world outside the hotel rooms appears to become more catastrophic, Leila actively incorporates John into more neoliberal behaviours: for example, 'transforming' him with a new, expensive set of clothes that he re-clothes himself in under the gaze of her and the audience. Lewenstein seems to invite the audience to witness Leila's performative actions as part of a scene in a widespread catastrophe of globalized neoliberalism: a contemporaneous world in which cataclysm has already happened and is ongoing.[2]

Alistair McDowall's *Pomona* is a fitting final example here of apocalyptic-dystopian theatre that responds to neoliberalism, being one of the most critically and academically celebrated British plays of the 2010s. Commissioned by the Royal Welsh College of Music and Drama and debuting at The Gate Theatre with direction from Ned Bennett in April 2014, *Pomona* went on to be revised and produced at the Orange Tree in November,[3] then transferred in 2015 to both the National Theatre and Manchester's Royal Exchange. The cyclical narrative of *Pomona* focuses on several intermingling plots including a search through Manchester for a lost twin sister, an immersive role-playing game and an organ-harvesting, baby-farming secret facility. Relating to Girard's theories of ritualistic violence and Butler's critique of the utilitarian production of neoliberal citizens where 'a body is hyper-instrumentalized for a brief period of employment and then arbitrarily deemed disposable' (Butler in Butler and Athanasiou 2013: 147), the performative 'oiling' of the neoliberal machine by bodily violence, dehumanization and commodification is compared in *Pomona* to occult sacrifice via Lovecraftian horror and *Indiana Jones and the Temple of Doom* (1984). Ian Farnell, who analyses McDowall's sci-fi elements in his earlier work *Brilliant Adventures* (RE, 2013) and the later *X* (RC, 2016), writes that the 'radical approach' McDowall takes in presenting vital socio-political concerns through methods counter to standard 'theatrical orthodoxy' raises 'intriguing questions of how the iconography of twenty-first century culture [...] can be best represented onstage' (2019: 137).

In the case of *Pomona*, the 'iconographic elements' litter its nightmarish urban landscape to create a sense of contemporary catastrophe through dystopian performatives. References from *Indiana Jones* to *Dungeons and Dragons* to McDonald's to Cthulhu imbue the bodily commodification of neoliberalism with the cataclysmic and identify it in the narratives of a pop culture permeated with capitalist realism while, as Rebellato writes, its 'jagged dramaturgical experiments [...] suggest a situationist disrupting of the spectacle, as we lurch [...] between comedy and horror, urban thriller and Lovecraftian fantasy' (2017: 46). While envisioning an all-too contemporary dystopia then, *Pomona* is focused on the perception of both its characters, and its audiences. *Pomona* depicts neoliberalism as an apocalypse in that it is a mass of violent acts that changes the perception of its citizens, or at least encourages them *not* to perceive anything alternative to its dictates: to perpetuate the smooth functioning of systemic violence. This is most evident in the dialogue of the enigmatic oligarch Zeppo, who advises to 'choose what you educate yourself about' (14); citing his own wilfully ignorant love for McDonald's chicken nuggets: 'if I look into the nuggers, if I open that door, am I gonna find out like, positive things? Or am I gonna maybe find out horrible things' (McDowall 2014: 14 [*sic*]). Despite Zeppo's ideology, the characters of *Pomona* variously 'look inside', even though many of them financially benefit from the suffering that takes place in the underground facility. As in Plato's *Cave*, bringing the truth to light is not comfortable – and is even violent for *Pomona*'s characters – yet the neoliberal encouragement to *not look* allows acts of violence to persist unperturbed. Fittingly, the initial productions of *Pomona* did not feature an interval.

Though *Pomona* does not make explicit political statements, it presents active spectating as political, but sacrificial of comfort. Rather than inviting the audience to 'imagine how the story ends', or that the audience should themselves imagine the end of neoliberalism, its cyclicity and lack of clarity instead poses that to imagine the end is to think through the logic of capitalist realism. As Angelaki continues, '[a]t a time of emotional and fiscal austerity, the theatre no longer relies on the extravagant spectacle, or even plot, to make its point' (2013: 74). Indefinite repetition, on the other hand, is a continual act of leaving meaning, and therefore totality, open. The conclusion of *Pomona* seems to suggest this: like a game, the narrative effectively 'restarts'. Indeed, arguably more so than theatre of the 1980–2000s that critiqued neoliberalism, the apocalyptic-dystopian plays of the 2010s espouse a malaise towards neoliberalism and a wariness towards combating it head-on – while still possessing a wry suspicion of its collapse. The cyclicity of *Cougar* and *Pomona* also seen in *Oil*, for example, comprehend neoliberalism's ability to repetitively sustain itself while simultaneously acknowledging its unsustainability. They stalk around neoliberalism: they do not directly critique it, instead representing it in ways that seek to burst free of the incorporative nature of capitalist realism.

Though the terms apocalypse and dystopia may appear excessive to apply to an economic system, British theatre of the 2010s illustrate neoliberalism's often systemic and invisible operations of violence in the realm of the seen through experimental dramaturgical methods. Its totalizing influence is such that it is enmeshed in concerns of protest, the environment, and gender and racial inequality. Although Rebellato above jokes about the relation of the 'apocalyptic tone' to the 'self-destructive tendencies' of Brexit, considering 2010s apocalyptic-dystopian theatre in the light of the referendum and its phenomena certainly warrants thought (and he does give this further consideration in 'Nation and Negation'; 2018). Although some surface-level comparisons can be made between the wilful ignorance of *Pomona*, the dystopia of *1984* and the 'post-truth' arguments of the Leave campaign, Brexit represented for many how British society may not be heading into an upward trajectory but sliding into dystopian insularity – while the confidence of the Remain vote demonstrated a perceptual blindness towards the hurt of those communities most affected by neoliberal policy. The tension between Leila and John in *Cougar*, the oligarchs and those they command in *Pomona*, the elites and the revolutionaries of *Wolf from the Door*, or the oppression felt by the characters of *If You Won't Let Us Dream, We Won't Let You Sleep* perhaps invite a different reading of these apocalyptic-dystopian plays: of societies torn apart by oppressive class relationships that those hierarchically 'higher up' – such as the standard make-up of theatre audiences – may not be themselves fully aware of.

Cross-Cultural Dramaturgies of Violence and *Three Kingdoms*

Both Brexit and the mode of British identity that its proponents galvanized seem to represent a general failure of a broader sense of European identity in 2010s Britain, certainly in England and Wales if not Scotland (where the Remain vote stood at 62 per cent). European identity and 'Europeanness' have historically proven very difficult to define, having to account for the shifting values, cultures and histories of dozens of diverse nations. Nevertheless, contexts of violence have often urged such a shared identity, or resulted in reactive articulations of one: notably, the social traumas of the World Wars (Habermas 2001)[4] and the Holocaust (Beck 2003) or, as Milija Gluhović suggests, '[s]tressing the colonial past' as 'a useful check on Euro-centrism' (2013: 9). These were apparent in cross-cultural theatre between Britain and the rest of Europe through the 2010s, particularly with the centenary of the First World War, seen in the German playwright Rolf Hochhuth's *Sommer 14: A Dance of Death* (1989) produced with a new translation by Gwynne Edwards (Finborough, 2014) and the Belgian theatre-maker Valentijn Dhaenens's *SmallWaR* (Traverse, Fringe, 2014).

Yet the depiction of such shared contexts of violence were not only historical: Belarus Free Theatre's *Minsk 2011* (YV, 2012) presented the contemporary authoritarianism of their native government; while Katie Mitchell's production of *Atmen* represented issues of climate crisis on the stage of Berlin's Schaubühne; and in Greece, *How to Hold Your Breath*, counter to its lukewarm debut at the Royal Court, 'played for over a year and clearly touches a nerve [...] they get that it is a play about refugees and it's a conversation they want to have', as Zinnie Harris stated (Gardner 2018). Though the violence represented by these works appears broad, they can all be understood through the theatre-makers' use of violence as a relatable 'stage language' for the distinct socio-cultural connections between Britain and Europe. This is argued here through the case studies of the Royal Court Theatre's International Department, which developed and debuted several European writers' works in the 2010s, and Simon Stephens's collaborative *Three Kingdoms*. Additionally, the dramaturgical use of violence in these works is suggested as being influenced by earlier British-European theatre, such as in the wide influence exerted by the work of Sarah Kane. These theatricalized reiterations of cross-cultural violence in the 2010s – in both the narratives and their representations in cross-cultural production – are posed as performatively reinforcing the presence of violence in British-European relations.

The Royal Court's International Department was founded in 1996 by the theatre's then-artistic director Stephen Daldry and its former Young People's Theatre director Elyse Dodgson. Although European plays concerned with violence certainly played on the Court's stages prior to this, the International Department arguably strengthened and proliferated this aspect. Dominic Cooke expressed some anxiety on there being 'a danger that the writers feel encouraged to report from the front line and give us the shit bits from the lives of their countries' (Aston and O'Thomas 2010: 97). Such 'frontline reporting' was apparent in the three full productions of new European writing at the Court in the 2010s. The first was Aleksey Scherbak's *Remembrance Day* (2011), which focuses on the socio-political divisions between Latvians and Russians in Riga, with the difficulty of being implicated in both Nazi and Soviet histories and the competing forces of neoliberalism and nationalist populism. Anna Wakulik's *A Time to Reap* (2013) is concerned with female agency – specifically through abortion rights – within the Catholic-inflected politics of Poland, queried through a more neoliberal, potentially 'immoral' London. The last was Natal'ya Vorozhbit's *Bad Roads* (2017), directed by Vicky Featherstone and made up of several women's experiences of the war in Donbas, influenced by Vorozhbit's own travels in the warzone. Interestingly here, there is no narrative of cohesive pro-Europeanism in the face of 'the Russian threat' – both sides appear culpable in the violence. As a pro-Russian solider claims: 'under the beautiful pretence of their "European values" they're making wars and making nations like ours – like brothers – fight' (2017: 51).[5] So, all three plays contain, to extents, what Cooke describes as 'the shit bits' of their countries.

With the inescapable histories of *Remembrance Day*, the 'traditional' values of *A Time to Reap*, and the broken literal and social infrastructure of *Bad Roads* – '[t]he road was like this before the war […] it's got nothing to do with the war' (32) – the plays represent how the old wounds of existing socio-political issues, rather than being repaired by European 'togetherness', have persisted and perpetuated contemporary contexts of violence. There is evidence to suggest that the Court has encouraged the development of such international 'frontline' plays: one anecdote gathered by Elaine Aston and Mark O'Thomas cites the International Department's frustration when a promising playwright 'dropped an idea of writing about a 12-year-old assassin in favour of a play about an elephant who escaped from the circus' (2010: 38). As Jen Harvie argues, guiding work in this way can be regarded as cultural imperialism (2003), a criticism which materialized in the Russian press when the Department introduced verbatim theatre at its Moscow workshops (Dugdale 2013). Though the Department was not the sole platform for European work on 2010s British stages (LIFT, the London

International Festival of Theatre, being one such example), its influential 'style' was detectable through the decade. For example, the Birmingham Repertory Theatre's trans-European collaboration *Europa* (2013) examined European identity through issues of immigration and the titular, foundational Greek myth of abduction and rape. Prompting the repetition of European work on the British stage that represents contemporary contexts of violence, the Court has been crucial in the construction of this association: a performative reiteration of what (violent) content should be represented in European plays staged in Britain.

The recourse to 'frontline' issues of violence in these plays may well inform the distaste of its detractors, even if their criticisms often seem to be focused more on *how* these issues are represented. For example, Anders Lustgarten, who engages in relatively direct political theatre, has expressed a wariness of European theatrical practices: 'There's a strong tendency in British theatre now (heavily influenced by a German dramaturgy which itself is played out and changing) to grandiose empty spectacle, to gesture politics onstage' (2016a: xi). David Hare, too, has been particularly hostile towards European theatre in the 2010s – infamously so in theatre reviewing and academic circles, as Lyn Gardner (2017), Duška Radosavljević (2017) and Chris Megson (2018a) attest. Hare contends that 'state-of-the-nation' plays are 'the strongest line in British theater' as opposed to what he calls 'an overaestheticized European theater [...] all that directorial stuff that we've managed to keep over on the continent is now coming over and beginning to infect our theater' (Sweet 2017: 68–9). Hare's language reflects xenophobic metaphors, characterizing 'European theatre aesthetics as a viral contagion', as Megson writes (2018a: 44). Lustgarten and Hare's detractions likely refer to what Rebellato calls a 'vast plurality of staging practices' generally coded as European theatrical techniques, identified through markers such as 'a certain scenic anti-realism, directorial auteurism, [and] the text not as the dominant signifying system, but one set of signs among others' (2017: 11). Though these dramaturgical tools are, of course, not inherently 'European' or 'violent' (or, as Hare might have it, violent in their invasive Europeanness), they became performatively coded as such due to the theatre-makers that used them and what was represented.

However, these techniques, counter to their critics' assumptions, are not so much 'European', but emergent from British-European theatrical exchange. A major influence on the cross-cultural nature of 'European practices' was the work of Sarah Kane: or, the responses to her plays from directors like James Macdonald and Thomas Ostermeier and, as Helen Iball writes, her overall impact on European theatre-makers, particularly in Germany (2008: 56). Productions of Kane's work were notable for staging her 'unstageable' or, at least, very difficult to stage images of violence: such as a vulture descending to feast on a corpse in *Phaedra's Love* or rats carrying off dismembered limbs in *Cleansed* (RC, 1998). The dramaturgical answers to staging such 'unstageable' images and actions were found in the implementation of practices that became considered in Britain as 'European', such as in Ostermeier's expressionistic rendering of *Zerbombt* (*Blasted*; Schaubühne, 2005), or Macdonald's debut production of *Cleansed*, of which he joked in interview that any attempt to stage it realistically would 'burst a blood vessel' (Christopher 1998).

A 2010s production of *Cleansed* by Katie Mitchell (NT, 2016) typified these 'European techniques'. It featured Mitchell's recognizable auteurism: certain stage directions were cut or amended, and she approached the text as a 'musical notation' rather than a play (Trueman 2016b). While being 'more realistic' than Macdonald, Mitchell did not 'burst a blood vessel' and still opted for a generally surrealist approach: despite the stark, laboratory setting, she prompted performers to understand character motivations through the logic of a dream (ibid.). Though Mitchell's *Cleansed* explicitly represented violence in a manner contrary to most of the plays analysed here,[6] Kane's influence returned more generally to British theatre in the 2010s through what became recognized as European practices: anti-realism, directorial auteurism, the text as relatively interpretative and reduced in its symbolic primacy, and imaginative representations of violence. And, of course, the irony of two of Britain's most influential contemporary directors (Macdonald and Mitchell) advancing and championing the 'European techniques' described by Rebellato and decried by Hare should not be lost here.

The reiteration of these practices from European theatre-makers on 2010s British stages and vice versa is certainly evident in the work of Simon Stephens. A vocal champion of cross-cultural theatre exchange, his most obvious example of this sentiment over the decade was *Three Kingdoms*: a joint production developed between his long-time directorial collaborator Sebastian Nübling, and the Estonian designer Ene-Liis Semper alongside her company Teater NO99. The production premiered at the latter's eponymous theatre in Tallinn (which, along with the company, ceased operation in 2019), toured to the Munich Kammerspiele, and concluded at London's Lyric Hammersmith in May 2012. The tour referenced narrative locations as well as the creatives' locales, as the London-based detective Ignatius leads a murder investigation which takes him to Hamburg and Tallinn to uncover a transnational sex-trafficking ring.[7] Balme notes that 'the *mise-en-scène* shifts with geography from the dialogue-based scenes in London to a more overtly visual and physical style in Central and Eastern Europe' (2014: 69; emphasis in original), likely referencing the generalized dramaturgies of these nations' theatres. As Ignatius's case progresses, the binaries between police/suspects and fantasy/reality start to collapse. The symbolic, dream-like nature of the narrative was accentuated in features like Semper's iconic deer and wolf heads which adorned the sex workers and their literalized predatory traffickers – exemplary of the anti-realism of European practices.

The production will most likely be remembered in British theatre history as being a crux of heated debate: there was a clear 'split between newspaper critics [...] resistant to the work, and online writers who embrace[d] it fervently' (Costa 2012); Balme even explores the production as central to a discussion about the public sphere and theatre reviewing (2014: 68–72). What is given less attention in this debate – along with the problematic aspects of *Three Kingdoms*'s representation of preyed-upon, dehumanized and underdeveloped female characters – is how the reviewers' respective opinions were predicated on the production's perceived 'Europeanness'. For example, Billington writes of *Three Kingdoms* that 'the venture makes me question the very concept of a European co-production [...] that displays geographical diversity but has no specific identity' (2012). This response aligns with Lustgarten and Hare's criticisms of European theatre's 'emptiness' and over-aestheticization; and, interestingly, reflects Theresa May's later description of pro-EU liberals as 'citizens of nowhere' in the wake of the Brexit referendum (2017; see also Rebellato 2018). Despite the specificity of the narrative's locations, Semper's set design appears 'placeless': Stephens describes that it 'seemed to understand the atomised, hallucinatory nature of sex and travel and money' (Bolton 2015: 4). These elements – the cross-cultural co-production, the tour, direction, scenography and narrative – productively and dramaturgically represented the placelessness of a contemporary, globalized, neoliberal Europe. The shadowy sex traffickers of *Three Kingdoms*, who become indiscernible from law institutions, predatorily profit from Europe's 'atomised' placelessness; slipping between nations to continue their violent practices.

Three Kingdoms critiques the 'neoliberal placelessness' of contemporary Europe specifically in how it maintains conditions for the violence of the cultural commodification of women. Yet, Billington's statement suggests an equation of the production's collaboration and its European theatrical practices with the very 'European neoliberalism' Stephens, Semper and Nübling critique.[8] In addition to *Three Kingdoms*, Stephens has explicitly engaged with this concern in *Carmen Disruption* (2014; after Georges Bizet's 1875 opera *Carmen*), directed by Michael Longhurst at the Almeida (2015). The production foregrounded the play's provocation of a 'dying' Europe, described by Angelaki as 'the abduction of Europe in the post-capitalist apocalypse of transience and fluidity' – like *Europa*, it evokes the Greek myth, but here specifically through a 'life-size prop of a bull that lies front- and centre-stage [...] and begins to bleed' (2017: 174). The European practices deployed here productively question European identity rather than create what Lustgarten derides as 'grandiose empty spectacle'. The anti-realism of *Carmen Disruption*'s gored, bleeding bull and the anthropomorphic costumes of *Three Kingdoms* symbolically and effectively defamiliarize the predatory nature of European neoliberalism to underline its violence. Indeed, these plays, much like the theatre explored in the previous section, depict a Europe 'abducted' by neoliberalism and made quasi-dystopian.

Rebellato identifies many such 2010s British plays that have 'a persistent pattern of dramaturgical displacement [...] whereby particularities of place are problematized or eliminated' (2018: 23), again referring to Kane's *Blasted* and its Leeds-cum-Srebrenica hotel room as a particular influence in this regard (29). Rather than view these plays as a symptom of theatre-makers being among the 'citizens of nowhere' of liberal, 'Remainer' Britain, Rebellato contests they are 'an intersection between imagined space and imagined non-space, within real non-utilitarian spaces that we must in turn connect to the utilitarian space of our daily lives and of the political realities that surround us' (35). Their dramaturgies, then, perhaps look to radically 'stage a community without boundaries' (36), a suggestion that emerges, in part, from Nancy's conception of communitarian space as never complete (1991), as the space inside the border as necessitated on the outside and therefore based on 'perpetual movement' (Rebellato 2018: 34). Applied to Europe, this would contest assertions of 'emptiness' with 'incompleteness', while also echoing Nancy's later writings on the 'truth of violence' as the (doomed) urge to tear something away – to make it distinct from all other things.

The theorization of such an expansive space gesturing towards 'infinite democracy' (36) counters the exclusivity of Brexit nationalism, or even that of the EU towards the Mediterranean refugee crisis. But it is difficult to delineate such an egalitarian, free movement of ideas and peoples from the deregulated, market-oriented movement of neoliberalism which, as *Three Kingdoms*, *Pomona* and *Cannibals* demonstrate, extends to the movement of people, goods and people *as* goods. Indeed, Angelaki's reading of *Carmen Disruption* above suggests that 'Europe' is elsewhere, imaginary and lacking not because of its utopian incompleteness, but because its identity is kept in constant deferment by the placeless individualism of neoliberalism. Perhaps the non-places and the 'nowhere-ness' of these plays are instead, as Stephens says of Semper's set design, an expression of neoliberalism's cross-cultural channels that, in their corrosion of communitarian values as well as nationhood and place, perpetuate individualism and exclusion rather than gesture beyond it.

Regardless of whether the plays discussed here wish to represent Europe as productively or nihilistically empty, Rebellato writes elsewhere that the generalized European practices described above are key to their representations:

> Europe figured as an imagined location in the mind of the characters or maybe of the author and *Carmen Disruption* stood in relation to *Carmen* like a complicated and intricate scaffolding placed around a building that has since disappeared. The production took its cue from this imagined, empty Europeanness, brilliantly evoking it through a kind of pastiche of an imagined European production, with no realist settings, [and] performers playing at the edge of actor and character.
> (2017: 12)

With the 'pastiche' of European practices here being, potentially, a satire of a formless Europe, it is intriguing that such practices are used to represent an 'empty Europeanness' rather than a more positive vision of Europe – also true of *Three Kingdoms*. Like the practice of 'the text not as the dominant signifying system', its three languages (and locations) are relatively inconsequential. The juridical co-operation between Ignatius and the other police forces are sometimes tense, and despite speaking German and having lived in Hamburg as a student, he dictates an Estonian with: 'I don't give a shit about what happens to your fucking country. I honestly don't care' (2015: 135). Being more individualist than communitarian, his apparent Europeanness dissolves into intolerance, just as the façade of European civility is stripped away through the play to reveal a neoliberalist nightmare of greed and violence emphasized by surreal choreography and dreamlike scenography. Such European practices, then, appear apt at creating a more tangible sense of contemporary neoliberalism.

Like the apocalyptic-dystopian plays cited earlier, these 'placeless' plays do not seem to overtly offer explicit political aspersions for themselves, though it may be reductive to claim them as either illustrating a neoliberal emptiness or a potential space for more expansive communitarian imagination. Instead, these visions can be regarded as interconnected in the plays' dramaturgies. *Three Kingdoms*, for example, presents a nightmarish vision of Europe but the material facts of its cross-cultural production show genuine intercultural connections. Like Kane's influence and the 'frontline reporting' that the Court's International Department encouraged, these British-European plays attempt intercultural bonding through expressing the various acts and structures of violence that their societies have suffered from neoliberal policy to which a counter-identity could potentially be formed. This is supported,

I contend, through Cathy Caruth's understanding of cross-cultural trauma: 'In a catastrophic age [...] trauma itself may provide the very link between cultures: not as a simple understanding of the pasts of others but rather, within the traumas of contemporary history, as our ability to listen through the departures we have all taken from ourselves' (1995: 11). Gluhović also writes that even his 'cursory look at some recent outputs in the field of theatre and performance studies dealing with historical traumas, violence and witnessing seems to fulfil this promise' (2013: 16). The cultural or societal trauma Caruth articulates here, when shared between nations, may provide an intercultural language of sorts: 'the very link between cultures'.

With the apocalyptic-dystopian aspect of neoliberalism, and with this ideology being the predominant governing system (and crisis) of 2010s Europe, this could well be described as a 'catastrophic age' that a relatable 'stage language' of violence could create cross-cultural links between. Plays like *Three Kingdoms* do not seem to champion a new mode of Europeanness beyond a predatory, deleterious neoliberalism that should be combated. Yet, like Nancy's understanding of the community as informed by what is outside it, perhaps they advocate that the corrosive forces of neoliberalism should be reconfigured through the affective bond of shared contexts of violence as Europe's 'other' in this regard, rather than as its dominant political ideology. Still, there are issues in these plays' representations of European identity as formed from the shared violence of neoliberalism. Caruth's conception of 'cultural trauma' as applied to neoliberal policy is, of course, vastly different – incomparable even – to the shared trauma of war, occupation and genocide that has informed European relations through the post-war period. Additionally, shared trauma as a cross-cultural link has been in effect in European relations for decades, yet division has still fostered between European states.

Though time and distance have certainly informed the renewal of these issues, the sharing of contexts of violence to form cross-cultural relations certainly has limitations. For example, notwithstanding *Three Kingdoms*'s critique of neoliberalism's commodification of women and exacerbation of violence against them – while simultaneously having minor female roles and representing these as dehumanized – what does the production's depiction of an 'atomized, hallucinatory', and violent Europe *do* for the fraught British–European relations of the 2010s, critique as this is? This concern can, of course, also be levied at the work and influence of the Royal Court's International Department. Does the performative reiteration of a 'violent Europe' on British stages, even if this has potentially communitarian aspirations, only encourage opinions such as Hare's with their regard of Europe's influence on Britain and its stages as a viral infection that, as Brexit seems to suggest, must be cauterized? So, both European theatre and European theatrical practices on the 2010s British stage have often related to issues of violence, which has created a reiterated association of what such plays and practices represent. In the case of European techniques, these have contributed to the overall trend of violence in 2010s British theatre argued in this work – that it is often shown as intangible, permeating and told rather than directly shown, which practices of anti-realism, abstraction and directorial auteurism, as evident in *Three Kingdoms*, enable.

Conclusion

If a definition of neoliberalism could be formulated from the examples of 2010s theatre explored through this chapter, it would be an ideology that espouses a commitment to deregulated capitalism and open, unimpeded markets to the extent that neoliberal economies and policies have permeated the cultural imagination of Britain and, more generally, Europe with capitalist realism. Neoliberalism has seemingly occupied and engineered the body; tolerated the exploitation and violence that occurs when human greed is encouraged to apocalyptic and dystopian levels; and affected a 'cultural trauma' where societies have been marked by losses of communitarian values. While suggesting audiences' ability to refuse these systems, much of the theatre cited here plays on their involvement within them: such as *Pomona*'s provocation of imagining the end of neoliberalism or, at least, the audience's inability to. Additionally, though *Three Kingdoms* potentially advances the dehumanization of 'preyed upon' women under neoliberalism, the material factors of its production demonstrate how cross-cultural artistic ventures can collaborate to create provocative visions of a Europe made 'atomized' and 'hallucinatory' through neoliberal policy.

These plays, then, draw on the theatre audience's shifting role between passive consumption and emancipated interpretation: perhaps creating spaces where individualism is questioned, and 'anti-neoliberal' communitarian values are posed as an actual alternative. In the context of the Brexit vote effected, among other reasons, by the abjection caused in great part by neoliberal policy, they arguably warn how the perceptual barriers of capitalist realism mean that apparently anti-neoliberal actions may be short-circuited, especially if they follow practices of exclusion. Indeed, in response to Hare's characterization of British theatre being 'infected' by European practices, Gardner argues that cultural interchange has been essential for the 'plurality [...] in terms of form and content' in 2010s British theatre (2017). The next chapter demonstrates this 'plurality' through three formally distinct plays which, nevertheless, are connected in how they make tangible for their audiences the 'traumas of contemporary history' – such as the violence of structural neoliberalism – in relation to Brexit, racism and British and European identities in the 2010s.

6

Racism

This chapter continues the general focus of the last by exploring productions that represented the structural violence connected to Brexit. Whereas the former inspected the ideology of neoliberalism, this chapter looks at the relation between Brexit and racism as made tangible by representations on the 2010s British stage. Of particular interest here is national and group identity – specifically European and British identities – and how they are factored in 2010s British theatre as constitutive of structural racism and influential of the conditions that resulted in Brexit. The first part of the chapter offers a close, comparative reading of two plays: Zinnie Harris's *How to Hold Your Breath* and Anders Lustgarten's *Lampedusa*. These both opened in 2015 in the context of, and in response to, the Mediterranean refugee crisis, which the plays use to consider European identity against (and through) questions of insularity, individualism, and representations of the 'Other'. The second section analyses Somalia Nonyé Seaton's *Fall of the Kingdom, Rise of the Foot Soldier* which, released in the wake of Brexit, explores British identity not only in the context of an apparent refusal of European identity, but as an intersectional expression of neoliberal capital deprivation and latent, structural racism.

The 2010s saw continued complications of British identity with reinvigorated independence movements in Wales and Scotland, the latter even holding an (unsuccessful) referendum on independence following the Scottish National Party's election in 2011.[1] Sociological research shows that 'over the last 40 years, a higher fraction of the British population has identified exclusively with their nationality', whether as a citizen of the UK, England, Scotland or Wales, 'and a correspondingly lower fraction has identified as European' (Carl, Dennison and Evans 2018: 289).[2] 'Britishness', which is 'relatively deep-rooted' and 'somewhat unique within the EU' (299), may in fact hamper a sense of European identity because of a constitutive Euroscepticism tempered by specific aspects of 'history, culture and geography' such as Britain's island status, its 'relatively strong cultural and political links with much of its former Empire', and being the only major European power to have not been occupied during the aforementioned traumas of the twentieth century (297). Jon Stratton even argues that the

English cultural imaginary has 'historically always resulted in an antipathy to integration with the continent of Europe', with specific concerns of 'invasion, occupation and sovereignty' (2019: 225) due to an 'unresolved cultural trauma of the Second World War' (247).

However, central to both contemporary questions of British identity and the Brexit vote is racism. This is related not so much to cultural trauma, but to the trauma of colonialism and assumed superiority historically inflicted by Britain, particularly on Black and Brown bodies. Indeed, in the context of Brexit – placed, for example, by Reni Eddo-Lodge within a broader history of structural British racism (2018: 119) – the artistic director of the Bush Theatre between 2012 and 2019, Madani Younis, noted that in 2016 'few of us could have predicted the steep rise in racially motivated hate crime, or the vitriol that was unleashed on the "immigrant"' (2017: iv). With the Bush's hosting of Reginald Edmund's 'Black Lives, Black Words' the next year, an international project of short plays by and about the Black diaspora, Black British playwrights like Seaton, Winsome Pinnock, Trish Cooke, Mojisola Adebayo and Rachel De-Lahay further represented how British society harboured structural racism in the context of Brexit.

Such xenophobia is also more widely relevant to questions of European identity. As Butler's theories on performativity demonstrate, identity is the performance of, (re)establishment of, and (re)iteration of socio-cultural norms, which become embodied through everyday routines and activities, moulding into (and ever-evolving as) a performative identity. Yet, oriented on a place that is itself vague, European identity is too 'zoomed-out' from citizens' everyday 'performances', with material markers being the most important signifiers of this identity: 'half of those who are citizens of eurozone countries cite the euro. Only half as many cite history and culture' (Green 2015: 4). This has proven a particular issue when creating a sense of European identity in Britain, where material, symbolic representations of Europeanness, not to mention proximity and land borders to other European nations, have generally been lacking in British citizens' routines.[3] With the concept of Europeanness being so complex on one hand or, on the other, 'so diluted that it means anything and nothing' (Stråth 2000: 44), it is often based on what the political scientist Patrizia Isabelle Nanz calls 'symbolic boundary-drawing and [...] different politics of inclusion/exclusion' (2000: 294). Despite Europe in the 2010s, as Gluhović states, 'still / again facing xenophobia, racism, and inequality' (2013: 4), European and, more specifically, British identity can instead be understood in the 2010s as constitutive of contemporaneous contexts of violence – in great part, because of the very 'politics of inclusion/exclusion' they attempted to define themselves by.

Europeanness and the Other in *Lampedusa* and *How to Hold Your Breath*

Though the last chapter posed that the placelessness, violent situations and supposedly European theatrical practices seen in many cross-cultural British-European plays were key in the representation of a deleterious, transnational neoliberalism felt by many Europeans over the 2010s, there were several other, more tangible crises faced by Europe across the decade which also raised questions of what it meant to be 'European'. These included the rising authoritarian tendencies of Andrzej Duda and Victor Orbán's respective governments in Poland and Hungary, the economic crash in Greece, and the annexation of Crimea by the Russian Federation and the war in Donbas. But among these, the Mediterranean refugee crisis stands as the most devastating for loss of human life. Although the contention in the last chapter that the placeless plays of the 2010s could be read in the context of Brexit as an open, communitarian arena for considerations of Europe, the refugee crisis demonstrated that 'openness' was something for Europeans alone. Despite a context of historical violence and the urgent death toll of the individuals attempting to reach Europe, these refugees instead became the 'Other' for European identity – dispossessed subjects dehumanized by their very existence outside the bounds and borders of European neoliberalism.

Due in great part but not exclusively to the collection of uprisings and civil wars that the media of the Global North homogenously called the Arab Spring – not to mention the effects of the UK and US' wars in Iraq and Afghanistan – many individuals were forced into exodus from their homes in North Africa, the Middle East and elsewhere. Though Europe had been generally celebratory of the Arab Spring, this support did not seem to extend to much material action or aid for its ramifications. With access to Europe sought out through several routes, the International Organization for Migration estimated that in 2014 alone 3,072 people died in the attempt to cross the most dangerous of these passages, the Mediterranean Sea. Despite Italy's appeal for assistance with humanitarian aid, Lustgarten writes that 'the EU's response, driven by the cruellest British government in living memory, was to cut the main rescue operation', which was replaced with one that received a third less in funding (2015). As Achille Mbembe states, Europe claims 'the largest marine cemetery in this century', and those refugees who survived their long journeys found themselves in a 'Europe of camps. Samos, Chios, Lesbos, Idomeni, Lampedusa, Vintimille, Sicily, Subotica – the list goes on' (2019: 102). These camps became, for many, detention centres of indefinite deferral, while for those who finally reached their destination they were met with bureaucratic indifference, hostility and racism.

The crisis, then, is in many ways a failure of Europe: but not for the reasons Nigel Farage's inciteful 2016 Leave campaign poster implied, which showed a long line of refugees appearing to walk towards the viewer's perspective, framed by the words 'breaking point: the EU has failed us all' (Stewart and Mason 2016). Instead, Europe's failure is in its institutions' and peoples' cultural and political identities as being apparently, in the contexts of colonialism and the traumas of the twentieth century, 'articulated around peace, democracy, and human rights' (Gluhović 2013: 9). Rather than European identity offering Nancy's ideal 'incomplete' community or a transcension of 'previous nationalist rivalries' as Nanz writes, it has been crafted 'by uniting against "outsiders" such as immigrants' (2000: 290) – which, in the 2010s, significantly consisted of those often dehumanized in mass media as 'boat people'. In the context of Europe's inability to construct a cohesive shared identity partially expressed through Brexit, and unable to live up to its apparent standards, it can be levied that 'Europeanism itself is a universal form (and rhetorical phrase) hollow on the inside' (Velikonja 2013: 256–7). Against the (at best) inefficient or (at worst) uncaring response to the crisis, European theatre-makers sought to represent it onstage and potentially generate action from their audiences. S. E. Wilmer writes that '[b]ecause the need for asylum has been increasing and the problem is not being solved by political means, artists have been using theatrical performance to intervene in the political arena to offer insight and new perspectives' (2018: 2). This was particularly true in Britain, whose governments were influential in the more 'fortress-like' practices of the EU's border control.

Emma Welton records that British theatrical institutions 'embarked upon nuanced representations of migration and exile, to proactively support immigration communities' (2020: 230), seen with the Theatres of Sanctuary programme, the 2016–17 Horizons programme at the Young Vic, and in dedicated companies such as LegalAlien, Phosphorous and Maison Foo (242). Plays that variously depicted the crisis and its effects included Hannah Khalil and Untold Theatre's *The Scar Test* (Arcola, 2015), David Greig's version of Aeschylus' *The Suppliant Women* (YV, 2016), Tess Berry-Hart's *Cargo* (Arcola, 2016) James Phillips's *Flood* (Hull, 2017) and Henry Naylor's *Borders* (Fringe, 2017). The most commercially successful of these was Joe Murphy and Joe Robertson's *The Jungle*, which premiered at the Young Vic in 2017 before transferring to the West End's Playhouse Theatre. The two writers drew on testimonies gathered from their work with Good Chance Theatre, which managed a temporary theatre space in 'The Jungle' – the nickname for the refugee camp at Calais destroyed by French officials in late 2016. *The Jungle*'s narrative revolves around the sometimes tense interactions between British volunteers and the diverse denizens of the camp. After various experiences of violence that have propelled and dogged their journeys, many of the refugees espouse an idealistic idea of Europe. Though this has been eroded by prosecution and harassment, many still hope the UK will fulfil their utopian vision.

Welton continues that the production used tactics of humour, identification and proximity (some of the audience appear to be seated in the central, purpose-built café of the camp, and even share food with the performers) to the ends that an 'empathetic understanding [...] may *do* something to redress the hostilities of British immigration' (2020: 231; emphasis in original). Though it is difficult to chart how performative affect can influence material doing, Welton specifically judges *The Jungle* for 'drawing spectators into emotional identification with individual characters, at the expense of broader systemic critique' (235). The West End run of *The Jungle* had donation buckets and supplied information on how audiences could help refugees – though a cynical reading could be that this merely provided an easy way for its relatively well-off audiences to relieve their guilt at the end of the play. Furthermore, the move from the Young Vic to the West End, and then to Broadway – targeting audiences of large metropolitan centres – seems ill-advised given the production's objective to garner empathy, when a tour that included venues in locations with stronger opposition to immigration may have potentially had better affective, performative socio-political impact. The immersive dramaturgy, then, is too 'zoomed-in' to offer its audience a critical reflection of the structures that maintain the conditions of the refugee crisis: Welton even contends that the individuation that immersive strategies encourage aligns with the neoliberal state's abdication of care, placing 'responsibility upon the individual spectator' (238). Therefore, she surmises, 'productions representing migration should maintain a critical distance from existing structures of political power, resist dramaturgies of proximity which simplify differences, and allow their audiences the creative and critical imagination to be politically mobilized' (242).

Two plays that move towards a fulfilment of these criteria are *Lampedusa* and *How to Hold Your Breath*. The former is by Anders Lustgarten, a self-defined 'anti-prop' playwright who looks 'at the effects of major systems on real people [...] in quite a realistic, practical way' (Doohan 2013). His extensive output over the 2010s included *A Day at the Racists* (Finborough, 2010), which depicts the 'conversion' of working-class Labour voters towards right-wing, racist parties like the BNP; *If You Don't Let Us Dream, We Won't Let You Sleep* (mentioned in the last chapter); and an expansive representation of the lives affected by drone warfare in the Middle East in *Shrapnel: 34*

Fragments of a Massacre (Arcola, 2015). Lustgarten believes his plays offer '[t]he possibility of agency, of emotional connection with other people in an economic system predicated on fragmented isolation and comfort shopping. And it's that hope, perversely, that really offends certain people' (2016a: x). Indeed, a lukewarm review of *Lampedusa* from Susannah Clapp notes that 'apparently first-hand accounts are looped into an improbably hopeful plot', though she admits the production put her 'on the verge of weeping' (2015). *Lampedusa* was developed with the artistic director and co-founder of the HighTide theatre company and festival, Steven Atkinson, who notes that the refugee crisis 'started to headline the TV news' as the play opened at London's Soho Theatre in April 2015, before transferring to the HighTide Festival in September as 'public opinion finally shifted away from the growing fear and xenophobia' with the widely reported image of Alan Kurdi, 'a three-year old Syrian boy, washed up ashore in Bodrum, Turkey' (2016: xiii). As Clapp mentions, *Lampedusa* comprises two overlapping monologues from the Italian fisherman-turned-lifeguard but, mostly, body retriever Stefano (played by Ferdy Roberts) and the British-East Asian debt collector Denise (Louise Mai Newberry).

How to Hold Your Breath is by the prolific Scottish playwright Zinnie Harris, whose major works over the 2010s were revisions of classics including the *Oresteia* adaptation *This Restless House* (Citizens, 2016), the Orpheus and Eurydice-myth-inspired *Meet Me at Dawn* (Traverse, 2017), the Ibsen-filtered-through-#MeToo *(the fall of) The Master Builder* (West Yorkshire Playhouse, Leeds, 2017), and the ghostly, feminist retelling of John Webster's *The Duchess [of Malfi]* (Lyceum, Edinburgh, 2019). *Hold Your Breath*, too, is something of a 'riff' on European classics, being as Rebellato describes 'a kind of anti-*Faust*, a play about a woman refusing a pact with the devil, and being pursued across Europe' (2018: 35–6). Directed by Vicky Featherstone at the Royal Court in February 2015, it opens with Dana (played by Maxine Peake) waking up with Jarron (Michael Shaeffer) after he has mistaken her for a sex worker. When Dana refuses Jarron's money, the self-confessed demon/ UN employee appears to place a physical mark and curse on her. After she receives a job offer in Egypt, Dana and her pregnant sister Jasmine (Christine Bottomley) travel from their home in Berlin as Europe goes into economic collapse. Hounded by another demon, the enigmatic Librarian (Peter Forbes), the sisters eventually attempt to cross the Mediterranean Sea on an ill-equipped boat, during which Jasmine drowns. Dana is only saved by the demons when they judge that she will forget the horrors of her journey, stating that 'people like Dana [...] live in a hazy afternoon' (Harris 2015: 158). The implication here is that 'people like Dana' – Europeans – can easily 'wash off' the tumultuous events they witness in their lives.

Both plays, then, offer a more 'zoomed-out' observation of the refugee crisis than *The Jungle*: in *Hold Your Breath* through magic realism and an imaginative reversal of those affected; and in *Lampedusa* through the implicit connection of British austerity to underfunded Italian/EU rescue operations. Though Clapp's emotional experience of *Lampedusa* (which was not distinct to her review) may signal the 'blinding' individualistic empathy Welton criticizes, this is balanced by the distance between Denise and Stefano. This equilibrium between criticality and empathy can be described through the term 'touching tales'. This is applied by Liesbeth Minnaard (2020) to *Lampedusa* and taken from Leslie Adelson's description of cultural narratives that connect different social groups which 'evoke a culturally residual, referentially non-specific sense of guilt, blame, and danger' (Adelson 2000: 102). The associations between marginalized groups then 'touch' epistemologically – but are *touching* in that they channel cultural anxieties and cause emotional affect to champion the multicultural incorporation of others/Others. In *Lampedusa*, the two narratives are brought into proximity with one another, making constructive connections between callous social attitudes in Britain and the refugee crisis; drawing it closer to the innocuous functioning of contemporary society for British audiences and so increases the crisis' affect through touching these tales. As Atkinson reports, '[s]ome audiences cried. Some were motivated to action. Others were affronted' (2016: xiii).

The production's methods of direct address and actor-spectator closeness engendered affect, particularly during the HighTide shows, which were performed in a temporary wooden, domed amphitheatre designed by Lucy Osborne. As Atkinson continues: 'with the wind rushing the dome and the sound of the sea outside [...] the audience sat on benches corkscrewing upwards, and the cast sat amongst them' (xiii). This was alike to *The Jungle*'s staging then, albeit more intimate and evocative, but the balance of simultaneous distance and proximity in *Lampedusa*'s narrative voices demonstrated the encompassing neoliberalism that exacerbated the crisis. On the other hand, *Hold Your Breath* attempted to balance affect and critical distance by transplanting its metropolitan audience into an alternate version of the refugee crisis – implicitly asking, 'what if it were us?' Its critical distance, as with *Lampedusa*, was made through wider connections: to neoliberalism as represented by the finance-driven and self-help advocating demons and, like *Three Kingdoms*, to neoliberalism's exacerbation of gender inequality and commodification more specifically: it being telling that, like Kane's *Blasted*, the play opens with oppressive gender dynamics before disintegrating into catastrophe.

Still, perhaps *Hold Your Breath*'s dramaturgy was too 'zoomed-out': Harris stated that it 'didn't hit home' for audiences (Gardner 2018) and it received unenthusiastic reviews. For example, Billington writes that 'what you get, dramatically, is repetition rather than development or debate' and that it 'feels as it were illustrating a thesis rather than exploring a conflict' (2015). Again, as with *Three Kingdoms*, Featherstone's direction and Chloe Lamford's design connote 'European practices': the performances appeared dreamlike, particularly Peake's Dana, and the set was a major signifier in critiquing 'the imbrication of consumerism and structural violence' as Tom Cornford writes, 'resembling a furniture showroom which was gradually stripped away to nothing, and billboards of lifestyle imagery and advertising that were removed to reveal a tattered public information poster from the 2014–2015 Ebola outbreak' (2018: 105). The climax then took place on an abstract representation of a boat, with the characters precariously perched as the stage floor itself diagonally arched upwards. Again, these scenographic techniques created a vision of an empty, neoliberal Europe – but may have been too distancing to fully motivate any affective action for the audience or demonstrate their own performative implication in the structural violence on display.

This performative implication, specifically, is how individuals may foster a sense of Europeanness that maintains structural violence and the conditions on which violence like the Mediterranean refugee crisis occurs: in other words, being European through exclusion and exploitation of Others. Not only does this refer to how (European) neoliberalism is enacted through embodied behaviour as articulated by the plays explored in the previous chapter, but how Europeanness may combine with neoliberal attitudes to Other those beyond its free-market boundaries, or those who threaten to cross them and would seem to demand European responsibility. In *Lampedusa*, Denise and Stefano both espouse individualism, weariness and wariness, reflecting the contemporary malaise of European society and politics, particularly towards migrants and refugees. Though such attitudes would not usually be thought of as pertaining to a European identity, Denise and Stefano's similar demonstration of them seem to suggest they are nevertheless a commonality among contemporary Europeans. As the latter states of his titular community in response to the crisis: 'Why are we, a little dusty island you've never ever heard of, left to deal with all this alone? / And do the migrants not understand Europe is fucked?' (Lustgarten 2016b: 266–7). Denise, too, dismisses those she collects from – 'you ant got the money, do without' (265) yet is initially unable to theorize her occupation as a debt collector as connected to the 'breathtaking cruelty' (274) that inhibits the state from allowing welfare for her disabled mother, or, indeed, as part of the same ideology that informs the reservation of funds for the rescue operations Stefano is a part of. It is their close embeddedness in these violent situations that keeps them from recognizing the suffering of others/Others in the various ideological cruelties of European neoliberalism, and therefore their attitudes and behaviours continue to foster this structural violence of neoliberal-Europeanness.

Meanwhile, *Hold Your Breath* poses Europeanness as hollowed out by its structural violence. Dana and The Librarian mention literature including Shakespeare, Proust, Milton, Dante and Goethe with the implication that European culture is built upon 'demons': of colonialism, imperialism, feudalism, religious intolerance, xenophobia and other forms of exploitation and violence. The demons of the play themselves are incarnations of the neoliberalism of contemporary history, representing the finance-oriented ideology through a necessity for commodification as 'the original transactional creature' (Harris 2015: 45), and offering a stream of self-help guides such as '[h]*ow to Get a Good Seat at the Theatre* [and] *Which Charity You Should Give to to Make you Feel Better*' (158; emphasis in original). Seemingly demonstrating a demonic heart at the centre of Europeanness, the production depicts an absence of European identity corroded by its contextual violence – a lack of ground for Europe to solidly exist on, as even the hazardous, unstable stage floor seems to suggest. Dana, who speaks of the privilege of her Europeanness – 'because we live in Europe, because nothing really bad happens' (92) – does not share any solidarity with other Europeans aside from her sister. This is brutally depicted when Dana must perform sex work to raise funds to make the Mediterranean crossing, being assaulted by other women in the same situation who, to easily steal her money, fool her into a sense of camaraderie. The attackers' conversation refutes the stance that experiences of violence can inform shared identity: 'Marta: give her a minute [...] she's hurt / Clara: we're all hurt' (139). Dana refuses money for sex at the play's start, and by the conclusion has, out of necessity, performed sex work, lost the remainder of her family and had her memory wiped.

Hold Your Breath, then, illustrates a European 'non-identity'. Rather than enhancing any sense of European identity, Dana's journey across a violent Europe seems to efface it. As she describes the catastrophe around her: 'it's hell then / it might have been Europe yesterday' (122). This apocalyptic-dystopian interpretation of contemporary Europe depicts a cultural landscape and identity eroded by a lack of commitment, continual contexts of violence like neoliberal policy and the refugee crisis, and a historical context of violence as symbolized by the demons. The creeping destruction of Dana's identity is visualized by the mark left on her by Jarron, which slowly grows across her body. In contrast to her agonizing, identity-destroying odyssey, the demons seemingly appear at will – demonstrating the apparently unsolicited movement afforded to the neoliberal market and to Europeans more generally (Mbembe 2019: 103). Like the pernicious, free-travelling sex traffickers of *Three Kingdoms*, the demons can at once appear anywhere in the production's neoliberal-permeated vision of Europe while remaining dissociated from their space of residence and are uncaring of contemporary catastrophes: 'Jarron: I didn't do a single thing. / Librarian: alright, but you watched. You didn't stop it' (155). In many ways the demons represent archetypal, neoliberal Europeans, granted free movement and a lack of obligation to place and peoples not unlike Theresa May's 'citizens of nowhere'. If 2010s Europeanism is defined by transnationalism, *Hold Your Breath* poses that they are in a state of constantly 'leaving behind' the reality of Europe, inconsequentially effacing their point of origin and being disinterested in the spaces they pass through – which appear, like them, atomized and disconnected.

Though *Lampedusa* too initially demonstrates this fragmented, individualistic Europeanness in its characters, it optimistically poses that, like Nancy's ideal, open community, a European identity unbound from neoliberalism and violence can be performatively constructed through the respect and incorporation of alterity – of the Other. Denise and Stefano both begin to enact positive behaviours and attitudes through burgeoning friendships with two such characters: Carolina, a Portuguese migrant in debt who comforts Denise after the loss of her mother and encourages her studies in politics; and Mobido, a refugee who Stefano reluctantly bonds with before searching for, and saving, his wife Aminata. Denise, given support and perspective from her friendship, abandons her job as a debt collector; while Stefano ends the play as the guest of honour at Mobido and Aminata's 'second wedding', '[t]heir "European wedding", they called it. To celebrate her coming back from the dead' (290). The implication is that their respect of the Other has resulted in perceptual criticality for Denise, and something of a minor revival of the 'essence of Europe' for Stefano. Denise concludes with a summary of her completed politics essay on 'untrammelled materialism', in which she argues for 'our ability to walk away from delusions, from traps. To save ourselves from our baser instincts' (289–90). These baser instincts, as in Denise's story, include the material greed that encourage debt, propagate racist scapegoats, and shut individuals off from others and their realities. As she confesses: 'I'm not a giver. A confider. I cling on to what I am [...] because I've had to fight so bloody hard for every last inch of it' (279). In their respective situations of violence, both characters became apathetic in response to their vulnerability. Once they lose their prejudices and confide in others/Others, they begin to enact positive change.

The version of European identity that *Lampedusa* appears to advocate, then, is one in which citizens/audiences understand how experiences of interconnected violence 'touch tales' with one another, conforming with the assertion in the last chapter that the presentation of socio-cultural, cross-European trauma can generate a reactionary sense of identity that opposes the adoption of neoliberalism. The embodied vulnerability and precarity that come from its structural violence encourages insularity and self-reliance – characteristics of the model neoliberal citizen. Rather than allowing these 'baser instincts' to take over, *Lampedusa* argues that accepting this vulnerability and recognizing it in others/Others can productively generate a more communal sense of identity without Welton's concern of simplifying differences. Though *Lampedusa* appears to fulfil her criteria then, there are still representational issues in Lustgarten's advocacy for a more open, cosmopolitan European identity. Namely, the secondary characters of Carolina and Mobido are never physicalized onstage, instead being 'suppliant' to the development of Denise and Stefano. This issue is even more prominent in *Hold Your Breath* which, in its more pessimistic perspective on European (non-)identity, did not seem to fulfil Welton's third standard of mobilizing action to the extent that descriptions of *Lampedusa* attest – at least in Featherstone's Court production.

Hold Your Breath 'seeks not to expose the condition of migrancy so much as the structural violence of privilege' (Cornford 2018: 104), therefore its depiction of refugees suffer from self-reflection – like *Lampedusa*, being foils to the representational primacy of its central characters as well as the dramaturgical arguments on European identity. Though Cornford praises the 'thoroughly justified critique of the structural violence of global inequality' in the play, there is an abjection of 'racialised migrant-figures' (105) which appear as extras throughout, dressed in dark clothing and being more diversely cast than the white, European central characters. Like those plays discussed in the last chapter that performatively reiterate visions of a violent Europe, *Lampedusa* and *Hold Your Breath* are implicated in representational suggestions that the refugees are subaltern to Europeans, as is the crisis itself to considerations of European identity. So, unlike *The Jungle*, both plays allow a measure of critical distance that makes the refugee crisis more salient as linked to structural violence. Whereas *Hold Your Breath* suggests that this structural violence has hollowed out any notion of European identity, *Lampedusa* poses that a genuine, interdependent one can be forged out of a respect and duty of care towards those that neoliberalism and xenophobia would Other. Both also depict how individual behaviours – specifically, privilege in *Hold Your Breath* and insularity in *Lampedusa* – performatively engender the status of an empty, neoliberal-Europeanness that is especially uncaring to the dispossessed. Still, despite these productions' representations of the Mediterranean refugee crisis, they both seem to utilize it as a crux for considerations of European identity rather than foregrounding the refugees' subjectivities which, despite Welton's critique, *The Jungle* better exceeds at.

Cornford states that accounts 'of theatrical representations of nationhood' should come with a consideration of 'who will tell the other[ed] stories' (2018: 111; brackets in original) and finds more satisfactory conveyances of this in work from theatre-makers outside the normative borders of European identity in Zodwa Nyoni's *Nine Lives* (Òran Mór, 2014) and Isango Ensemble's *A Man of Good Hope* (YV, 2016). As he continues, 'the engagement of such differential experiences' is crucial in the predominantly white, Eurocentric British theatre – both for theatre institutions, and academics (111–12). Indeed, diverse as the dramaturgies of the plays analysed here are, they come from creatives with relative privilege and 'belonging' in British culture. It is, of course, difficult to gauge what the 'nodes' of these performances contributed to the British public sphere in relation to Brexit, with both plays preceding the referendum. The next section continues by inspecting 2010s British identity within these questions of Europeanness which, informed by the ramifications of Brexit, are interconnected with structural racism. The case study is a production that unsettles 'the predominantly white, Eurocentric British theatre' from a writer whose identity exists as 'suspect' by the structural, racist violence her play critiques.

Racism and British Identity in *Fall of the Kingdom, Rise of the Foot Soldier*

Like other right-wing movements across the Global North in the 2010s, such as France's Front National, Trump's US administration, and the politics of Duda and Orbán, the anti-neoliberal stance of Brexit was enacted in great part through nationalist populism (Corbett and Walker 2019: 87–8): a collection of political ideologies that commonly unleash racist sentiment to garner support, while often being themselves covertly neoliberalist. As Nadine Holdsworth writes on British identity and social abjection: 'Brexit, like the Windrush Scandal, revealed deep anxieties around the relationships that immigrants and their descendants have with the host nation and lifted a veil on how the immigrant, no matter how long they have lived in Britain or how integrated they are or appear to be, is always suspect, is the stranger' (2020: 170). While informed by issues of wealth inequality, Brexit was nevertheless engendered by, and engendering of, the overt and systemic racism that has festered within 'Britishness'. One theatrical articulation of British identity informed by structural, racist violence was Somalia Nonyé Seaton's *Fall of the Kingdom, Rise of the Foot Solider*. Seaton is a British theatre-maker of Jamaican and Nigerian descent, being the founder and artistic director of No Ball Games Allowed, a company that creates work with, and for, young people. Her plays over the 2010s included *Crowning Glory* (Theatre Royal Stratford East, London, 2013), which focuses on female agency and oppression, the familial trauma-concerned *House* with Clean Break (Assembly Rooms, Edinburgh, 2016), and *Mini Me* (Bunker, London, 2019) which was part of Rachel De-Lahay and Milli Bhatia's 'My White Best Friend (And Other Letters Left Unsaid)' festival.

Directed by Nadia Latif, *Fall/Rise* was part of the 'Making Mischief' season which debuted in July 2016 at the RSC's Other Place in Stratford-upon-Avon twinned with Fraser Grace's *Always Orange* (noted in the last chapter). In the spirit of Shakespeare's works that 'spoke truth to power', the RSC's deputy artistic director Erica Whyman stated that the plays would lay 'bare some of the most uncomfortable aspects of being alive in the United Kingdom now' (2016: xxi). Holdsworth writes that Seaton 'particularly wanted to address the nation's failure to find the appropriate language to openly discuss issues of race and national identity' (2020: 179). *Fall/Rise*'s set, designed by Madeleine Girling, consisted of a multitude of stacked boxes: some metal, some plastic and some filled with water 'which would show ripples at times of great emotion' (Baxter-Derrington 2016). Projections from the lighting designer Claire Gerrens would also illuminate these boxes with England flags or show news clippings of far-right politicians like Nick Griffin and Nigel Farage. A three-person Chorus intermittently occupied the stage, wearing cardboard boxes on their heads with drawn-on faces and eschewing nationalist populist and racist platitudes such as 'political correctness is causing our country irreversible scars' (Seaton 2016: 8). Their headpieces explicitly demonstrate the caricature-like nature of their words – many of which had been said by contemporaneous politicians – while identifying them as an embedded subsection of society: 'part of the scenery'.

Against this scenography, the teacher Sally Hawkins (played by Laura Howard) harbours Aisha (Donna Banya), a Black student who has killed a racist attacker in self-defence. It is later revealed that Hawkins had reported Aisha's incendiary blog explaining her experiences as a young Black woman living in London – 'set against the background of the government's Prevent strategy' as Gardner writes (2016b), which expected teachers to report 'extremist behaviour' exhibited by students. With Hawkins's boyfriend Archie (Ifan Meredith) freely making xenophobic comments at social gatherings and Aisha sent to trial, Hawkins's Pakistani-British friend Shabz (Syreeta Kumar) calls Hawkins out for enabling structural racism. The play ends with Aisha offering a rousing, revolutionary call to arms to a group of protesters. Debuting just a month after the Brexit referendum results, *Fall/Rise* presented a blistering critique of the systemic racism embodied in white, liberal attitudes in an area that voted in favour of Leave by 51.6 per cent ('EU Referendum' 2016). Audiences were faced with a discomforting vision of contemporary Britain: whether they were, perhaps, international tourists visiting the 'home of Shakespeare' in a country that would now seem less welcoming; residents shown the racist implications behind their majority Leave vote; the white, liberal theatregoers that make up much of the RSC's audiences given a mirror to their own innocuous biases; or Black and Global Majority spectators who were presented with a tangible image of the structural violence of British culture and society.

With its stylized set and Chorus sections, *Fall/Rise* moves towards the European practices discussed in the last chapter rather than strictly adhering to social realist theatre; the Chorus's box-masks are even reminiscent of the dehumanizing animal heads of *Three Kingdoms*. Yet, it is arguably more of a 'state-of-the-nation' play than most other British productions in the 2010s – including those within David Hare's dogmatic anti-European boundaries. As Holdsworth writes, state-of-the-nation plays see 'some sort of rupture, crisis or conflict' and 'comment directly or indirectly on the ills befalling society, on key narratives of nationhood or on the state of the nation as it wrestles with changing circumstances' (2020: 39). Though examples of British theatre later reflected on Brexit's ostensibly inherent racism such as Roy Williams's

The Death of England (NT, 2020), *Fall/Rise* was initially distinct in this regard as, after the surprising referendum result, the British theatre establishment generally began to question the lack of theatrical representations of Euroscepticism. As James Doeser reports, '96% of members of the Creative Industries Federation indicated they wanted to stay in the EU' (2016), and so theatres felt they had been biased towards Remain attitudes. Such a reflection was certainly warranted, especially if Brexit is understood 'as an expression of capital deprivation' as Rebellato writes (2018: 20; see also Pettifor 2017: 130).

Brexit could be viewed as a staple for further abjection of the working-class: Doeser continues that it 'was a grand expression of a long-standing yet previously muted philistinism' (2016). Such a perspective was criticized by Aleks Sierz, as it reduced Leave voters to being 'politically wrong' and 'culturally ignorant' (2017: 5). Still, theatre-makers who sought to pander to this Euroscepticism arguably perpetuated this sentiment: if Leave voters are 'culturally ignorant', theatre would have to be catered specifically for them as, otherwise, it would be unrelatable and beyond their understanding. The most notable expression of this was the commission of a 'Brexit play' by the artistic director of the National Theatre, Rufus Norris, which became Carol Ann Duffy's verbatim play *My Country; a work in progress* (2017), later broadcast as a short film on BBC2. Sierz records that it 'expressed[ed] the verbatim opinions of ordinary people: some reasonable, some racist, some frankly stupid' and, overall, 'has a good claim to be the worst new play of that year' (2018: 62). His damning critique of *My Country* is in part informed by its unnecessariness, as plays such as Rachel De-Lahay's *Routes* (RC, 2013), Carla Graul's *Occupied* (Theatre503, 2014), Andrew Muir's *The Session* (Soho, 2015), Stephen Laughton's *Screens* (Theatre503, 2016), and Tess Berry-Hart's *Cargo* had all previously offered nuanced depictions of Euroscepticism without transplanting racist sentiments onto a public stage. Though *My Country* shows commitment from the National Theatre towards a better representation of abject voices in the 2010s, it also shows how such projects can fail when these voices are 'pandered' to, or their racist statements are platformed to abject other less-represented groups.

Perhaps informed by the reiteration of an empty, placeless Europe on British stages, Sierz concludes that the 'failure of successive governments to "sell" the idea of being European to the British public at large is matched by theatre's failure to convince a mass audience that a European identity – as well as a British one – might be worth having' (2017: 11). This may additionally correspond with Balme's critique of contemporary British theatre as having etiolated into a 'black box of artistic absorption' (2014: 14). Though some productions like Rob Drummond's *The Majority* (NT, 2017) sought better engagement following the Brexit vote (albeit only through its dramaturgy and form), others like Gary Owen's *Iphigenia in Splott* (NT, 2016) seemed to take it for granted that theatre audiences would, generally speaking, be predominantly made up of white, middle-class individuals and so only represent the public to a limited extent. However, the very assumption of theatre spaces as being white and liberal arguably fed this perspective, as well as the marginalization of certain voices. As Emma Dennis-Edwards states, 'excuses of "risk" and "sales" that venues have tried to fob black people off with have been proven to be nonsense, and are in fact racist' (Minamore 2019). This racialized assumption also speaks to the class and political marginalization detected by Sierz in the discourse around theatre institutions' lack of Eurosceptical theatre.

With the successes of Inua Ellams's *Barber Shop Chronicles* (NT, 2018), Lee-Jones's *seven methods of killing kylie jenner*, and the West End transfers of Natasha Gordon's *Nine Night* (NT, 2018) and Arinzé Kene's *Misty* (Bush, 2018) supported by the crowdfunded Black Ticket Project, even by neoliberal standards, as Dennis-Edwards claims, '[t]he idea of black work being a "risk" is redundant – the numbers don't lie' (ibid.). Though these examples may well be an indication of representational improvement towards the end of the 2010s, the assumption of theatre as a white, liberal 'box' through much of the 2010s perhaps explains its apparent inability to generate identity coherence – European or British – because of the perpetuation of reductive ideas of *who* theatre audiences were, and what determining work would be programmed to attract such consumers. Though as Chapter 3 argues, *ear for eye* uses this assumption as a productive part of its dramaturgy – taking a similar approach to *Fall/Rise*. Both productions offer a zoomed-out perspective on structural, racist violence, but where tucker green brings audiences into an assertive reckoning with Black witnessing and historical trauma, Seaton presents a more 'contemporary trauma' of British racism – intersected here with the capital deprivation of neoliberalism and gender inequality which she indicates in interview are 'part of the same beast' of 'structural racism' (Marsh 2016; quoted in Holdsworth 2020: 179).

Fall/Rise was perhaps too temporally zoomed-in to the events of Brexit to be as widely recognized to the same extent as *ear for eye* or the productions mentioned above – responding with a 'knee-jerk' but productive anger evident of a playwright herself affected by the structural oppression it represented: as Seaton writes in her foreword, '[w]e must get angry. We must stay angry. We must get organised' (2016: 3). Reviews were middling (Gardner 2016b), with one even noting *Fall/Rise* was 'unfortunately hampered by the intensely pretentious production' (Baxter-Derrington 2016), perhaps levied at its more 'European' dramaturgical aspects, with Holdsworth even recording that 'Dominic Cavendish noted Seaton's "combative" stance and patronisingly suggested that "this is the generation of hurt feelings and self-reinforcing ire. Grim, really["]'' (2020: 182, quoting Cavendish 2016). *Fall/Rise* may have been hampered by the white, liberal racism that it castigates, appearing as it did in majority-Leave Stratford-upon-Avon, somewhat obscured from the metropolitan audiences of London (in which the narrative is based) or nearby central Birmingham. This is not to say that these important concerns should not be presented on more regional or tourist-oriented stages, but the 'organized anger' directed at a large portion of the RSC's audience here may have been too unsettling for many – their implication in the structural violence onstage made most explicit when Shabz tries to make Hawkins aware of her own part in it: 'you're the problem' (66).

Other depictions of structural racism in the 2010s were found in Roy Williams's *Sucker Punch* (RC, 2010), Natasha Marshall's *Half Breed* (Fringe, 2017) and Dennis-Edwards's *Funeral Flowers* (Fringe, 2018). *Fall/Rise* is distinct, though, in that like Žižek's iceberg model, Seaton poses whether 'the nut jobs out there, flying their St George' (67) who seem to initially appear as 'the background' or 'the landscape' of structural racism in Britain are simply the tip above water – the subjective violence – and it is the innocuous, liberal attitudes of individuals like Hawkins (and arguably a large portion of the RSC's clientele) that are performatively maintaining the systemic violence of racism. This violence is pronounced through staging specific performative behaviours and attitudes that sustain contemporary British racism – evidenced in the relationship between Aisha and Hawkins. Initially appearing as a caring figure who shelters Aisha after her attack, Hawkins is later shown to attempt to hamper Aisha's self-identity and her protestations to British race relations: as Shabz states, '[y]ou let them take that girl's voice away from her, she wrote about her experiences, as a young woman having been born into a country that she does not feel safe in, and it made you uncomfortable' (63). Qualifying Shabz's criticisms, Hawkins tells Aisha that 'one must be cautious about how one's passion is displayed' (32), calling her comments 'inflammatory' (37) – seeming to advocate her activism but only, as Aisha states, in 'a nice neutral colour palate […] an acceptable level of discomfort' (32).

Alike to the 'pattern-identifying' of Richardson (2020) and Eddo-Lodge (2018: 64), Holdsworth describes Aisha as 'exemplary' of Sara Ahmed's 'wilful subject' (2014), 'who keeps putting her head above the parapet to highlight social injustice or to locate her experience in a broader history of racial oppression' (2020: 181). Meanwhile, Hawkins is an example of a white liberal who comfortably backs 'good causes' – as Shabz says, '[g]ive to charity during Children in Need, fill out those change.org petitions' (67) – only to the extent that it does not alter the societal structure in which her position is benefited by her race. To use the language of *ear for eye*, Hawkins believes in 'progress' rather than 'change', duplicitously informing on Aisha's blog in accordance with the Prevent strategy. Later, when visiting Aisha in her cell, Hawkins tells her 'the world owes you nothing' (55), and when confronted by Shabz, Hawkins seems to view what has happened to Aisha individualistically – with self-pity, and as 'something bad' that has happened to herself rather than her student, unhelpfully 'wallowing in guilt' as Eddo-Lodge puts it, rather than actively tackling racism (2018: 215). These solipsistic, neoliberalist behaviours intersect with racial prejudice: as Shabz tells Hawkins: 'do you see how easy it is for you to become the victim?' (64).

These performative behaviours and attitudes, as *Fall/Rise* depicts, constitute contemporary notions of British identity. This is suggested by Madeleine Girling's set, which is littered by boxes of different sizes showing both far-right politicians and England flags – alongside the connotation of rigid 'identity boxes' which can become oppressive and confining, literalized when Aisha is imprisoned (51). Laura Howard's measured performance as Hawkins, which represents professional, pastoral concern, means that her hypocrisies must be made explicit by Shabz's dialogue to underline the harmfulness of her otherwise innocuous actions:

Shabz And I hope all of this has helped to open your eyes a little bit

Hawkins To what?

Shabz Well things maybe you don't ordinarily notice

Hawkins Like?

Shabz You're silent. You're always silent when you should speak up.

(62)

The 'silent' and polite Britishness of Hawkins in this regard connects to the provocations of the Chorus: 'At the core of British values we hold mutual respect and tolerance of different faiths and beliefs at the forefront of all we stand for as a nation' (29). Holdsworth notes that Seaton understands the liberal impairment to discuss racism as due 'to a heady combination of English reserve, fear of causing offence and an uncertainty of how to address complex and inflammatory topics with deeply ingrained historical roots' (2020: 179). As Hawkins demonstrates with her relationships, this 'tolerance' appears to allow more credence for racist views as with Archie's generalized xenophobia and less for genuine structural criticism.

Such tolerance, like the white haze which opens *ear for eye*, is described in *Fall/Rise* as an obscurement. As Aisha states, 'world's full of smoke' (40), and as Shabz says to Hawkins, comparing her to the overt racist 'nut jobs': 'People like you, well you're a bit harder to make out through the mist' (67). Eddo-Lodge also uses this metaphor: 'In a world where blunt, obvious acts are just the tip of the iceberg of racism, we need to describe the invisible monolith [...] We need to see racism as structural in order to see its insidiousness. We need to see how it seeps, like a noxious gas, into everything' (2018: 222). Similarly, Arinzé Kene's *Misty* symbolizes white, liberal gentrification specifically as a 'virus'. The 'smoke', 'mist' or 'virus' of the performative attitudes and behaviours constituting British identity tolerates racism to be fostered within it, while making hyper-visible anyone that stands out from its normative whiteness. In his preface for the playtext, for example, Kene questions what is meant by a 'black play' (2018: 3), why theatre is often denoted this way if it has a Black director or Black performers, while there is no common use of 'white plays'. *Fall/Rise* looks to 'zoom' its audience out of this 'mist' to understand Brexit – though necessarily intersected with issues of neoliberalism and capital deprivation – not as an anomaly of British identity, but as a revelation of a specific, deleterious part of it. As Shabz states: '2016, a year for exposing the beast that lies dormant in the belly of our country' (49).

Fall/Rise depicts a British identity fractured by contexts of violence: at once too 'silent' to defend any of its multicultural aspirations; too intertwined with neoliberalism to grant genuine social reform to those made abject by capital deprivation (and who look to abject others/Others in turn); and too 'tolerant' to offer a productive alternative to racism and populism. With the 'smoke' let out, Aisha believes society is unable to 'put it back once the lid's popped off' (40), therefore the play ends with revolutionary 'change': Aisha leading a demonstration, and the stage directions reading '[t]*he city burns. The people remain ...*' (69). Despite this fiery call to arms – not unlike the final question of *ear for eye* – *Fall/Rise* was perhaps 'too close' to Brexit and ill-situated in Stratford-upon-Avon for wider success; and assumed and challenged its audiences as part of a white, liberal structure which, as Dennis-Edwards states, has arguably proliferated the marginalization of certain voices on the 2010s British stage (Minamore 2019). Holdsworth contends that the 'English nation is blighted by a number of internal rifts and fissures that pit people against each other in ways that cast particular groups as threats to the nation', and theatre 'is implicated in both counter-hegemonic and resistant narratives that question and challenge' as well as potentially contributing 'to the recirculation of problematic cultural imaginaries that become attached to groups that fuel the kind of "cultural atmosphere" that fuelled Brexit' (2020: 3). Indeed, the most unsettling elements of *Fall/Rise* are the questions it poses to theatre audiences and institutions: how complicit are we in the structural violence that performatively oppresses identity groups?

With an assumed clientele, other theatre-makers and audiences have less space; as Camilla Whitehill puts it, '[w]hen white male is the status quo, everything else is shunted into tiny spaces' (2017). This apparently monopolized cultural capital of the theatre industry intersects with actual capital, as Rebellato poses in the context of understanding Brexit 'as an expression of capital deprivation' (2018: 20). With statistics supporting this, as he continues: 'In the theatre […] we have been accustomed to seeing ourselves as politically on the left, in opposition to the capitalist class, but these figures entitle us to ask ourselves, which side are we on?' (ibid.). With *Fall/Rise* describing the explicit, overt racism of some Leave voters as 'they know who they are and they know what they believe in' (Seaton 2016: 67), their actions and behaviours are construed as emergent from the landscape that surrounds them. Additionally, Eddo-Lodge identifies the neoliberal 'scarcity mentality' deployed on 'the white working classes' that 'shifts the focus of the problem on to black and brown people' (2018: 203). So, has the 'neoliberalization' of British theatre and its exacerbation of a white, liberal space – in some ways, a microcosm of capital control in society more widely – steered through the cultural capital of the theatre's 'node' in the public sphere a very partial construction of what Britishness is, and who is included in it? With identity groups beyond the white liberal make-up of British theatre 'put into little boxes', *Fall/Rise* and its scenography perhaps asserts, despite the subjective, obvious racist violence of the Chorus, that it is the 'box-creation' – the 'structure' – that benefits some through the abjection of Others/others.

Conclusion

The phenomena around Brexit, tied as they are to notions of British identity and relations to Europe and European identity, are themselves connected to the contexts of violence mentioned above – but also intersect with specifically British structural violence and its own national racism. *Fall/Rise* demonstrates these failings inherent in British identity as structured by the predominance of white, liberal attitudes – which push abject voices into compartmentalized 'boxes'. The performativity of (white, neoliberal) Britishness engenders the racism seen around Brexit, as well as the reactionary anti-establishment Leave vote which, fostered by issues of capital deprivation, scapegoats the immigrant, the Other and even British citizens of Black and Global Majority descent. All the productions discussed here share an understanding that in the violent contexts, respectively, of Brexit and its inescapable connection to structural racism; the 'cultural trauma' of European neoliberalism; and the wider crisis of European identity as articulated by that which it is not (the dispossessed refugee), group identity constructed in a context of violence is self-defeating, destructive and in desperate need of performative change.

This change is depicted in *Fall/Rise* as coming from plurally performative, revolutionary action; in *Lampedusa* as necessitated on interconnectivity over individuality, and in *Hold Your Breath* cannot occur until Europe's 'demons' or, in *Three Kingdoms* its 'wolves', are expunged. For these last two productions' monstrous characterizations of Europe's contemporary ills – to which can be added the box-wearing Chorus of *Fall/Rise* – the plays analysed over this and the last chapter show that the contemporary violence of racism, nationalist populism and neoliberalism felt across Britain and Europe is not contained within distinct individuals or events, but within the performative behaviours of its citizens. This is seen in the commodification and dehumanization illustrated in *Pomona*; the internal turmoil of Ignatius in *Three Kingdoms*; the defensiveness of Louise and Stefano in *Lampedusa*; the privilege of Dana in *How to Hold Your Breath*; and the unnoticed biases of Hawkins in *Fall/Rise*. Such behaviours and attitudes, as demonstrated in the last, are often innocuous and every-day, ranging across a spectrum of acts affiliated to differing extents to contexts and structures of violence. This 'continuum' approach to violence is explored in the next chapter, which analyses how 2010s British theatre represented and interrogated gender-based violence and oppression.

7

Gender

Speaking about her direction of Sarah Kane's *Cleansed* at the National Theatre in 2016, Katie Mitchell mentions that she was influenced by an essay which 'proposes that violence is a gendered activity [...] that it's men who do violence' (Trueman 2016b). She then suggests that Kane may have framed violence in the torturous extremities evident in *Cleansed* because 'if it is a gendered activity and you're a feminist, then you're going to portray it very particularly [...] [M]aybe the feminist rage *at that* is why the violence is so intense' (ibid.; emphasis in original). Though Kane's stance on feminism has remained ambivalent,[1] Mitchell's dramaturgical consideration of this theory highlights a key facet of feminist discourse over the decade: that normative gender identities can enable the perpetuation of gender-based violence.

The essay Mitchell refers to is by Rebecca Solnit, who argues that: 'We have an abundance of rape and violence against women in this country and on this Earth, though it's almost never treated as a civil rights or human rights issue, or a crisis, or even a pattern. Violence doesn't have a race, a class, a religion, or a nationality, but it does have a gender' (2014: 21). Solnit, then, articulates that much violence is a symptom of reiterated gender identities that have been affirmed so continually that the systemic violence they create is rendered invisible. This invisibility and the silence it often affords were vehemently challenged by many examples of British theatre over the 2010s. The focus of this chapter is to chart and examine the ways in which gender-based violence was depicted onstage over this decade, with special accordance given to feminist scholarship and practitioners. But first, it is important to define what is meant by gender-based violence, especially in relation to *gendered* violence, as well as briefly expound on the relevance here of performativity and 'fourth-wave' feminism.

Gender, Violence and the Fourth-Wave Onstage

Returning to Solnit, her essay has twin contentions: firstly, that violence's many forms are typified as homogenously gendered when they should, in fact, be understood as predominantly masculine since they are overwhelmingly perpetrated by men globally (2014: 25–6) and enacted along conventional traits of masculine identity – so, gendered violence. Secondly, there is a pattern of gender-based violence (GBV) – of men that are violent to women (as well as trans* and non-binary individuals) and *can be* violent to them because of the established genders of the victim and perpetrator (20–1). GBV is defined as violence committed on individuals because of their gender or gendered behaviour, most often by perpetrators whose violence is somewhat culturally authorized by their own (cis-male) gender. In the case of *Cleansed*, particularly through Mitchell's Solnit-inspired reading, the institutional violence is meted out through the authoritative, male Tinker (played by Tom Mothersdale) and applied to the female characters – such as Grace (Michelle Terry), whose gender is symbolically effaced by Tinker's procedures on her sexual organs – as well as the male characters who stray from traditional masculinity, whether in their sexuality or their behaviour.[2] So, the violence is gendered *and* gender-based.

As with the embodied, performative attitudes and behaviours that constitute forms of structural violence already discussed, such as racism in the last chapter, GBV does not always constitute a set of clear-cut actions. Karen Boyle argues that specific attention should be paid to the terminology used around GBV, refuting the claim that 'conflating gender inequality more broadly with violence against women specifically runs the risk of stretching the definition of violence so far that nothing is not violence' (2019: 28). Therefore, she advocates 'continuum thinking', drawn from Liz Kelly's influential argument (1998) that 'the pervasive nature of men's sexual violence means that women make sense of individual actions in relation to a continuum of related experiences across a lifetime' (Boyle 2019: 21; see also Moser 2001; McGlynn, Rackley and Houghton 2017); similar to Richardson's Black witnessing. Solnit too identifies this continuum, as her essay 'began with an amusing incident and ended with rape and murder', demonstrating 'the continuum that stretches from minor social misery to violent silencing and violent death' (2014, 16).[3] In other words, though actions on the GBV continuum are not all violent per se, they are all *performative* of a reiterated, structural oppression based on gender, a cultural reiteration of which genders can be oppressed.

The performative aspects of GBV – what assumptions, ideologies and behavioural structures are made through its actions – can be theorized as being twofold. Firstly, violence can be a performative action of identity formation. For example, as research on the online abuse of feminists shows, 'the motivation and impact may be not only to demean or exclude the individual victim, but thereby to build up the identity and status of the communicator' (Lewis, Rowe and Wiper 2016: 1478). Actions on the continuum of GBV are performative of certain normative identities, 'depicting' certain genders as victims and asserting masculinity in a feedback loop where violence is predominantly male because men perpetrate it, and perpetrating violence performatively constitutes men as men. This relates to the hierarchical taxonomies discussed by Wolfe (2018), where assumed superiority is performatively reiterated – indeed, links between masculine domination/consumption of women and animals have been thoroughly explored in ecofeminist discourse (see Adams 2015). It is also not to say that men are *only* constituted by violence – but the enacting of violence is normatively ascribed as a masculine activity.

Secondly, the reiteration and performance of actions on the GBV continuum performatively invokes and maintains their existence, powering the structural violence of gendered oppression. This pertains to Boyle's description of a 'representational continuum', also informed by Kelly (2005; 2016), specifically her notion of a 'context for additional, material acts of sexual violence: legitimating and supporting a culture of male sexual entitlement, dominance and coercive control' (Boyle 2019: 29). So, many acts of GBV can performatively establish who is culturally authorized to perpetrate and who can be perpetrated. To take *Cleansed* again as an illustrative example, Tinker's tortures performatively assert who he and his victims are, as well as his own hegemonic entitlement to perform these tortures. The fact that this is being witnessed by an audience raises questions of how these representations can be critical of GBV, rather than authorizing it.

Through the 2010s, concerns of GBV and performative behaviours were touched on by the discourses and movements that came to be known as 'fourth-wave' (Anglo-American) feminism. Commonly viewed as beginning around 2012,[4] fourth-wave feminism has been characterized by its shift in focus from legal equality to systemic discrimination; its challenge of normative, traditional behaviours; its connection to issues of racism, neoliberal exploitation and the environment; and is combative of sexual violence, the accountability of its perpetrators, and the questioning of systems that make perpetration permissible (Abrahams 2017). Furthermore, with its use of humour, pragmatism and utilization of social media, fourth-wave feminism is regarded as being highly accessible (Cochrane 2013). This is not to say that fourth-wave feminism was a strictly defined ideology or movement, with many of its concerns being advancements of past 'waves', as well as it being a coalescence of sometimes contesting viewpoints and objectives. Arguably, the fourth-wave's interconnectivity, and potential generalization, was engendered by another of its aspects: the technological and communication advancements of social media. Indeed, its proliferation and endorsement by high-profile figures arguably led to a perception of feminism as 'trendy, simple and nonthreatening' (Gray 2019). Though feminism gained wide exposure then, this has been queried as reducing it to 'its most benign interpretation' (Hess 2015).

Another aspect of the fourth-wave was the widespread adoption of 'intersectionality'. Intersectional feminism is, for the most part, understood as *de facto* when referring to the fourth-wave; being coined by Kimberlé Crenshaw (1991) 'to describe the interconnectivity of oppressive societal and institutional structures and their effect on individual and collective experience [...] investigating the relationships between different oppressive systemic forces (e.g., racism, classism, sexism, homophobia)' (Koch and Matsuzaka 2019: 32). As well as inviting allyship with the LGBTQI+ community, intersectionality advocates a feminism less dominated by the experiences of middle-class, white women. This has been especially crucial in terms of race, with intersectional feminism seeking to redress the peripheral status mainstream feminism has historically allotted to Black and Global Majority women. This was still an issue through the 2010s, with Lynette Linton, the current artistic director of the Bush Theatre, stating that 'the #MeToo movement was slow to embrace the stories of women of colour' (Akbar 2019a), though the examples of such work recorded here demonstrate the necessity of such perspectives.

With understandings of reiterated normativity, performative identities and inquiries into various modes of violence, considerations of fourth-wave feminism and its associated movements are crucial to understanding the context of 2010s British theatre (Akbar 2019a; Fallow and Mullan 2021). Just as fourth-wave features are not fully distinct from preceding 'waves', broadly feminist 2010s British theatre shares concerns with playwrights from previous waves/decades. For example, the intertwining of capitalist exploitation with gender dynamics and the performative link of subjective actions to systemic violence evidenced in *Oil* and *How to Hold Your Breath* are similar to the more 'second-wave-responsive' concerns of Churchill's *Top Girls* and Sarah Daniels's *Masterpieces* (RE, 1983).[5] A 'feminist lineage' in British theatre has indeed been identified by Elaine Aston, though she perceives this as having generally transformed since the 1970s when 'although women playwrights [...] may have had mixed feelings about feminism, it generally had an enabling effect, creating unprecedented opportunities', to the 1990s where playwrights had 'to contend with a false impression of feminism as an unfashionable "ism"' and so dramaturgical strategies were employed to make audiences affectively 'feel the loss of feminism' (2010: 577). Aston sees Kane's *Blasted* as indicative of this, which 'experientially figured the "crisis of living" through rape and war' (584): the world it depicts is devoid of feminism and is all the more horrific for it. As shown above, however, there was clear evidence of feminism in British culture no longer being perceived as an 'unfashionable ism' as the 2010s progressed.

Feminist dramaturgies on the British stage could be placed into two broad categories: those that generally adhere to the wide range of practices understood as theatrical realism and those that actively divert away from it. Realism is one of the most widespread forms of theatre, defined by Raymond Williams as possessing the characteristics of 'social extension' (characters representing relatable members of society); contemporaneousness ('emphasis on the actions of the contemporary world'); and secular action (human action 'played through in specifically human terms'; 2002: 107–8). Linear narratives, as well as sets, costumes and speech that are mimetically close to what they represent are also common markers of realism. Williams surmises that realism is mutable and changes over time: its 'methods and intentions are highly variable and have always to be taken to specific historical and social analyses' (114), though, is generally used to describe a certain adherence to non-surrealist, non-expressionist methods. Of the productions analysed in this work so far, *The Children* best demonstrates what is commonly referred to as realism – but even here, this supports Williams's definition of realism as being 'highly variable', with the action set in a proposed not-so-distant future, and its human, secular action consciously existing in tension with broader ecological concerns. As the plays explored here look to represent, perceive and theorize violence in alternative ways, it is no coincidence that they have few shared characteristics with traditional realism; and, indeed, British playwrights who used realism (in all its formal looseness) to represent GBV often actively considered the relevance of realism to tell such narratives.

There has been a long-standing debate on the relationship between feminism and realism; predominantly arising at the turn of the 1980s–90s from scholars like Sue-Ellen Case (1998), Jill Dolan (1990) and Elin Diamond (1990) who describe realism as a 'conservative force that reproduces and reinforces dominant cultural relations' (Dolan 2012: 84) and is 'more than an interpretation of reality passing as reality; it produces "reality" by positioning its spectator to recognize and verify its truths' (Diamond 1990: 61). Just as Nevitt (2013) writes of staged sexual violence that normative, assumptive representations can performatively reiterate such acts and the attitudes that authorize them, Case, Dolan and Diamond contend that the patriarchal, capitalist 'reality' of society both informs realism and is performatively affirmed by it. Their understandings of realism see it as a relatively fixed, 'conservative' form, but their criticisms of realism as being mimetically close to normative comprehensions of reality do not necessarily contradict Williams's definition of it as being 'highly variable'. Sheila Stowell, cognizant of Suffragette plays and their use of realism to present socio-politically progressive women (1992a), counters that 'dramatic forms are not in themselves narrowly partisan' (1992b: 87). Though Aston (1995), Diamond (1997), Jeanie Forte (1995) and Serena Anderlini-D'Onofrio (1999) advanced on arguments against realism, Stowell's contentions warned against easy equations of realism as anti-feminist.

Around the turn of the millennium the increasingly all-encompassing forces of globalization and neoliberalism – which were invariably tied to feminism and sought to 'hollow' its meaning as Aston writes of Kane (see also Bumiller 2008) – saw realist aspects being reformulated by playwrights. Aston, who revised her earlier stance on realism (2016), records that '[o]n the one hand, this reactionary climate saw experimentalists such as Churchill or debbie tucker green form innovative dramaturgies', and on the other, it 'injected social energies into the (re)turn to the realist tradition of showing the world as it really is' (24). But with the reservations of meticulously depicting the 'real world' with its attendant unjust systems, not to mention the formal advancements made by feminist playwriting, 'realist' playwrights through the 1980s into the 2010s increasingly approached the form from a tradition of reiterated 'looseness'. As the playwright April de Angelis concludes in her radio documentary *Theatre of the Abused* (2014), which also explores the representation of GBV in British Theatre, realist depictions – particularly by female theatre-makers – are often more nuanced than simply performatively reasserting patriarchal reality. In looking to explore the representation of what I refer to as the 'performative continuum' of GBV, this chapter proceeds with close analyses of two plays with different modes of staging GBV. With space in the 2010s public sphere carved out for numerous representations of feminist stances and female experiences in general, if still not proportionally enough, British theatre increasingly saw concerns of GBV articulated onstage, which, as Lisa Fitzpatrick states, is suggestive of 'a common life-experience for women across cultural and social groups' (2018: 75). With this chapter focusing later on the lineage of the 'experimentalists', next I look at 2010s playwrights who represented the GBV continuum through 'fluid realism': a term that underlines the variable aspect of the form as cultivated by feminist British playwrights.

The Performative 'Reality' of Gender-Based Violence in *Bird*

The term 'fluid realism' comes from Dolan, who writes that the 'feminist critique of realism [...] can now expand its terms and criteria as the genre also becomes more fluid' (2008: 455; quoted in Aston 2016: 19). This informs Aston in her contention that by the end of the 2000s playwrights concerned with centring female experiences were becoming 'more fluid' in their 'applications of realism', perceiving this as reflective of 'a shift away from those conservatively formed, phallocentric uses of the genre' (32).[6] Aston notes how Fiona Evans's *Scarborough* (RC, 2006), Anupama Chandrasekhar's *Free Outgoing* (RC, 2007), Kirkwood's *NSFW* and in a later article (2017) Harris's *How to Hold Your Breath* and Penelope Skinner's *Linda*, all exemplify how feminist and female playwrights could mould realism around their dramaturgies; with the last two challenging the dominance in the theatre industry of the male (tragic) lead – a criticism levied by Vicky Featherstone (Hutchinson 2015).

Fluid realism, then, ranges from subversions of realist narratives often linked to critiques of associated socio-political dogmas, to formal shifts away from conventional perceptions of reality such as the magic realism in *Oil* and *How to Hold Your Breath*, but is defined by a departure from realism's conventional phallocentrism, seeking to represent the world 'as it is' while offering critiques of this 'reality' and/or glimpses of alternatives. Aston notes how both *How to Hold Your Breath* and Kane's *Blasted* 'depart from a private sexual encounter that descends into global atrocities; both formally defy the logic of realism's mimetically structured world' (2017: 304), and so could also be said to show different connective 'ends' of the GBV continuum. Other plays include formal shifts by twisting the ordinary workings of realism's linear structure to represent time in alternate ways. For example, Chloë Moss's *Fatal Light* (Soho, 2010), Rose Lewenstein's *Now This is Not the End* (Arcola, 2015), and Alice Birch's *Anatomy of a Suicide* (RC, 2017) all contort Williams's rules of contemporaneousness and reactive human action to articulate narratives of intergenerational trauma and violence between mothers and daughters.

Fluid realism can also be applied to realist plays that self-referentially criticize their own form to puzzle the troubling way the mode contributes to reality-production. Kirkwood's *NSFW*, for example, seeks to dramatize the social totality of the GBV continuum; focusing on the staff of a Playboy-like magazine as the father of an underage model (unknown to the editors) challenges its editor-in-chief, before being reasoned into accepting a large sum and informed that teenage girls making themselves sexually available is 'the way things are': 'We did not go round to her house, with a gun, threatening violence [...] They come to us' (2012: 46). Rather than offering a feminist rejoinder to this climate, Kirkwood instead mirrors the narrative with a look inside a fictional 'woman's magazine' where women in positions of power themselves criticize and objectify female bodies. As Aston notes, *NSFW* 'provides a telling codicil to the prophetic *Top Girls* as it dramatizes the individual conditioned and consumed by neoliberalism' (2016: 25). That this is done through the mode of realism satirizes how 'reality' is informed by knowledge production: in these cases, print media.

Nina Raine's *Consent* (NT, 2017) too adheres closely to traditional realist techniques, focusing on a lawyer, Edward, who successfully defends a prosecution from Gayle, a victim of rape, only for her to commit suicide and, as their marriage unravels, Edward rapes his wife Kitty. As the couple show signs of reconciliation in the narrative's denouement, this again satirizes how normative structures (such as marriage, or indeed realism itself) can support such violent perpetrations, highlighted by the supernatural presence of Gayle's haunting ghost (2018: 117). The use of 'haunting' characters to disrupt traditional narratives is another hallmark of fluid realism: also seen, for example, in Harris's *The Duchess [of Malfi]*, in which murdered female characters persist on the stage in an 'afterlife of violence'. Encompassing the formal shifts of *How to Hold Your Breath* and the narrative subversion of *NSFW* and *Consent*, fluid realism situates itself in a position of ambivalence: self-effacingly accepting its (arguably) 'patriarchal' structure even as it considers and skirts with alternatives. It tackles the GBV continuum by demonstrating its 'reality' while short-circuiting what Aston views as the standardized phallocentrism of realism. The subject of my close analysis here is the Welsh playwright Katherine Chandler's *Bird*, which uses fluid realist techniques of disrupted linearity, hauntings and critiques of the structures which constitute 'reality' to represent the systemic and subjective violence affecting a young woman on the brink of leaving the care home system.

As mentioned in the previous chapter, Wales saw a pronounced push of national identity and even calls for independence – though its mobilizing political party, Plaid Cymru, never gained the majority that the SNP did in Scotland. Yet, the launch of the English-language National Theatre of Wales in 2009 garnered further vitality and exposure for Welsh theatre. Welsh playwrights through the 2010s like Brad Birch depicted a 'preoccupation with the modern displacement of the human soul and the forceful reclaiming of this through transgression and violence' (Price 2014: xvii), and Chandler specifically 'dramatises incisively how a politics based on fear damages the lives and hopes of working-class and middle-class characters alike, by demanding complicity and silence' with institutions becoming 'hierarchies of systematic repression' (Price and Wasserberg 2014: xiv). After winning the 2013 Bruntwood Prize for Playwriting, Chandler's *Bird* became a joint production between Sherman Cymru, Cardiff – directed by its artistic director Rachel O'Riordan – and the Royal Exchange: debuting at the former in May 2016 before transferring to the latter. Her earlier plays *Before it Rains* (Bristol Old Vic, 2012) too takes place in a 'left behind' Welsh community, and *Parallel Lines* (Chapter Arts Centre, Cardiff, 2013) explores the after-effects of an illicit student–teacher relationship from both perspectives. Her later plays *Thick As Thieves* (Theatr Clwyd, Mold, 2018) and *Lose Yourself* (Sherman, 2019) saw Chandler return to issues of care in a neoliberal climate in the former, and sexual violence in the latter.

Bird takes place in a Welsh coastal community, likely around Bridgend, where Chandler conducted her research (2016: 2). It focuses on the teenagers Ava (played by Georgia Henshaw) and Tash (Rosie Sheehy), both on the brink of no longer being able to be supported by their care home as blamed by their social worker on the 'government [...] and capitalism and Fucking Thatcher' (11). Ava has been in care following sexual assault from her stepfather; she meets her estranged mother Claire (Siwan Morris) with hopes of living together, only to find her in denial of her partner's abuses and unwilling to rehouse her daughter. Tash and Ava discuss their options, with the latter becoming increasingly anxious about potential homelessness. Ava then encounters the older teenage Dan (Connor Allen) in a park, who euphemizes to her '[t]hey say to come here. You're known [...] And I thought. Why not. I'll give it a try' (23). Viewing her as a commodity – a perception Ava apathetically, but submissively responds to – she gives him oral sex: an act the production does not frame as violent, but one that is certainly fixed on the GBV continuum in the power dynamics performatively established by the two teenagers.

Later, Ava meets Lee (Guy Rhys), a 40-year-old taxi driver who often spends time with the two young women, supplying them with alcohol. It becomes apparent that Lee is manipulating them, with the implication being that he will offer them accommodation in return for sex – a continuation of the dynamics of structural violence witnessed earlier. Ava again meets with her mother and learns she has a sister; Claire has accepted her partner may be abusive and reveals to Ava she has left him, but is as yet unwilling to take Ava back. Ava then informs Claire that Tash has been dead for three months after committing suicide. Dan later shows some remorse for his earlier solicitations and the play ends with him and Ava fishing and playing on the beach. The fluid realism of *Bird* can be seen in its narrative, dramaturgy and structure. The story reiterates the dire straits of social services in 2010s Britain, which here impacts the options available to young people in care, threatening substance addiction, homelessness, suicide and sexual exploitation.[7] Kenny Miller's set design too evidences fluid realism with its lack of detailed time or place: the sparseness of the white wall, blue floor and twin ladders at the back of the stage (seemingly to nowhere) evoke the precarity of funding cuts in children's care and the isolation of a forgotten coastal community.

Chandler's narrative structure, emphasized by O'Riordan's direction, is also fluid: Ava's encounters with the neglectful Claire, exploitative Dan and manipulative Lee blend into one another as her opportunities appear increasingly limited and compromised. This is best expressed by the periodic memories or 'hauntings' of the deceased Tash segued across Ava's otherwise linear experiences – the magic realism of which suggests at something beyond the structures in which Ava finds herself ensnared. *Bird* is also arguably reiterative of the realist tradition, not only of Aston's proposed advancers of fluid realism such as *Top Girls* which also features 'left behind' young women but, through its central metaphor, plays like Ibsen's *A Doll's House* and Anton Chekhov's *The Seagull* (1896). For example, the young women's opportunities are related to a bird shown 'how wonderful it was to fly and then [given] a room ten-foot square to do it in' (58); Tash's suicide is described by Ava as '[s]he flew' (67); whereas Ava's name literally 'means [...] [b]ird' (8).[8] *Bird*'s connotations to Ibsen's 'caged bird' and Chekhov's oscillating symbol of freedom and dependence which, too, connects to a suicide, performatively reiterates these plays' concerns with female subjugation in a contemporaneous context: alerting to the long history of this violence, its social and historical specificity, and its continued representation by (fluid) realism.

Ava and Tash's experiences on the GBV continuum are central to *Bird*. The narrative opens on them playing at the top of a cliff and pondering the '[f]ree' birds around them (5–6) while they are themselves in a literally precarious position. This symbolic image carries through Tash's haunting of Ava, as the former's belief in parallel universes – '[t]here are other worlds, Ava. Other places than this' (30) – is manifested in the 'freedom' of her suicide: 'If it all gets too much / We'll fly' (51). Tash's lingering presence, then, both serves as a reminder of the casualties of GBV and an ominous consideration that the only freedom from oppressive structures may be in death. O'Riordan states that the play 'puts the voices of vulnerable young women at the centre of the narrative. It makes us, as the audience, acknowledge that we allow the disadvantaged young to be ignored, marginalised and disregarded' (2016: ii). Chandler explicitly places female experience at the centre of her representation of the GBV continuum which differs, for example, from *Mr Incredible*, while demonstrating a similar message as perceived by Aston in its realist form of 'patriarchal entrapment' (2016: 32). In *Bird*, the perpetrator of sexual violence against Ava – referred to only as 'him' – is absent, though his dissociated presence colours the stage with oppressive, hegemonic masculinity. As Ava states to Claire, 'it seems to me. It feels to me that he's here. Telling you what to do and you don't even know it' (38).

Ava's abuse from 'him' is the central act of violence in the narrative but occurs long before the action begins – its repercussions being felt throughout. The disembodied GBV that he represents threatens to manifest in Ava through her passive satiation of Dan's exploitative desires (her history of abuse having likely coloured her understanding of sexuality), and indeed in the embodying acts of Dan and Lee themselves. The latter most notably physicalizes this through his coercive, violent behaviour:

Lee Drink it.
       LEE *holds the bottle to her mouth and forces her to drink.*

Ava I don't want any more, Lee.
       LEE *gets a knife from out of his pocket and slowly slices it into his palm making it bleed.*
       Lee. Your hand, Lee.

Lee If you don't come it feels like this.
       This is what it feels like.
       Do you understand?

(50)

While Lee's actions and his exploitation of Ava and Tash more generally are symptomatic of systemic GBV, they also demonstrate the intertwined violence of neoliberalism. Even as he mourns 'them houses there. Twenty year ago. They had windows, not boarded up like that' (28; [*sic*]), he fails to see that his manipulation of the young women is performative of the 'neoliberal continuum' – not unlike the initially limited perspectives of *Lampedusa*'s characters, for example. With his coercion symbolized as indissociable from his act of self-harm, his oppression of Ava and Tash is connected to the systemic violence that also affects him.

The magic realism of the onstage presence of the deceased Tash, the invisible but permeating presence of 'him', and the behaviour of Lee are all indicative of the GBV continuum which intertwines with the neoliberal ravages of 'left-behind' Welsh communities and makes women such as Tash, Ava and Claire particularly vulnerable (Ishkanian 2014). Though Claire's tentative turn to protective motherhood and Dan's repentant offering of companionship to Ava show small steps within their community towards interdependence rather than neoliberalist individualism, the production's conclusion, with Ava once again '*standing at the tip of the cliff*' (72) seemingly at peace, suggests that the precarity and potential violence of her position have changed little – she has merely come to accept them. *Bird*'s fluid realism then represents the *reality* of the plight of whom O'Riordan calls 'vulnerable young women' especially precarious to the convergent issues of GBV. Yet, its form and narrative imagine an improved, alternate situation, as physicalized by the presence of the absent Tash. As Aston writes, this manner of realism further 'open[s] up realist conventions to humancentric ends' (2016: 32). In its simultaneous mimesis of reality and aspirations for performative change, fluid realism serves as a fitting form to inspect the reverberations of violent acts and a potential blueprint for better perceiving the intersections of the GBV continuum.

Breaking (Violent) Form in *seven methods of killing kylie jenner*

As Aston mentions, an increased understanding around the turn of the millennium of feminism as deeply connected to, or hollowed out by, neoliberalism resulted in 'innovative dramaturgies' by 'experimentalists' who sought new ways to represent this increasingly all-encompassing landscape (2016: 24). Experimentalism here broadly refers to those extreme modulations to traditionalized forms which pushed standardized conventions even further than fluid realism. Such experimentalism was symptomatic of the continued discourse from (feminist) scholars and the innovations of playwrights like Churchill, Kane and tucker green. Their works represented violence as no longer contained to the personal – or even the national – but caught in a larger, globalized series of networks. As *Blasted*, *How to Hold Your Breath* and *Escaped Alone* espouse for example, the network of neoliberalism is intertwined with the GBV continuum. Fourth-wave movements in the 2010s identified and advocated potential strategies to begin to unravel structures of GBV, which was found to be deeply ingrained in many processes and institutions. Notably, Emma Willis connects real-life sexual assaults to realist acting practices (2019) – with method acting seemingly encouraging a permissiveness to 'lose oneself' in the craft and in some cases validate exploitative and unacceptable behaviour.[9] Willis, then, indicates that realism's adherence to reality creates a troubling ground between representation and real-world GBV, which allows for a justification of assault while in character and, furthermore, authorizes acts of assault as 'part of the business'.

Willis's writing here bears similarity to earlier contentions by Sue-Ellen Case, who stated that realism's sexual othering of women made the form a 'prisonhouse of art […] both in their representation on stage and in the female actor's preparation and production of such roles' (1988: 124). Like Nevitt's contentions on performativity and depictions of violence then, these perspectives understand deleterious representations as performatively affecting normative, sometimes oppressive assumptions. Willis refers to Elin Diamond's term 'realism-without-truth' (1990), which describes 'realism without the patriarchal truth claims that underlie it, and that construct and shape female subjectivity' (Willis 2019: 261). Contending that 'the ability or willingness on the part of female actors to be emotionally and sexually vulnerable is considered a part of professional practice', realism-without-truth 'provides one way of beginning to unknit the interweaving of the language of naturalistic acting, including its gendered aspects, and the justification of abuse' (ibid.). Willis's analysis prompts a consideration of 'what the emotional realism that naturalistic acting aims towards might look like if the so-called truths of the "real world" that underpin it were challenged' (268) and highlights an urgency to demonstrate abuses of GBV while performatively attempting a 'corrective vision'.

The manner through which realism-without-truth is fulfilled onstage is through practices of 'feminist mimesis'. As Serena Anderlini-D'Onofrio states, traditional mimesis has largely been understood in masculine terms: forms that arguably adhere closely to 'phallic mimesis' such as realism therefore 'cannot be feminist because [...] it homogenizes the two sexes to one [...] it reduces women to copies of men' (1999: 175). Though later scholars revised their stance on realism and feminism as evidenced in the last section, Anderlini-D'Onofrio highlights the necessity of strategies that look to represent non-male experiences without homogeneity or the logic of patriarchal truth, and indeed the broad incorporation of capitalist realism. Central to this consideration is how form was employed as a dramaturgical strategy. The primary analysis here, of Jasmine Lee-Jones's *seven methods of killing kylie jenner*, poses that the disruption and alteration of conventional theatrical form could be an imaginative surrogate for the unravelling and abolishment of modes of systemic GBV.

Lee-Jones's widely celebrated play came at the end of a decade where many female-led plays and playwriting moved away from more conventional forms. Some examples are cited by Laura Bissell, who also employs Diamond to interrogate (re)performances 'that attempt not to "reproduce the same", but to incite reflection and action' (2018: 523), including Duffy's *My Country*, Junction 25's *A Bit of Bite* (Tramway, Glasgow, 2016), Nic Green's *Cock and Bull* (Arches, Edinburgh, 2014) and Femme Feral's *Theresa May Smackdown* (Hackney Showroom, London, 2017). These performances repurpose, parody, or defamiliarize political figures and hegemonic positions 'through heightened, queered, and feminist means' (525), re-reflecting the real through feminist mimesis to construct realism-without-truth. Practices of feminist mimesis suggested by theorists include placing a female duo 'at the center of the dramatic structure usually occupied by the phallic hero' (Anderlini-D'Onofrio 1999: 175), whereas Diamond explores 'wedging a space between the body and the text of the body, [to] displace the imaginary wholeness of the actor in realism, making her truth provisional, contingent' (1990: 87). Such acts of feminist mimesis can be posited as performative exercises that look to iterate reality in a reformulated way; as Willis theorizes, perhaps providing a GBV-combative representational goal for disentangling patriarchal truth from reality itself.

One of the most notable formal innovators of the decade whose works displayed these strategies to represent GBV was Alice Birch. These include

Revolt. She said. Revolt again. (RSC Stratford, 2014). Inspired by Crimp's *Attempts on Her Life*, Rebellato writes that this comic, apocalyptic play 'systematically tries both to revolutionise the world and to revolutionise the writing of plays' (2017: 32). It opens in relatively realist fashion, with a heterosexual couple returning from a dinner party and initiating sex, but their titillating talk is continually examined and reformulated to remove any connotations of hegemonic masculinity or symbolic GBV: 'I'm kissing you and and pressing you to me – can I say pressing?' (2014: 50). The play becomes increasingly experimental as it seeks further ways to dissociate GBV from language, representation and reality. However, its conclusion has a sense of resignation, with four women casually discussing the overthrow of the patriarchal, capitalist system, before mourning the project's actual lack of existence: 'It failed. The whole world failed at it. It could have been so brilliant' (101). The indication appears to be that the totalizing systems of GBV and neoliberalism are potentially too monolithic and deep-seated to be erased, both in theatrical form and reality itself, despite Birch's formal experiments.

Birch continues these concerns in her collaboration with RashDash, *We Want You to Watch* (NT, 2015), which focuses on the characters Pig and Sissy as they seek to 'de-pornify' and disentangle patriarchal oppression from reality. The doubled protagonists adhere to Anderlini-D'Onofrio's practice of feminist mimesis, and the jostling between text and movement for primacy – noted in Birch's preamble, 'sometimes words are the best medium to articulate what we think and feel, and sometimes movement/image is' (2015: 10) – speaks to Diamond's positing of a representational 'wedge' between the body and the text. But in similar fashion to *Revolt. She said. Revolt again.*'s conclusion, the characters' project and their position is challenged throughout, such as when they ask a hacker to 'turn off' the internet: 'PIG I believe in our ability to make something better / SISSY I believe in the human capacity to change and do something / HACKER Well we haven't fucking done it so far' (62). With Pig and Sissy's anti-porn crusade consistently called into question, *We Want You To Watch* seems to reflectively interrogate the performative potential of feminist mimesis. This perhaps emerges from an apparent stratification of what feminism itself *is*, as also playfully examined in Rose Lewenstein's *Fucking Feminists* (Theatre503, 2016). Taking the form of a debate between '*an all-female cast of roughly five actors*' (Lewenstein 2016: 44) any certainty of what the term stands for is made increasingly unsure, with one viewpoint posing that 'it's about choice' (55). This indicates that contemporaneous feminism veers dangerously close to being a hollow market 'brand' (Hess 2015; Gray 2019); short-circuiting the radical performative potential of feminism and incorporating it into the dictates of neoliberalism's smooth functioning.

This wariness is perhaps best seen in Birch's Clean Break-commissioned *[BLANK]* (NT, 2018), a text of sixty scenes from which performance makers can create their own piece on the 'structural' relation between criminality, the justice system and women rendered particularly vulnerable partly due to the social ravages of neoliberalism (Birch quoted in Jones 2019). Specifically, Maria Aberg's 2019 Donmar Warehouse production features a 45-minute 'liberal dinner party' scene in which #MeToo is discussed over cocaine and vogue Middle Eastern cuisine. The implication here is that vocalizations of increased societal justice often come as 'lip-service' from those who comfortably benefit from the machinations of systemic violence, owing to the apparent stagnation of radical (feminist) change under neoliberalism. Birch mentions in interview that 'she is aware that the play will be seen largely by people like herself', surmising that theatre can't 'really' effect change (ibid.). Identifying 'an arrogance that suggests that theatre can change the world', she instead seems to position herself as a slow agent of gradual performative transformation – 'a much longer process' than 'immediate change' (ibid.). Like the plays critiquing neoliberalism examined in Chapter 5, Birch's theatre simultaneously holds value in the performative exercise of attempting radical change while understanding the difficulty of shaking the entrenched positions that structural violence places both theatre and citizens more generally in.

The re-attempting, reformulating, and reiterating of 'freeing' form and narrative is central to Diamond's realism-without-truth; though the acknowledgement of the (theatrical) limitations to do so are arguably characteristic of the 2010s. This is also seen in Hickson's *The Writer*, which opens on a young woman admiring the stage – in this case, that of the Almeida – after a production has ended. She comes across the older, male director, who asks her opinion on the play. In dialogue evocative of Solnit's essays and feminist arguments against realism, she surmises the play's likeness to:

> hearing from old men [...] patting the back of your hand gently as they explain what they consider to be the truths of the world [...] like his truth and my truth are anywhere near the fucking same when it's you that gets to make the world and me that's got to live in it.
>
> (2018: 14–15)

After she agrees to write a play for him, the 'real' writer and director enter the stage for a post-show discussion. The proceeding scenes routinely undermine one another, including a set-piece in which the writer goes to a folkloric, female utopia where 'the possibility of new constructions' exists (64), only for the director to disparage 'all this breaking-form shit' (71). Though readable as an autofiction where the sovereign creativity of the artist is undermined by patriarchal, capitalist demands, Hickson notes in interview that the idealist writer and pragmatic director represent the duality of her considerations as a playwright (Angel-Perez and Rousseau 2023).

Though *The Writer* demonstrates a similar, potentially undermining self-reflexivity alike to Birch's work then, it indicates how more experimental playwrights concerned with GBV used cyclicity, reiteration and a compulsive (re)breaking of form as a source of creativity that could approach the issue from multiple angles, as Bissell suggests with her case studies (2018: 523). Additionally, Ellie Kendrick's *Hole* (RC, 2018) takes a form akin to a cabaret or music hall performance, with various choreographies, readings and actions performing around ideas of circularity and repetition to suggest such forms as being distinctly feminine, with mythical and astronomical imagery equating 'black holes' with the dissolution of (patriarchal) structures. Also celebratory of form-breaking is Outbox's *And The Rest of Me Floats* (Rose Lipman Building, London, 2017), 'a play about the messiness of gender' which features trans*, non-binary and queer performers autobiographically relating their experiences through reflective 'text, imagery, movement, and form' (Burratta 2018: 5). Like Travis Alabanza's *Burgerz* (explored in the Conclusion), the performance makers here productively use past recollections of GBV and homophobia that took forms such as subjective attacks or symbolic effacements to reassert themselves through performance. Outbox's dramaturgy takes explicit aim at traditional theatrical conventions as a node of structural GBV: 'swerving realism means that the linear, causal narratives that see trans and queer people victimised, in trauma and in danger could be re-authored' (ibid.). Outbox's queering of form relates to feminist mimesis, and the play pointedly, joyfully envisages an attempted representation of realism-without-truth as its conclusion disavows conventional theatre and '*the whole theatre becomes a dance floor*' (64). Just as, for example, tucker green brought to British theatre her own set of influences and styles, the perspectives of Alabanza and Outbox bring their own specific divergencies to both theatrical and socio-cultural 'realism' through productive new forms.

A new perspective and representation of GBV is also offered by Jasmine Lee-Jones's *seven methods of killing kylie jenner*, which debuted with direction from Milli Bhatia at the Royal Court in July 2019.[10] Focusing on two female friends in their early 20s – Cleo (played by Danielle Vitalis), who is Black, cis and heterosexual, and Kara (Tia Bannon), who is Black, mixed-race and queer – *seven methods*' title relates to a series of protest tweets by Cleo (known on Twitter as @INCOGNEGRO) in response to a real *Forbes* article titled 'At 21, Kylie Jenner Becomes The Youngest Self-Made Billionaire Ever' (Robehmed 2019). Cleo tweets:

> YT [whitey] woman born into rich American family, somehow against all odds manages to get more rich [...] Kylie has only reached billionaire status by stealing BW [Black women] sauce and reselling it to wypipo [white people] like the shit's new - meanwhile the pay gap for BW in the States + UK continues to widen ...
>
> (2019: 2–3)[11]

Satirically challenging this article, Cleo tweets various ways through which Jenner can be killed relevant to its racial, capitalist and gendered issues: 'METHOD #1/#DEATHBYPOISON/Kinda like the temporary lip fillers that helped you gain/Acclaim [...] But when Mac [Cosmetics] instagrammed a picture of a Black model with lips of the same width/She was called ugly/Defiled/Reviled' (4). As Cleo's tweets gain traction and notoriety, she begins to receive online racist and misogynistic abuse. When an unearthed, earlier post of hers reveals homophobic tendencies (56), Cleo's (past) problematic views become both highly criticized online and generate significant friction between her and Kara.

Cleo, increasingly isolated, later apologizes online and relates Jenner's beauty empire to the colonial exploitation of Saartjie (or Sarah Baartman) – a Black South African woman born in the late eighteenth century who was displayed as a curiosity across Europe, with even her remains exhibited in a museum (Lee-Jones 2019: 87). Cleo and Kara reconcile and conclude the play performing a ritual to invoke Saartjie's spirit, before perplexedly, then assertively regarding the audience: 'What are you gonna do now ... clap?' (85). Like Eve Leigh's *Midnight Movie*, which also debuted on the Jerwood Upstairs Theatre in the same year, *seven methods* has an idiosyncratic form that emerges in no small part from the online world and veers significantly away from conventional realist practices. Emily Davis remarks in her own gif-filled review of the piece that its references and terminology render much of the script 'incomprehensible to an older person' – a somewhat generalizing statement, but one that highlights the specificity of the playtext's 'brilliant patchwork of GIFS, twitter threads and acronyms [...] originated, curated and developed by young black women' (2019).[12] In interview, Bhatia mentions of her direction that 'every person in our rehearsal room is a black or a brown woman, so there's no [white/male] gaze' (Wong Davies 2019). In both form and process then, *seven methods* envisions a realism-without-truth as elaborated on by Willis, as it challenges the 'so-called truths of the real world' and looks to expunge patriarchal influence from the rehearsal room.

seven methods represents aspects of the GBV continuum by exposing the audience to the rampant GBV of the online world, which is 'increasingly recognized as a major human rights problem' (Suzor et al. 2019: 96), and its intersection with racism. Though Cleo initially criticizes the Forbes article's manifestation of socio-cultural racial and gender exploitation ('[i]nside that tweet is hundreds of years of anti-blackness, positive affirmations of capitalism, cultural appropriation ...'; 15), her activism leads to online vitriol against her. These expletive performative 'speech' acts could be defined as both subjective and symbolic violence as per Butler, as well as plottable on a continuum of image-based abuse (McGlynn, Rackley and Houghton 2017) as Cleo's Black womanhood is virulently slurred: the playtext includes blacked-out image boxes, with the overlaid descriptions 'A PICTURE OF A GORILLA' and 'AN IMAGE OF A BLACK WOMAN BEING LYNCHED' (42). This relates both to Richardson's exploration of the web as a simultaneous site of anti-racist resistance and oppression (2020) and to how online feminist activism more generally has also been targeted (Lewis, Rowe and Wiper 2016). In the case of the latter, such abuse has been identified as resultingly limiting women's civil engagement (Citron and Norton 2011) and their cyberspace presence overall (Halder and Jaishankar 2009).

Though initial scholarship regarded online harassment as a self-contained phenomenon, studies in the 2010s increasingly saw it as linked to the wider GBV continuum: the internet is 'an extension of offline gendered realities, where violence and abuse is the "wallpaper"' (Lewis, Rowe and Wiper 2016: 1479). Just as Lewenstein's *Darknet* depicts the web as a fiefdom of neoliberalism, for example, *seven methods* and *Midnight Movie* represent it as having been permeated by the GBV continuum, with the form of the latter also matching the disorienting online world and its all-too-common exploitation and degradation of women. Research evidences the 'most commonly used social media for feminist debate was Twitter', yet 88 per cent of their respondents 'had been abused on it' (ibid.: 1469). Arifa Akbar's review draws attention to the fittingly represented 'real danger and psychological darkness' of Twitter, conveyed significantly through 'Twitterludes' in which the performers' caricature memes and gifs set to 'smoke, flashing lights, electronic voice distortion and thrillerish music' (2019b). Samantha-Louise Hayden's review describes these as the play's 'most stylistically inventive moments' that are experimental in terms of conventional theatrical form, but representative of how 'the way our online language has seeped into our IRL vocabulary' (2019). Both this permeation of the virtual world and the matrices of systemic violence are literalized by Rajha Shakiry's set and Jessica Hung Han Yun's lighting design, which Hayden describes as 'a canopy of entangled ropes and netting, its trailing cords simultaneously symbolising the Twitter threads on which this play is centred; the global system of computers that make up the internet; the noose' (ibid.; this can be seen on the front cover, which was photographed by Helen Murray). These varied yet connected connotations literalize the link of online harassment to long-seated practices of systemic racism and GBV.

The two female leads adhere to Anderlini-D'Onofrio's practice of feminist mimesis, and their ontological status when 'really' regarding the audience somewhat conforms to Diamond's push to make their truth 'provisional' and 'contingent'. These practices of feminist mimesis – of duality and reality – also connect to Lee-Jones's understandings of 'what it means for women of colour, and in this case black women, to exist between two spaces, and what that does to your psychological framework' (Wong Davies 2019) – best expressed through the relationship between IRL-Cleo and TL-@INCOGNEGRO.[13] Rather than self-multiplicity being anti-patriarchal as some (white) feminist scholars have advocated then, Lee-Jones demonstrates it as being specifically 'exhaustive' for someone like Cleo (ibid.). Diamond's suggestion of creating a dramaturgical 'wedge' between body and text to productively disrupt the 'contingent truth' of characters and realism is also absent in *seven methods*. Instead, the literal text/code of the online world threateningly looks to close the gap between itself and Cleo's lived reality – seen in the vocalization of Twitter-speak and the embodiment of performed memes. Though this is claimed by Cleo and Kara as their own language, this encroachment of the virtual world often becomes insidious and symbolically violent as they enact prejudicial memes and gifs in what Lee-Jones's directions call 'digital blackface' (xxiii). The internet – just as 'IRL' – is a space through which the systemic racism and GBV so often found on its platforms incorporates, mobilizes and defamiliarizes bodies.

Both young women face – or have faced – a certain divorce from themselves. Kara has only relatively recently come to terms with her own queerness, having been initially reviled by Cleo for it as a teenager: 'I was like I think I like girls [...] and u looked like u were gonna throw up and then pushed me off and were like never ever say that ever again. So I didn't. Not for a very very long time' (65). Cleo's latent homophobia alongside Kara's own hesitance to support her activism demonstrates how structural violence can performatively operate through those who are themselves oppressed by it. Just as *The Writer* and Birch's work suspiciously critique the ability of radical change, the fissure in Cleo and Kara's friendship seen in their repetitive bickering suggests that such change may be stalled by the 'in-fighting' of partisan, pro-feminist groups. Cleo too shows an estrangement with herself, seen not only in the duality with her online avatar but – as Lee-Jones mentions via Hansberry and Dubois – with a self-conscious regard of herself in a structurally racist and misogynistic society:

> I don't wanna look angry and cry
> and sometimes I'm scared it will make me look crazy if I get angry and cry
> and no one will listen to me or ppl [people] will just think I'm weak
>   or just a mewling girl or some old archaic female stereotype which
>   might not apply to me anyway bcos [because] I'm a black woman
>   and sometimes people don't really see me as a woman anyway
> or as much of a woman
> or even human.
>
> (74–5)

Cleo's understanding here of how others may perceive her in a dehumanized way, seen in the online abuse directed towards her, has infected her own sense of self; her identity markers are 'robbed' from her while she herself is marginalized.

Though Cleo initially projects her systemic oppression onto a figurehead of this socio-cultural prejudice and exploitation – namely, Kylie Jenner – and states (titular) numerous ways to dispatch her, by the end of *seven methods* it becomes apparent that such an act of retributive subjective violence is not enough: systemic violence is not so easily solved and such embodiments fall short of its totality. Though the play opens as '*KARA and CLEO drag something on resembling a body*' (1) this is revealed to be a '*life-size sacrifice*' of material possessions at the conclusion (80); offered in ritual to conjure the spirit of Saartjie following Cleo's invocation of her to '*explode*' the Twittersphere (79). Rather than a sacrificial killing then, the play concludes with an altogether different kind of ritual that pays tribute to the silenced voices of (Black) women, connects the strands of modern-day racism and GBV to long-seated patriarchal and colonial exploitation – an inverse of the ritualistic violence theorized by Girard.

Lynette Goddard contends that Selina Thompson's *salt.* (Southbank Centre, London, 2017), Juliet Gilkes Romero's *The Whip* (RSC, 2019) and Winsome Pinnock's *Rockets and Blue Lights* (RE, 2020) are examples of Black British female writers drawing on Saidiya Hartman's concept of the 'afterlife of slavery' (2007) to offer empowered representations of (historical) Black women: a performative strategy that grants them an agency in the present that they would not have been afforded in the past (2020b). The references to Saartjie in *seven methods* similarly serve as a performative strategy to retrospectively empower Black women in the past and cyclically affirm them in the present. This performative invocation follows the symbolic destruction of the Twittersphere; represented in great part through Shakiry's webbed construct hanging above, which itself alludes to the continuums of systemic violence. Its matrix of ropes suggest the ways in which Black women have been (and continue to be) literally and figuratively bound, not to mention the historical implications of lynchings, hangings and slave ships.

The representation of the GBV continuum in *seven methods* demonstrates it as intertwined with other forms of violence – specifically neoliberalist and racist violence – and exacerbated by the internet, which itself is thoroughly indoctrinated into the everyday lives of British citizens. Yet it also productively draws from the internet, notably the vernacular of Black Twitter, to bring a new, experimental form to British theatre from which the play derives much of its satirical power and social critique; as well as locating it as a source of the systemic issues facing the two women, which they themselves foster. To purge themselves of these oppressions, Cleo and Kara performatively evoke Saartjie and 'explode' the Twittersphere altogether – offering a realism-without-truth in which the structures of violence are obliterated by an invocation of (Black) female solidarity. As Bhatia states in interview – referring to *seven methods* as well as her other work in 2019 on Rachel De-Lahay's curated 'My White Best Friend (And Other Letters Left Unsaid' festival at the Bunker and the collaborative *Dismantle This Room* at the Court – '[t]here's something in doing these shows which is about inheriting or not inheriting structures – why do we have to inherit structures in order to make stuff?' (Wong Davies 2019). Like other experimental feminist theatre representing the GBV continuum such as *Revolt. She said. Revolt again*, *We Want You To Watch* and *The Writer*, *seven methods* locates the perpetuation of this violence in the patriarchal-designed structures that govern reality – including theatrical forms themselves. As Bhatia implies then, *seven methods* rejects traditional theatrical structures as it symbolically destroys the systemic conduits hanging above the action, performatively re-affirming the characters' humanities and attempting to disentangle systemic GBV both onstage and in the rehearsal room.

Conclusion

This chapter has offered an overview of broadly feminist playwriting in 2010s Britain, with a focus on those plays that looked to represent the GBV continuum. As with depictions of violence onstage during this decade more generally, GBV remains largely 'unseen' in physical, subjective manifestations. This is something of an inverse of Early Modern theatre, for example: whereas Solga notes its effacement from culture and spectacularization on stage, in 2010s Britain, GBV was widely discussed in culture but not physicalized onstage. Instead, the strands of this continuum are referred to – whether through its structural intersection with neoliberalism seen in Chandler's *Bird*, or its permeation through online spaces and corporeal bodies as with Lee-Jones's *seven methods of killing kylie jenner*. As mentioned, however, 2010s British theatre had its own continuum-based limitations. Despite the appeals of fourth-wave feminism for inclusivity, British feminist theatre in the 2010s was largely written by white, middle-class, cis-female playwrights, with Black and Global Majority, multi-ethnic, working-class non-binary and trans* perspectives on gender concerns gaining little exposure in non-fringe venues. This was surely a fault of the theatre establishment more widely, even if the primacy of hegemonic masculinity in theatre was increasingly queried by the dramaturgies discussed here as well as by the creatives steering these on the level of production.

These plays articulate GBV as a continuum of performative acts, transmitted and enacted through attitudes, behaviours, actions and structures. Like the challenge of depicting the climate crisis then, representing the GBV continuum is a phenomenological quandary. With strategies of demonstrating effects, behaviours and structures over explicitly subjective acts, these plays begin to outline the shape of a performative continuum rather than a series of isolated incidents. The continuum-thinking advocated by feminist thinkers can, arguably, be applied to other forms of violence to better understand the interrelation between subjective and objective (symbolic, systemic) modes, linked by a 'connective tissue' of performativity: applied in the Conclusion through an illustrative exploration of Alabanza's *Burgerz*. This production, like those discussed here, focuses on the necessity to perceive violence through a consideration of performativity, and the potentiality of performativity to dismantle the continuum.

Conclusion

Theatrical Critiques of Violence

This study has surveyed a wide variety of 2010s British theatre that engages with issues of violence: with predominant concerns raised here being protest, climate crisis, neoliberalism, European and British identity, racism and gender-based violence. What connects the productions explored here is a dramaturgical commitment to representing violence as structural rather than as a series of unconnected acts – showing the shape of the whole 'iceberg', rather than what only appears above the surface. This manner of depicting violence onstage has been informed by wider socio-cultural understandings, with broader debate and dissemination on ultra-objective, 'invisible' forms of violence facilitated by movements like BLM and #MeToo. These movements, as with the productions analysed here, demonstrate an understanding that violence is structural; maintained by a Möbius strip of subjective and spectacular acts as well as innocuous behaviours and attitudes – or, through implicit social contracts of plural performativity. While this Conclusion looks to summarize the research of this work, one last production is explored here to draw together and illustrate three summative contentions.

Encapsulating many of the concerns seen in the plays examined over the past chapters, Travis Alabanza's *Burgerz* can be described as a mixture of solo performance, participatory theatre, monologue theatre and autobiographical performance. Alabanza is a Black non-binary writer, performer and theatre-maker who established themselves as one of the leading trans* voices in 2010s British performance. Among other accolades, they published a 2017 poetry book, led a 2017 Ted Talk on silence and victimization, and starred in Chris Goode's adapted *Jubilee* (RE, 2017) and Scottee's *Putting Words in Your Mouth* (Roundhouse, London, 2016). Opening for previews in October 2018 at the Ovalhouse, before playing at the Hackney Showroom, the Royal Exchange and Hope Street Theatre in Liverpool, *Burgerz* was directed by Sam Curtis Lindsay and performed by Alabanza, who wrote the script after an incident where, as the first lines state, '[a] burger was thrown at me in broad daylight in April 2016 on Waterloo Bridge whilst someone yelled the word tranny. I think over one hundred people saw and I know no one did anything' (2018: 7).

The performance consists of Alabanza relating and theorizing the experience including requiring 'a cis white man ... to help me. / Make a burger' (19). With assistance from the participant, who speaks lines from a 'recipe book', Alabanza proceeds to cook and construct a burger onstage – shaping the patty, chopping vegetables and organizing the packaging – while relating the incident to broader structural violence, and symbolizing the coercive construction of gender through the creation of a burger. This use of the audience as participatory performers reading from a script was also used in Tim Crouch's *Total Immediate Collective Imminent Terrestrial Salvation* (Fringe, 2019) to represent the gathering of a cult whose leader, following the death of his son, is convinced of the world's imminent end. Like this and other works by Crouch, Alabanza also uses the 'ritual' of performance, the implication of the audience within it, and the experience of shared imagination as productive components of the dramaturgy.

The central act of harassment done to Alabanza that informs the show is approached by them through 'continuum-thinking'. *Bird* and *seven methods of killing kylie jenner* both depict how the proliferation of certain attitudes and behaviours that are in themselves not 'violent' per se still maintain gender-based violence. Indeed, I contend that violence in its many forms and guises was generally represented in new British playwriting over the 2010s in adherence to 'continuum-thinking': that is, violence as not a strict definition of acts and phenomena but a spectrum covering certain acts, behaviours and events ranging from the normalized to the spectacular. Understanding violence through this continuum-thinking can be retrospectively applied to the other forms of violence represented by plays analysed earlier: such as racism in *Fall of the Kingdom, Rise of the Foot Soldier* and climate crisis in *The Children*. This adheres to the definitions of violence explored in Chapter 1 – namely, that the term is not fixed, but has vague boundaries troubled by relatively 'ordinary' acts. Taken separately, these are not violent, yet in reiterated multiplicity they can constitute a context of violence. This creates an atmosphere where, as in *Some People Talk About Violence*, subjective acts of violence are not explicitly apparent, but violence can nevertheless be affectively felt. Such continuums of violence then – made up in great part by relatively everyday acts – create wider networks of violence.

Though *Burgerz* revolves around a central act of subjective violence, Alabanza rationalizes it through the acknowledgement of the continuum it emerges from. In the playtext's foreword, they note how the production 'has become an emblem for so many other incidents, deaths, acts of violence and harm, that the trans and gender non-conforming community have to face every single day' (xi). The incident suffered by Alabanza on Waterloo Bridge is contextualized as one of many oppressive actions:

> Anti-trans billboards go up around Liverpool the same week that one of our sisters is murdered in the streets.
>
> They're debating our existence on the television again, whilst a trans friend was held up at knifepoint the day before […]
>
> Harassment isn't just one moment. It doesn't just start and stop.
>
> (43–4)

Informed by Alabanza's lived experience, the conception of harassment not being a series of anomalies – something that 'doesn't just start and stop' – is an example of continuum-thinking. Though different forms of violence are certainly not easily reducible or comparable to one another, the transphobia recounted here by Alabanza as well as, for example, the neoliberal attitudes of *Three Kingdoms* and the misogyny and racism of *seven methods of killing kylie jenner* demonstrate how structural violence is supported by a continuum of acts, behaviours and attitudes that are performatively 'weaved' into culture and society.

Indeed, I also contend that acts on the continuum of certain kinds of violence – 'continuums' of GBV, climate crisis, etc. – performatively maintain structural violence. For example, the 'doing' of acts on the continuum of racist violence, whether these are overt acts of subjective violence, or innocuous systemic or symbolic behaviours, maintain a structure of racism. This corresponds to Balibar's understanding of violence as a Möbius strip: a structure perpetuated by the 'performance' of ultra-subjective and ultra-objective violence. Furthermore, like this Möbius strip, structural violence *informs* continuums of violence; for example, the existence of microaggressions is due to structural racism, while aiding in the continuation of structural racism. This 'weird loop' can be seen in *ear for eye*, where the classification of racially motivated murderers is connected to both historical and contemporaneous racism. The structure of the violence of neoliberalism, too, is discerned through the 'touching tales' of *Lampedusa*: the reiteration of certain performative attitudes and behaviours enabling the maintenance of an ideological structure that affects – and is maintained by – a debt collector in Leeds, a lifeguard in the Mediterranean and others/Others more explicitly made abject by its smooth functioning.

Burgerz also expresses how continuums of certain acts, attitudes and behaviours maintain forms of structural violence. Much like *Fall of the*

Kingdom, Rise of the Foot Soldier, Alabanza articulates how even a 'neutral' stance on trans* and gender non-conforming individuals feeds into their structural oppression. As Alabanza states of those who witnessed the assault, 'I'm not going to say anymore that no one did anything, because walking away is action [...] doing nothing is not neutral' (57–8). The indifference displayed in such actions essentially validates the occurrence of the violence: it presupposes that structural violence against individuals like Alabanza is part of the everyday functioning of society. Most likely, many of those present would not endorse the attack, but their lack of 'performance' to suggest anything but indifference authorizes the structural violence of transphobia and GBV. Alabanza even admits to being 'kind of not shocked' at the incident: 'To be trans and Black and gender non-conforming is to both be accustomed to the violence whilst also dissociating from its reality' (54). The performativity of actions, behaviours and attitudes that inform structural violence maintains its existence and normalcy – '[t]he world was working exactly how it had been made to' (56). As *Burgerz* represents, this is to the extent that those afflicted can become 'dissociated' from its reality, and those who unknowingly preserve it do not feel obliged to assist certain individuals when in an abject position of harassment or danger.

A third and final contention here is that much 2010s British theatre uses dramaturgical techniques concerned with visibility, invisibility and scale to gesture to these continuums and structures of violence; and, indeed, these productions demonstrate how these concerns are essential to understanding violence in this structural way. This adheres to Paavolainen's theories of theatricality ('zooming-out') and performativity ('zooming-in') which have been referred to throughout this work, and is related to Richardson's Black witnessing, Nixon's slow violence (taking a temporally and spatially broad standpoint to discern environmental damage), and Fisher's capitalist realism (how normative perception inhibits the ability to 'look beyond' capitalism and neoliberalism). *Escaped Alone*, for example, situates its audience at different perceptual levels: zoomed-in to the summer garden or zoomed-out through Mrs J's cataclysmic orations. Between these two standpoints, connections can be made to the innocuous acts on the continuums of violence and their overarching structures. Indeed, structures of violence can persist in great part because of their phenomenological obscurement: the techniques of the 2010s British theatre explored here look to enable audiences to see the 'bigger picture', to make invisible violence visible.

Burgerz utilizes questions of scale, visibility and invisibility to question, critique and represent normative perceptions of violence onstage. Alabanza figures the incident on Waterloo Bridge as 'invisible': 'I had to touch the mayonnaise on my shoulder for me to make sure that it was real, because if you looked at everyone else, it would have you thinking nothing in the world had changed' (55). Informed by the innocuousness and indifference of systemic violence, the harassment was somewhat invisible or normalized, in that it was a symptom of the smooth functioning of structural violence. Alabanza masterfully guides their audience through different approaches to the incident: zooming-out to relate it to broader structural violence, and zooming-in to the minutiae of the construction of a burger – the object thrown at them. The burger itself becomes a symbolic visualization of the coercive establishment and policing of heteronormative gender and its socio-cultural norms: 'As if the burger isn't violent in its creation. As if violence doesn't happen to hot dog and burger-choosers, as if it starts when you are choosing between hot dog and burger' (14). As mentioned in Chapter 2, this understanding is theorized by Butler, who similarly argues that '[w]e are at least partially formed through violence. We are given genders or social categories, against our will' (2009: 167). This process of having to learn the correct acts, gestures and behaviours to normatively, performatively ascribe gender is visualized by Alabanza's moulding of unformed meat into a patty to be then categorized and 'boxed' – a metaphor like that used through *Fall of the Kingdom, Rise of the Foot Soldier*. Again then, violence is illustrated in *Burgerz* as being closely tied to (normative) perception.

Overall, *Burgerz* is at once exemplary of the contentions I have formulated from my research on 2010s British theatre and the representation of violence, while still being among the most distinct productions of the decade. Towards its conclusion, Alabanza notes how immediately after the incident they caught a woman's eye 'for two seconds […] And she carried on walking' (57). They then gesture for a woman in the audience to join them onstage and read from the 'recipe book' a 'vow' on behalf of the audience:

> I vow to protect you, as in the plural, as in more than just you. I vow to realise that in my safety, in my comfort, in my silence, comes your danger, hurt, and entrapment. I vow to know that I cannot possibly be free, whilst you, the plural, are still hurt […] [T]here cannot be singular anymore […] we have tried singular, and we continue to fail.
>
> (60–1)

The participant then throws the burger at Alabanza to end the show, in an act of reclamation 'to bring this vow of words into action' (60). This action – and vow in action – is something like the performative rituals explored by Austin and explicitly acknowledges plurality.

Not only does *Burgerz*'s participatory finale acknowledge the authorizing, plural performativity of those gathered, but directs this plural performativity towards the directive of 'protecting the plural', going beyond individuality or partisanship to recognize interdependency as a necessary tool to dismantle structural violence. As Effie Samara argues:

> the power of a performative collective can and does act to consolidate a political entity, which, even in total silence, asserts its presence as a plural and unyielding organism in the performative of a body politic. The political significance of assembling as physical bodies deconstructs the metaphysics of absence by negating presence, not in individual subjectivity, but as a social movement.
>
> (2021: 62)

As shown through the analyses of many of the case studies here, Alabanza's appeal to the plural performativity of the audience – seen in many other examples of 2010s British theatre – looks to not only 'make visible' the structural violence in their lives, then, but makes visible the revolutionary power of such an assembly.

Final Remarks

While there is certainly much scope to inspect how other playwrights and productions staged structural violence in relation to performativity, further queries that arise include how the movement in 2010s British theatre to represent systemic rather than subjective violence correlated to similar mediums like dance, live and performance art, music and opera. Though the Introduction generalizes theatre as more proficient in this approach than film or television, did examples of other performing arts also succeed at such representation? Another question for further study would be how did work from theatre companies and institutions – such as educative programmes – actively, materially combat issues of structural violence in specific communities? And a major question, which will take some years to deduce, is how the dramaturgical advancements of this decade impacted future theatre – especially in a new decade that began with a truly deadly and destabilizing pandemic of 'invisible violence'?

Still, this study has offered among the first historicizations of British theatre in the 2010s – contextualizing this decade of work which has, at the time of writing, not yet seen sustained critical attention as a complete decade of playwriting. Furthermore, many examples of British theatre of this time have been noted here, whether as part of a larger thematic body or through close analysis, which can be used as a resource for future evaluations of 2010s British theatre. My research's elaboration on theories of 'invisible' forms of violence in conjunction with performativity will hopefully complement other studies on theatre's representation of violence. Yet, its distinction in this regard may see this book used as a useful touchstone for stagings of violence in (contemporary British) theatre, as well as an illustrative guide for violence studies and representations of violence more generally. The arrangement of this work's concerns into distinct chapters on protest, climate crisis, neoliberalism, racism and gender-based violence means that studies in these areas can utilize the research of these parts which, taken individually, are extensive enough to offer findings on these subjects.

By way of some final remarks, I would contend that the examples of 2010s British theatre explored here – depicting, querying and challenging the proliferation of violence – generally advocate for more interdependent and communitarian modes of being in contemporary, neoliberal-inflected British society. Even the more nihilistic among the examples here such as *Three Kingdoms* or *Pomona* offer such interpersonal connection, in both these productions' cross-cultural reach as well as their offering of what Rebellato calls 'real non-utilitarian spaces' (however constricted by institutionalization or insularity) to dissect 'the political realities that surround us' (2018: 35). With Chapter 1 suggesting that the productions analysed here can be read as 'theatrical critiques' of violence, such interpersonal engagement and radical optimism is necessary for any such critique, as Evans and Giroux state:

> should we take the performative nature of violence seriously, what is demanded is not accepting the inevitability of injustice, but a pedagogical confidence to imagine another world is both possible and desirable. Oppressive power does not fear vulnerable subjects. It produces them. What it fears is the courage to counter its spectacles of violence with the belief, despite the horror, that there are still enough reasons to believe in this world and transform it for the better. Holding on to that confidence seems key to our critique of violence today.
>
> (2015: 140)

This returns to the 'weird loop' of the performative potential contended by Butler, of making visible the performative constitution of structural violence: even as plurally performative actions establish and maintain the contexts of violence that plagued the 2010s and will, most likely, continue to exist, so too does this signal the weakness of such violence. As the expansive and imaginative dramaturgies of the productions explored here suspect – which 'take seriously' the performative nature of violence – the plural performativity generated by collectives such as those sitting in a theatre space can potentially eradicate the structural violence represented. These 2010 British plays, then, demonstrate how the articulation of violence in such a medium shows that the performative role of theatre is one of making violence visible, while making visible the gathered plurality that can combat it.

Notes

Introduction

1 This relates to one of the playtext's epigraphs, from the blog of a top UK barrister, David Osborne: 'If the complainant (I do not refer to her as the victim) was under the influence of alcohol or drugs, or both, when she was "raped", this provides the accused with a complete defence' (quoted in Whitehill, 2016b: 53).
2 This Code appeared to respond to allegations directed at the former artistic directors of London's Old Vic (Kevin Spacey) and the Royal Court (Max Stafford-Clark).
3 Though, of course, violent in its own accord, the COVID-19 global pandemic has also been symbolically used to illustrate structural violence. For example, 'racism is a virus' became a popular phrase in BLM demonstrations after 2020.
4 For example, two of the most well-recognized TV drama serials of the 2010s – *Breaking Bad* (2008–13) and *Game of Thrones* (2011–19) – on one hand espoused the dangers of crime and war, while on the other provided images of visceral and spectacular violence.
5 Indeed, although British theatre certainly made some advancements in diversity, emergent and professionally successful playwrights through the 2010s overwhelmingly came from southern England and particularly from regions close to London.
6 Fitzpatrick draws on the work of Sharon Marcus here, who 'proposes that rape can be understood in terms of a "script"' (2018: 11); 'enabled by narratives, complexes and institutions which derive their strength [...] from their power to structure our lives as imposing cultural scripts' (Marcus 1992: 388–9; quoted in Fitzpatrick 2018: 11–12).
7 Nevitt does not overarchingly criticize Kane's play – or onstage representations of sexual assault overall – but the staging choices specifically made in the Bristol Old Vic's 2005 production. As she writes, 'performers and directors have a responsibility to make their choices in such a way that the image of rape they create serves the narrative and political needs of the play but does not empower rapists or disempower their victims' (33).
8 I have referred throughout to the earlier VAULT version of the play; the later Fringe version concludes with a voice-over from Holly: 'What do people do now / When it's over' (Whitehill 2016c: 42), echoing dialogue from Adam at a new opening scene, which features a dislocated, dominating male voice. This concluding, open question is arguably inserted to further confront the audience with their attained knowledge of the subject matter, and to not completely remove Holly's trauma and voice from the story.

9 Kelly's theatre has consistently dealt with violence – as mentioned regarding his work in the 2000s. Although *Girls & Boys* takes a formal turn away from explicitly representing violence onstage, his contributions to theatre in the 2010s were significantly less than in the previous decade (focusing on television, film and adaptations). Therefore, his plays are not closely examined in this work, in favour of analysing more emergent voices.

Chapter 1

1 Mahesh Upadhyaya, who in 1968 'became the first person in the UK to bring a racial discrimination case to court using the recently introduced Race Relations Act', records that at the time, '[w]hen I went looking for digs it was standard to see signs saying "No blacks, no dogs, no Irish"' (Verma 2018).
2 It should be noted that the 2010s saw increased research and debate on the unfair treatment suffered by women who kill their abusive partners in self-defence (see, for example, Howes et al. 2021).
3 Mrs J's monologues are full of such varied connotations: there are echoes elsewhere to novels such as John Christopher's *The Death of Grass* (1956) and J. G. Ballard's *The Drowned World* (1962), films like *The Day After Tomorrow* (2004) and *The Wizard of Oz* (1939), and the disasters of Hurricane Katrina (2005) and the Rio de Janeiro floods and mudslides (2011).
4 Many of these terms are developed from previous work by Johan Galtung, Étienne Balibar and Pierre Bourdieu.
5 The term, coined by Chester M. Pierce (1970), is used for seemingly everyday and often unintentional speech and behaviour that can communicate prejudice or hostility to social and cultural groups.
6 I elsewhere compare these metaphorical 'dark matters' in Harold Pinter's work (Watson: 2021a).

Chapter 2

1 This ties into Austin's conception of 'infelicitous' performatives: that 'a performative utterance will, for example, be *in a particular way* hollow or void if said by an actor on the stage' (1962: 22; emphasis in original). Austin's prejudice of performed language being 'non-serious' was later challenged by Derrida (1988: 17).
2 Several psychological and neurological studies in the 2010s evidenced this latter effect (McGreenery et al. 2010; Berman et al. 2011; Cacioppo et al. 2014).
3 As Althusser writes, before a child can recognize its name it is 'appointed as a subject in and by the specific ideological configuration in which it is "expected"' (2001: 119). Interpellation does not so much describe an individual as inaugurate them into an ideology.

4 Though McDonagh's plays have comedic elements – often veering into gallows humour (literally with *Hangmen*) – the 'Irishness' of his earlier plays has been criticized as bordering on caricature (Wallace 2006).
5 Indeed, though this study contends that new British plays of the 2010s generally did not represent explicit, subjective violence onstage, that is not to say that there were no such examples. Marjory's 'comedic' gunning down of Dirk and Barry bears similarity to Rory Mullarkey's *Pity* (RC, 2018) where, in one scene, two rival factions continue to shoot each other to death in unrealistic perpetuity as a neon sign flashing the word 'violence' was lowered onto the stage. More visceral, realistic representations were also seen in, for example, Gary Owen's *Violence and Son* (RC, 2015) which focuses on toxic masculinity and domestic abuse. However, as contended, such representations were the exception rather than the rule in 2010s new writing.

Chapter 3

1 These include the International Labour Organization; Armed Conflict Location and Event Database project; and Global Database of Events, Language and Tone.
2 Although an Arts Council review in 2016 identified that there were ongoing issues and concerns with audience diversity in terms of socio-economic background (as well as ethnic diversity and disability accessibility), it also concluded that evidence suggests 'the theatre sector is increasingly invested in its audience development role' (Naylor et al. 2016: 56).
3 Other examples of protests against theatre across Europe included Romeo Castelluci's *On the Concept of the Face before the Son of God* (2011), which was heavily protested against by Christian groups in Paris for its interpreted blasphemy (Balme 2014: 157). Additionally, Frljić's *Klątwa* (*The Curse*; 2017) saw heated protests in Warsaw that took place in a 'context of political censorship and moral panic' (Lease 2018).
4 As Leah Bassel paraphrases from Gus John's keynote at the 'Media and the Riots' conference (2011), such reporting 'arguably served to divide people into "good" and "bad" members of society' (2011: 3).
5 David Cameron's stance on the riots – '[t]hose thugs we saw last week do not represent us […] This is a great country of good people' (2011) – was particularly ignorant of any such nuance.
6 The Egyptian protests deployed nonviolence effectively to not only convince the national populace to the revolutionaries' cause, but to garner the sympathy of the global stage. Still, that the protesters had to fight to be 'coded as civil' speaks to Butler's conception that certain populaces and individuals are represented and reiterated in (Global North) media as more 'recognisable' than others.
7 Johan Galtung's granddaughter was present, and survived, Breivik's attacks. Despite his emotional stake in these events, Galtung stated that this violence

was informed by structural Islamophobia rather than being the isolated actions of a 'lone wolf' radical (Galtung et al. 2011).
8   Two other works perhaps influenced by this are Neil Bartlett's adaptation of Albert Camus's *The Plague* (1947; Arcola, 2017), which used microphones to suggest the characters being at a tribunal and appeared to assist them in compartmentalizing their difficult narratives; and Robert Icke's version of Ibsen's *The Wild Duck* (1884; Almeida, 2018), where characters would soliloquize to the audience with a microphone and so visualize distinctions between metaphor, reality and personal interpretation.
9   Michael Brown was an 18-year-old who, in 2014, was shot by police in Ferguson, Missouri despite having his hands raised.
10 Richardson identifies this in conversation with Ferrell: 'black male leaders within the movement have called her troublesome for highlighting their sexism – especially in terms of hoarding media opportunities or only doing certain kinds of work' (2020: 102).
11 Sloane's imperialistic ties were explicitly noted in another Court production, Sabrina Mahfouz's *A History of Water in the Middle East* (2019).
12 This draws on several incidents through the 2010s such as the Sandy Hook Elementary School shooting (2012; Newtown, Connecticut), the Emanuel AME Church shooting (2015; Charleston, South Carolina) and the Stoneman Douglas High School shooting (2018; Parkland, Florida).

Chapter 4

1   These terms were not new to the 2010s but became more widely accepted. Al Gore, for example, was using 'climate crisis' since the 1980s (Sobczyk 2019). Climate crisis is the preferred term in this chapter, as it reflects the urgency seen in many of the plays discussed here. That said, it should be noted that 'climate change' was the dominant term earlier in the 2010s (Zeldin-O'Neill 2019).
2   In 'Contemporary Catastrophes: 2010s British Climate Crisis Theatre and Performativity' (2022), I denoted this as CCT: climate crisis theatre. Here, I identify several different symbols and themes that theatre-makers in 2010s Britain used to represent the climate crisis onstage: these being temporally 'zooming-out'; children; 'cli-fi'; posthumanism; the legacy of slavery; and productions' material conditions.
3   This likely references Dunwich, a Scandinavian town of which much disappeared due to coastal erosion in the Middle Ages (Whiteley 2016). Furthermore, a few miles south is the decommissioned Sizewell plant in Suffolk – which nearly caused a major disaster due to a nuclear leak in 2007 (Gould 2009) – and bears similarity to the play's description of the station's 'great white dome' (Kirkwood 2016: 13).
4   This otherwise offhand comment may reference accounts of infants born with severe mutations due to radiation poisoning, such as the 'jellyfish babies' birthed following nuclear tests around the Marshall Islands (Nixon 2011: 7).

5 Kirkwood responded to a concern that Hazel was 'selfish' with the position that, on the contrary, it is inferred that Hazel has been doing 'everyday' environmentally friendly and community-engaged activities; her frustration at Rose's venture is that she must continue to 'give more' (Morrison 2016).

Chapter 5

1 Throughout this chapter and the next, 'Europe' will be generally used to mean non-British-European nations: particularly those represented by the European Union. This is not to say that my use of 'Europe' only relates to EU member-states; only that, particularly in British theatre, 'European' describes prominent EU member-states like Germany and France more strongly than, for example, Moldova or Serbia.
2 See 'Neoliberal (Dis)Possession in Rose Lewenstein's *Cougar*' (Watson 2021b) for a full analysis of this production.
3 As Ian Farnell writes, '*Pomona* is accredited, not entirely apocryphally, with restoring the fortunes of the Orange Tree' (2019: 123) after the Arts Council dropped its funding of the theatre in 2014 (Watson 2021b).
4 Of course – as noted later – the Second World War has often been deployed in the British national imaginary as a recourse to cultural exceptionalism rather than broader European co-operation; being used, for example, in pro-Brexit discourse (Stratton 2019).
5 Following the renewed invasion of Ukraine by Russian forces in early 2022, *Bad Roads* played at the Court again as a rehearsed reading.
6 The violence was depicted as surgical and horrifically banal. For example, a character's limbs were attached to a large machine and routinely dismembered; informed both by the Bosnian War and Mitchell's own experience of a dental implant operation (Trueman 2016b).
7 The protagonist's name – along with the play's title – perhaps refers to St Ignatius of Loyola, a sixteenth-century Spanish priest who devised spiritual exercises including 'Three Kinds of People', which advocates incarnating the values of the kingdom of God on earth. This perhaps relates to the dissonance between Europe's ideal image and its (in the play) violent reality – as explored in the next chapter.
8 The 'neoliberalization' of Europe has been represented in theatre across the continent, as tracked by Marilena Zaroulia and Philip Hager (2015), for example.

Chapter 6

1 The Scottish 'Indyref' came during a 'golden age for theatre production in Scotland' (McMillan 2011): following the establishment of the National

Theatre of Scotland in 2006, and with new work from upcoming and established playwrights like Alistair Beaton, Rob Drummond, David Greig, Zinnie Harris, Kieran Hurley, Morna Pearson and Anthony Neilson.
2 In the case of Scotland, however, renewed calls for a second independence referendum have been motivated by the country's majority Remain vote – suggesting that Scottishness in the 2010s had stronger ties to Europeanness and European identity than the rest of the UK.
3 This, of course, applies only to Britain rather than the UK overall – with the borders of Northern Ireland and the overseas territory of Gibraltar being major concerns following the Brexit referendum.

Chapter 7

1 Though Kane did not explicitly mention any commitment to feminism in her writing – stating, for example, in interview that 'I have no responsibility as a woman writer because I don't believe there's such a thing' (Stephenson and Langridge 1997: 134) – this potentiality is explored by Elaine Aston (2010).
2 It is notable too that Mitchell's production deviates from Kane's text when Tinker executes his female lover, perhaps to exorcise his 'feminised', romantic attachment to her, or to demonstrate her disposability all along, or both.
3 The incident which Solnit refers to is when an older man at a party mistakenly explains her own book to her, not considering that she was the author (2014: 1-4) – inspiring the term 'mansplaining'.
4 This year is notable for when Laura Bates began her Everyday Sexism Project, as well as campaigns including No More Page 3, One Billion Rising, and Free the Nipple. Additionally, the Slut Walks began the year before (2011), the same year as Chimamanda Ngozi Adichie's viral TEDx talk.
5 Second-wave feminism has been generally characterized as focusing on equal pay, self-determination and double standards (Evans and Chamberlain 2015) as satirized in *Top Girls*, and 'revealed the oppression of women in the entertainment media in terms of obsession with the portrayal of women as sex objects' (Iannello 1998: 316), as *Masterpieces* centres on.
6 Though Aston ends her article by introducing the term 'viral realism – realism as infectious, contagious and spreading from a "host" of playwrights' with a 'capacity for genetic mutation' (2016: 33), I use 'fluid realism' here to emphasize the 'variable' nature of realism identified by Williams, as well as the tradition of 'looseness' pioneered by the female British writers noted in this chapter, among others.
7 In 2018, an open letter from a coalition of 120 organizations warned the government that funding was desperately needed for children's services (Butler 2018). Research also revealed that between 2010 and 2018 there

was a 29 per cent cut in government funding for children's departments. Chandler herself states that the play was inspired by an incident reported in the news of two young women in care who committed suicide (2013).

8   Gardner's positive review of the production does nevertheless note that it 'overdoes the bird metaphors' (2016c).
9   Willis's primary case study here is the New Zealand acting coach Rene Naufau, who claimed his 'sexual offending in the classroom was simply preparing his students for the "real world of acting"' (2019: 259).
10 The production was also due to be performed at the Birmingham Repertory Theatre in December 2020 but was postponed due to the COVID-19 pandemic. It did, however, return to the Court in June 2021 to re-open the theatre after national lockdown.
11 Without looking to efface Lee-Jones's use of (Black) Twitter acronyms and portmanteaus, I have clarified their meanings for those unfamiliar with the terminology.
12 Lee-Jones provides a bibliography '*of all the memes, gifs and Twitter references made in the play, lest our labour and records be swept away again …*' (2019: 88).
13 Lee-Jones states her that she was influenced by both the playwright Lorraine Hansberry's essay 'Twice Militant' (1957; see Clements 2014), which offers a 'proto-theory' of intersectionality in the statement that women of colour are 'twice oppressed' but can be 'twice militant' in reaction to it, and W. E. B. Du Bois's theory of 'double-consciousness', or the sense of looking at oneself through the eyes of others – particularly through the lens of race (1999). This is explicitly challenged at the play's conclusion, as the audience's 'gaze' is returned by the performers.

Works Cited

'EU Referendum: Results' (2016), *BBC News*, 23 June. Available online: www.bbc.co.uk/news/politics/eu_referendum/results (accessed 25 March 2021).

'Fulke Rose: Profile & Legacies' (2021), *Centre for the Study of the Legacies of British Slavery*, UCL, n.d. Available online: wwwdepts-live.ucl.ac.uk/lbs/person/view/2146650539 (accessed 20 November 2020).

Abrahams, J. (2017), 'Everything You Wanted to Know about Fourth Wave Feminism – But Were Afraid to Ask', *Prospect*, 14 August. Available online: www.prospectmagazine.co.uk/magazine/everything-wanted-know-fourth-wave-feminism (accessed 14 November 2020).

Adams, C. J. (2015), *The Sexual Politics of Meat: A Feminist-Vegetarian Critical Theory*, 3rd edn, London: Bloomsbury.

Adelson, L. (2000), 'Touching Tales of Turks, Germans, and Jews: Cultural Alterity, Historical Narrative, and Literary Riddles for the 1990s', *New German Critique*, 80 (1): 93–124.

Adiseshiah, S. (2012), 'Political Returns on the Twenty-First Century Stage', *C21 Literature*, 1 (1): 99–117.

Adiseshiah, S. and J. Bolton (2020a), '"change ain't fuckin polite, scuse my language": Situating debbie tucker green', in S. Adiseshiah and J. Bolton (eds), *debbie tucker green: Critical Perspectives*, 1–19, Basingstoke: Palgrave Macmillan.

Adiseshiah, S. and J. Bolton (2020b), 'debbie tucker green and (the Dialectics of) Dispossession: Reframing the Ethical Encounter', in S. Adiseshiah and J. Bolton (eds), *debbie tucker green: Critical Perspectives*, 67–88, Basingstoke: Palgrave Macmillan.

Ahmed, S. (2014), *Willful Subjects*, Durham, NC and London: Duke University Press.

Akbar, A. (2019a), 'Theatre and #MeToo: "There's a new anger in women's stories"', *The Guardian*, 27 August. Available online: www.theguardian.com/stage/2019/aug/27/women-theatre-metoo-movement-sexy-lamp-bitter-wheat-harvey (accessed 21 January 2020).

Akbar, A. (2019b), 'Seven Methods of Killing Kylie Jenner review – social media storm lit up', *The Guardian*, 9 July. Available online: www.theguardian.com/stage/2019/jul/09/seven-methods-of-killing-kylie-jenner-review-royal-court-theatre (accessed 7 January 2021).

Alabanza, T. (2018), *Burgerz*, London: Oberon.

Alexander, J. C. (2017), *The Drama of Social Life*, Cambridge: Polity.

Althusser, L. (2001), 'Ideology and Ideological State Apparatuses (Notes Towards an Investigation)', in *Lenin and Philosophy and Other Essays*, trans. by B. Brewster, 85–126, New York: Monthly Review.

Anderlini-D'Onofrio, S. (1999), 'Is Feminism Realism Possible? A Theory of Labial Eros and Mimesis', *Journal of Gender Studies*, 8 (2): 159–80.

Anderson, K. (2011), 'Person of the Year 2011: The Protestor', *Time*, 14 December. Available online: http://content.time.com/time/specials/packages/article/0,28804,2101745_2102132,00.html?xid=newsletter-daily (accessed 28 December 2018).

Angel-Perez, E. and A. Rousseau (2023), 'Feeling a Responsibility to Art: A Conversation with Ella Hickson', in E. Angel-Perez and A. Rousseau (eds), *The New Wave of British Women Playwrights*, 227–38, Berlin and Boston: De Gruyter.

Angelaki, V. (2013), 'Politics for the Middle-Classes: Contemporary Audiences and the Violence of Now', in V. Angelaki (ed.), *Contemporary British Theatre: Breaking New Ground*, 57–78, Basingstoke: Palgrave Macmillan.

Angelaki, V. (2017), *Social and Political Theatre in 21st-Century Britain*, London: Methuen Drama.

Angelaki, V. (2019), *Theatre & Environment*. London: Red Globe.

Aragay, M. and E. Monforte (2013), 'Racial Violence, Witnessing and Emancipated Spectatorship in *The Colour of Justice, Fallout* and *Random*', in V. Angelaki (ed.), *Contemporary British Theatre: Breaking New Ground*, 96–120, Basingstoke: Palgrave Macmillan.

Arendt, H. (1963), *Eichmann in Jerusalem: A Report on the Banality of Evil*. New York: Viking.

Arendt, H. (1970), *On Violence*, Boston: Harcourt.

Aston, E. (1995), *An Introduction to Feminism and Theatre*, London and New York: Routledge.

Aston, E. (2010), 'Feeling the Loss of Feminism: Sarah Kane's *Blasted* and an Experiential Genealogy of Contemporary Women's Playwriting', *Theatre Journal*, 62 (4): 575–91.

Aston, E. (2013), 'But Not That: Caryl Churchill's Political Shape Shifting at the Turn of the Millennium', *Modern Drama* 56 (2): 145–64.

Aston, E. (2016), 'Room for Realism?', in S. Adiseshiah and L. LePage (eds), *Twenty-First Century Drama: What Happens Now*, 17–35, Basingstoke: Palgrave Macmillan.

Aston, E. (2017), 'Moving Women Centre Stage: Structures of Feminist-Tragic Feeling', *JCDE*, 5 (2): 292–310.

Aston, E. (2018), 'Enter Stage Left: "Recognition," "Redistribution," and the A-Affect', *Contemporary Theatre Review*, 28 (3): 299–309.

Aston, E. and M. O'Thomas (2010), *Royal Court: International*, Basingstoke: Palgrave Macmillan.

Atkinson, S. (2016), 'Introduction', in S. Atkinson (ed.), *HighTide Plays: 1*, ix–xiv, London: Methuen Drama.

Austin, J. L. (1962), *How to do Things with Words*, ed. J. O. Urmson. Oxford: Oxford University Press.

Balestrini, N. W. (2020), Interview with C. Bilodeau, 'Writing Plays That Are Climate Change', *JCDE*, 8 (1): 34–46.

Balibar, É. (2016), *Violence and Civility: On the Limits of Political Philosophy*, trans. G. M. Goshgarin, New York: Columbia University Press.

Balme, C. B. (2014), *The Theatrical Public Sphere*, Cambridge: Cambridge University Press.

Barrel Organ (2015), 'Some People Talk about Barrel Organ', *Exeunt*, 3 August. Available online: http://exeuntmagazine.com/features/some-people-talk-about-barrel-organ/ (accessed 4 June 2021).

Bassel, L. (2013), 'Speaking and Listening: The 2011 English Riots', *Sociological Research Online*, 18 (4): 111–21.

Baxter-Derrington, J. (2016), 'Fall of the Kingdom, Rise of the Foot Soldier – Making Mischief', *The Panoptic*, 7 August. Available online: https://thepanoptic.co.uk/2016/08/07/fall-kingdom-rise-foot-soldier-making-mischief/ (accessed 25 March 2021).

Beck, U. (2003), 'Understanding the Real Europe', *Dissent*, 50 (3): 32–8.

Benjamin, W. (2004), 'Critique of Violence', in M. Bullock and M. W. Jennings (eds), *Walter Benjamin. Selected Writings. Volume 1: 1913–1926*, trans. E. Jephcott, 236–52, Cambridge, MA: Harvard University Press.

Berlant, L. (2011), *Cruel Optimism*, Durham, NC and London: Duke University Press.

Berman, M. G. et al. (2011), 'Social Rejection Shares Somatosensory Representations with Physical Pain', *PNAS*, 108 (15): 6270–5.

Billington, M. (2012), 'Three Kingdoms – review', *The Guardian*, 9 May. Available online: www.theguardian.com/stage/2012/may/09/three-kingdoms-review (accessed 5 March 2020).

Billington, M. (2015), 'How to Hold Your Breath review – magnetic Maxine Peake is bedevilled in morality play', *The Guardian*, 11 February. Available online: www.theguardian.com/stage/2015/feb/11/how-to-hold-your-breath-review-maxine-peake-royal-court-theatre (accessed 20 March 2021).

Billington, M. (2016), 'The Children review – Kirkwood's slow-burning drama asks profound questions', *The Guardian*, 25 November. Available online: www.theguardian.com/stage/2016/nov/25/children-review-lucy-kirkwood-royal-court (accessed 28 January 2021).

Billington, M. (2018), 'Did Hans Christian Andersen keep a woman in a cage? A Very Very Very Dark Matter review', *The Guardian*, 25 October. Available online: www.theguardian.com/stage/2018/oct/25/a-very-very-very-dark-matter-review-martin-mcdonagh-wildly-inventive-jim-broadbent (accessed 5 July 2020).

Birch, A. (2014), *Revolt. She said. Revolt again*, in E. Whyman (ed.), *Midsummer Mischief: Four Radical New Plays*, 43–102, London: Oberon.

Birch, A. and RashDash (2015), *We Want You to Watch*, London: Oberon.

Bissell, L. (2018), 'There Is Such a Thing: Feminist Mimesis in Contemporary Performance in the UK', *Contemporary Theatre Review*, 28 (4): 522–36.

Blythe, A. (2014), *Little Revolution*, London: Nick Hern.

Bolton, J. (2015), Interview with S. Stephens, 'Preface to *Three Kingdoms*', in *Plays: 4*, 3–11, London: Methuen Drama.

Bond, E. (1997), 'On Violence', in *Plays: 1*, 9–18, London: Methuen Drama.
Boon, R. and P. Roberts (2012–13), 'On Writing for a Different Gender', *Exeunt Magazine*, 3 August Available online: http://exeuntmagazine.com/features/writing-different-gender/ (accessed 19 November 2020).
Bourdieu, P. (1991), *Language and Symbolic Power*, ed. J. B. Thompson, trans. G. Raymond and M. Adamson, Cambridge: Polity.
Boyle, K. (2019), 'What's in a Name? Theorising the Inter-relationships of Gender and Violence', *Feminist Theory*, 20 (1): 19–36.
Buchanan, J. B. (1971), 'Pollution by Synthetic Fibres', *Marine Pollution Bulletin*, 2 (2): 23.
Bumiller, K. (2008), *In an Abusive State: How Neoliberalism Appropriated the Feminist Movement against Sexual Violence*, Durham, NC: Duke University Press.
Bunch, M. (2012), 'Castration Anxiety and Traumatic Encounters with the Real in the Works of August Strindberg and Lars von Trier', in A. Westerståhl Stenport (ed.), *The International Strindberg: New Critical Essays*, 49–70, Evanston, IL: Northwestern University Press.
Burratta, B. (2018), 'A Note on the Play', in Outbox Theatre, *And The Rest of Me Floats*, 5–6, London: Oberon.
Butler, J. (1997), *Excitable Speech: A Politics of the Performative*, New York: Routledge.
Butler, J. (2006), *Precarious Life*, London: Verso.
Butler, J. (2007), *Gender Trouble*, London: Routledge.
Butler, J. (2009), *Frames of War: When is Life Grievable?*, London: Verso.
Butler, J. (2015), *Notes Towards a Performative Theory of Assembly*, Cambridge, MA: Harvard University Press.
Butler, J. (2020), *The Force of Nonviolence*, London: Verso.
Butler, J. and A. Athanasiou (2013), *Dispossession: The Performative in the Political*. Cambridge: Polity.
Butler, P. (2018), 'Children's services are at breaking point, experts say', *The Guardian*, 23 October. Available online: www.theguardian.com/society/2018/oct/23/childrens-services-at-breaking-point-experts-say (accessed 3 January 2021).
Cacioppo, S. et al. (2014), 'Toward a Neurology of Loneliness', *Psychological Bulletin*, 140 (6): 1464–504.
Cameron, D. (2011), 'PM's speech on the fightback after the riots', *Gov.uk*, 15 August. Available online: www.gov.uk/government/speeches/pms-speech-on-the-fightback-after-the-riots (accessed 5 November 2011).
Cardullo, B. and Knopf, R. (2001), *Theater of the Avant-Garde 1890–1950: A Critical Anthology*. London: Yale University Press.
Carl, N., J. Dennison and G. Evans (2018), 'European But Not European Enough: An Explanation for Brexit', *European Union Politics*, 20 (2): 282–304.
Carrington, D. (2016), 'The Anthropocene epoch: Scientists declare dawn of human-influenced age', *The Guardian*, 29 August. Available online: www.

theguardian.com/environment/2016/aug/29/declare-anthropocene-epoch-experts-urge-geological-congress-human-impact-earth (accessed 8 January 2021).

Carrington, D. (2020), 'Climate "apocalypse" fears stopping people having children – study', *The Guardian*, 27 November. Available online: www.theguardian.com/environment/2020/nov/27/climate-apocalypse-fears-stopping-people-having-children-study (accessed 10 January 2020).

Caruth, C. (1995), 'Introduction: Trauma and Experience', in C. Caruth (ed.), *Trauma: Explorations in Memory*, 3–12, Baltimore and London: The Johns Hopkins University Press.

Case, S.-E. (1988), *Feminism and Theatre*, New York: Methuen Drama.

Cavendish, D. (2016), 'The RSC's Other Place reopens with a double-helping of topical grimness', *The Telegraph*, 2 August. Available online: www.telegraph.co.uk/theatre/what-to-see/making-mischief-review-the-rscs-other-place-reopens-with-a-bleak/ (accessed 27 March 2021).

Chandler, K. (2013), 'BIRD by Katherine Chandler – Bruntwood Prize 2013 – Royal Exchange Manchester', *Royal Exchange Theatre* (YouTube), 4 December. Available online: www.youtube.com/watch?v=6QTQ8WZ1a2E (accessed 3 January 2021).

Chandler, K. (2016), *Bird*, London: Nick Hern.

Chaudhuri, U. (2016), 'Anthropo-Scenes: Staging Climate Chaos in the Drama of Bad Ideas', in S. Adiseshiah and L. LePage (eds), *Twenty-First Century Drama: What Happens Now*, 303–21, Basingstoke: Palgrave Macmillan.

Choudhury, A. R. (2019), 'Boris Johnson's Brexit deal is neoliberalism on steroids', *Peoples Dispatch*, 8 October. Available online: https://peoplesdispatch.org/2019/10/08/boris-johnsons-brexit-deal-is-neoliberalism-on-steroids/ (accessed 23 April 2020).

Christopher, J. (1998), 'Rat with hand exits stage left', *The Independent*, 3 May. Available online: www.independent.co.uk/life-style/rat-with-hand-exits-stage-left-1161442.html (accessed 15 April 2021).

Churchill, C. (2015), *Here We Go*, London: Nick Hern.

Churchill, C. (2019), *Escaped Alone*, in *Plays: 5*, 137–80, London: Nick Hern.

Citron, D. K. and H. L. Norton (2011), 'Intermediaries and Hate Speech: Fostering Digital Citizenship for Our Information Age', *Boston University Law Review*, 91 (1): 1435–84.

Clapp, S. (2015), 'Lampedusa review – moving tales of modern injustice', *The Guardian*, 19 July. Available online: www.theguardian.com/stage/2015/jul/19/lampedusa-review-moving-tales-modern-injustice-anders-lustgarten (accessed 25 March 2020).

Clapp, S. (2016), 'Escaped Alone review – small talk and everyday terror from Caryl Churchill', *The Guardian*, 31 January. Available online: www.theguardian.com/stage/2016/jan/31/escaped-alone-caryl-churchill-review-royal-court (accessed 7 June 2021).

Clements, A. (2014), 'The Private Life of Lorraine Hansberry: Letters, Lists, and Conversation', *HyperAllergic*, 29 January. Available online: https://

hyperallergic.com/104946/the-private-life-of-lorraine-hansberry-letters-lists-and-conversations/ (accessed 30 January 2021).
Cochrane, K. (2013), 'The fourth wave of feminism: Meet the rebel women', *The Guardian*, 10 December. Available online: www.theguardian.com/world/2013/dec/10/fourth-wave-feminism-rebel-women (accessed 14 November 2020).
Cohen, D. (1993), *Shakespeare's Culture of Violence*, Basingstoke: Palgrave Macmillan.
Connell, R. W. (2005), *Masculinities*. 2nd edn, Cambridge: Polity.
Corbett, S. and A. Walker (2019), 'Introduction: European Social Policy and Society after Brexit: Neoliberalism, Populism, and Social Quality', *Social Policy & Society*, 18 (1): 87–91.
Cornford, T. (2018), 'Experiencing Nationlessness: Staging the Migrant Condition in Some Recent British Theatre', *JCDE*, 6 (1): 101–12.
Costa, M. (2012), 'Three Kingdoms: The shape of British theatre to come?', *The Guardian*, 16 May. Available online: www.theguardian.com/stage/theatreblog/2012/may/16/three-kingdoms-shape-british-theatre-or-flop (accessed 5 April 2020).
Crenshaw, K. (1991), 'Mapping the Margins: Intersectionality, Identity Politics, and Violence against Women of Color', in M. A. Finemane and R. Mykitiuk (eds), *The Public Nature of Private Violence*, 93–118, London and New York: Routledge.
Crewe, J. V. (1990), 'The Violence of Drama: Towards a Reading of the Senecan Phaedra', *boundary 2*, 17 (3): 95–115.
Danan, J. (2013), *Entre théâtre et performance. La Question du texte*, Arles: Actes Sud.
Davidson, C. (2001), 'Violence and the Saint Play', *Studies in Philology*, 98 (3): 292–314.
Davis, E. (2019), 'Review: Seven methods of killing kylie jenner', *Exeunt*, 10 July. Available online: http://exeuntmagazine.com/reviews/review-seven-methods-killing-kylie-jenner/ (accessed 7 January 2021).
De Ambrogi, M. (2016), 'Black Gold, Dark Future', *The Lancet*, 388 (10059): 13–14.
de Angelis, A. (2014), *Theatre of the Abused*, original broadcast 4 December, London: BBC Radio 4.
Deacy, S., J. Malheiro Magalhães and J. Zacharski Menzies, eds (2023), *Revisiting Rape in Antiquity: Sexualised Violence in Greek and Roman Worlds*, London: Bloomsbury.
Derrida, J. (1984), 'Of an Apocalyptic Tone Recently Adopted in Philosophy', *Oxford Literary Review*, 6 (2): 3–37.
Derrida, J. (1988), 'Signature Event Context', trans. by Samuel Weber and Jeffrey Mehlman, in G. Graff (ed.), *Limited Inc*, 1–24. Evanston, IL: Northwestern University Press.
Diamond, E. (1990), 'Realism and Hysteria: Towards a Feminist Mimesis', *Discourse*, 13 (1): 59–92.

Diamond, E. (1997), *Unmaking Mimesis: Essays on Feminism and Theatre*, London and New York: Routledge.

Doeser, J. (2016), 'Brexit is just the Start of the War on Culture', *The Stage*, 5 July. Available online: www.thestage.co.uk/opinion/2016/james-doeser-brexit-is-just-the-start-of-the-war-on-culture/ (accessed 1 April 2020).

Dolan, J. (1990), '"Lesbian" Subjectivity in Realism: Dragging at the Margins of Structure and Ideology', in S.-E. Case (ed.), *Performing Feminisms: Feminist Critical Theory and Theatre*, 40–53, Baltimore and London: The Johns Hopkins University Press.

Dolan, J. (2005), *Utopia in Performance: Finding Hope at the Theater*, Ann Arbor: University of Michigan Press.

Dolan, J. (2008), 'Feminist Performance Criticism and the Popular: Reviewing Wendy Wasserstein', *Theatre Journal*, 60: 433–57.

Dolan, J. (2012), *The Feminist Spectator as Critic*, 2nd edn, Minnesota: University of Michigan Press.

Doohan, C. (2013), 'Anders Lustgarten', *Exeunt*, 20 February. Available online: http://exeuntmagazine.com/features/anders-lustgarten/ (accessed 20 March 2021).

Du Bois, W. E. B. (1999), *The Souls of Black Folk*, ed. H. L. Gates and T. H. Oliver. New York: Norton.

Dugdale, S. (2013), 'Preface', in B. Beumers and M. Lipovestsky, *Performing Violence: Literary and Theatrical Experiments of New Russian Drama*, 13–25, Chicago: University of Chicago Press.

Eddo-Lodge, R. (2018), *Why I'm No Longer Talking to White People about Race*, London: Bloomsbury.

Eliot, T. S. (2015), 'Seneca in Elizabethan Translation', in F. Dickey, J. Formichelli and R. Schuchard (eds), *The Complete Prose of T. S. Eliot: The Critical Edition, Volume 3: Literature, Politics, Belief, 1927–1929*, 195–234, Baltimore and London: The Johns Hopkins University Press and Faber & Faber.

Ellis-Peterson, H. (2015), 'Controversial Isis-related play cancelled two weeks before opening night', *The Guardian*, 4 August. Available online: www.theguardian.com/uk-news/2015/aug/04/controversial-isis-related-play-cancelled-two-weeks-before-opening-night (accessed 15 February 2019).

Enders, J. (1999), *The Medieval Theater of Cruelty: Rhetoric, Memory, Violence*, New York: Cornell University Press.

Esslin, M. (1980), *The Theatre of the Absurd*, 3rd edn, London: Penguin.

Evans, B. and H. A. Giroux (2015), *Disposable Futures: The Seduction of Violence in the Age of Spectacle*, San Francisco: City Lights.

Evans, E. and P. Chamberlain (2015), 'Critical Waves: Exploring Feminist Identity, Discourse and Praxis in Western Feminism', *Social Movement Studies*, 14 (4): 396–409.

Fakhrkonandeh, A. (2022), 'Oil Cultures, World Drama and Contemporaneity: Questions of Time, Space and Form in Ella Hickson's *Oil*', *Textual Practice* 36 (11): 1775–811.

Fallow, C. and S. J. Mullan (2021), 'The Royal Court in the Wake of #MeToo', in J. Rudakoff (ed.), *Performing #MeToo*, 123–40, Bristol: Intellect.

Farnell, I. (2019), 'Science Fiction and the Theatre of Alistair McDowall', *Contemporary Theatre Review*, 29 (2): 121–37.

Featherstone, V. (2017a) 'Code of Behaviour', *Royal Court Theatre*, 3 November. Available online: https://d19lfjg8hluhfw.cloudfront.net/wp-content/uploads/2017/11/06174357/A-Code-of-Behaviour-6Nov.pdf (accessed 27 May 2020).

Featherstone, V. (2019), 'A Statement from the Royal Court Theatre', *The Royal Court Theatre*, 15 December. Available online: https://royalcourttheatre.com/statement-royal-court-theatre/ (accessed 15 February 2019).

Finburgh Delijani, C. (2017), *Watching War on the Twenty-First Century Stage*, London: Methuen Drama.

Fisher, M. (2009), *Capitalist Realism: Is There No Alternative?* Portland: Zero.

Fitzpatrick, L. (2018), *Rape on the Contemporary Stage*, Basingstoke: Palgrave Macmillan.

Foakes, R. A. (2002), *Shakespeare and Violence*, Cambridge: Cambridge University Press.

Forte, J. (1995), 'Realism, Narrative, and the Feminist Playwright – A Problem of Reception', in H. Keyssar (ed.), *Feminist Theatre and Theory: Contemporary Critical Essays*, 19–34, London: Bloomsbury.

Foucault, M. (1991), *Discipline and Punish: The Birth of the Prison*, trans. A. Sheridan, London: Penguin.

Fragkou, M. (2018), *Ecologies of Precarity in Twenty-First Century Theatre*, London: Methuen Drama.

Fragkou, M. and L. Goddard (2013), 'Acting In/Action: Staging Human Rights in debbie tucker green's Royal Court Plays', in V. Angelaki (ed.), *Contemporary British Theatre: Breaking New Ground*, 145–66, Basingstoke: Palgrave Macmillan.

Fraser, N. (1990), 'Rethinking the Public Sphere: A Contribution to the Critique of Actually Existing Democracy', *Social Text*, 25/6 (1): 56–80.

Freshwater, H. (2009), *Theatre & Audience*, Basingstoke: Palgrave Macmillan.

Fuchs, C. (2016), 'Neoliberalism in Britain: From Thatcherism to Cameronism', *tripleC: Communication, Capitalism & Critique*, 14 (1): 163–88.

Galtung, J. (1969), 'Violence, Peace, and Peace Research', *Journal of Peace Research*, 6 (3): 167–91.

Galtung, J. et al. (2011), 'Norway's Johan Galtung, Peace & Conflict Pioneeer, on How to Stop Extremism that Fueled Shooting', *Democracy Now*, 29 July. Available online: www.democracynow.org/2011/7/29/norways_johan_galtung_peace_conflict_pioneer (accessed 22 May 2021).

Gardner, L. (2005), interview with d. tucker green, 'I was messing about', *The Guardian*, 30 March. Available online: www.theguardian.com/stage/2005/mar/30/theatre (accessed 15 November 2020).

Gardner, L. (2016a), 'Always Orange review - taut terrorism drama about society on edge of sanity', *The Guardian*, 3 August. Available online: www.

theguardian.com/stage/2016/aug/03/always-orange-review-the-other-place-stratford-upon-avon-fraser-grace (accessed 3 March 2021).

Gardner, L. (2016b), 'Fall of the Kingdom, Rise of the Foot Soldier review – England's green and unpleasant land', *The Guardian*, 2 August. Available online: www.theguardian.com/stage/2016/aug/02/fall-of-the-kingdom-rise-of-the-foot-soldier-review-rsc-making-mischief-festival (accessed 25 March 2021).

Gardner, L. (2016c), 'Bird review – a fragile teenage tale with a fiercely beating heart', *The Guardian*, 17 May. Available online: www.theguardian.com/stage/2016/may/17/bird-review-sherman-cymru-katherine-chandler-rachel-oriordan (accessed 3 January 2021).

Gardner, L. (2017), 'Why David Hare is wrong about the state of British theatre', *The Guardian*, 30 January. Available online: www.theguardian.com/stage/theatreblog/2017/jan/30/david-hare-state-of-british-theatre-europe (accessed 15 April 2021).

Gardner, L. (2018), 'What Draws British Playwrights to Europe?', *British Council: Theatre and Dance*, 28 March. Available online: https://theatreanddance.britishcouncil.org/blog/2018/cultureafterbrexit7/ (accessed 12 February 2020).

Garver, N. (2009), 'What Violence Is', in V. Buffachi (ed.), *Violence: A Philosophical Anthology*, 170–83, Basingstoke: Palgrave Macmillan.

Gilleman, L. (2010), 'Drama and Pornography: Sarah Daniels's *Masterpieces* and Anthony Neilson's *The Censor*', *Journal of Dramatic Theory and Criticism*, 25 (1): 75–97.

Girard, R. (2013), *Violence and the Sacred*, trans. P. Gregory, London: Bloomsbury.

Glencross, A. (2020), '"Love Europe, Hate the EU": A Genealogical Inquiry into Populists' Spatio-Cultural Critique of the European Union and its Consequences', *European Journal of International Relations*, 26 (1): 116–36.

Gluhović, M. (2013), *Performing European Memories: Trauma, Ethics, Politics*, Basingstoke: Palgrave Macmillan.

Goddard, L. (2020a), '"I'm a Black Woman. I Write Black Characters": Black Mothers, the Police, and Social Justice in *random* and *hang*', in S. Adiseshiah and J. Bolton (eds), *debbie tucker green: Critical Perspectives*, 109–28, Basingstoke: Palgrave Macmillan.

Goddard, L. (2020b), 'Evoking the Afterlife of Slavery in Selina Thompson's *salt*', The New Wave of British Women Playwrights: Experimenting with Form, online conference, 11–12 December, Paris: Sorbonne University.

Gould, M. (2009), 'Sizewell nuclear disaster averted by dirty laundry, says official report', *The Guardian*, 11 June. Available online: www.theguardian.com/environment/2009/jun/11/nuclear-waste-nuclearpower (accessed 28 January 2020).

Grace, F. (2016), *Always Orange*, in E. Whyman (ed.), *Making Mischief: Two Radical New Plays*, 71–133, London: Oberon.

Gray, E. (2019), 'In the 2010s, celebrity feminism got trendy, then women got angry', *HuffPost*, 26 December. Available online: www.huffingtonpost.co.uk/entry/celebrity-feminism-2010-taylor-swift_n_5dfbdc44e4b006dceaab16a7?ri18n=true (accessed 17 November 2020).

Gray-Hawkins, M. (2018), 'Collective Movements, Digital Activism, and Protest Events: The Effectiveness of Social Media Concerning the Organization of Large-Scale Political Participation', *Geopolitics, History, and International Relations*, 10 (2): 64–9.

Grech, S. (2020), 'The rise of performative wokeness', *@dolescent*, 16 March. Available online: www.adolescent.net/a/the-rise-of-performative-wokeness- (accessed 4 June 2021).

Green, S. (2015), *The European Identity: Historical and Cultural Realities We Cannot Deny*, London: Haus.

Habermas, J. (1991), *The Structural Transformation of the Public Sphere*, trans. T. Burger and F. Lawrence, Cambridge, MA: MIT Press.

Habermas, J. (2001), *The Postnational Constellation: Political Essays*, Cambridge, MA: MIT Press.

Haddow, S. (2014), 'History Will Eat Itself: Rory Mullarkey's *Cannibals* and the Terrors of End-Narratives', *JCDE*, 2 (2): 275–88.

Halder, D. and K. Jaishankar (2009), 'Cyber Socializing and Victimization of Women', *The Journal on Victimization*, 12 (1): 5–26.

Hales, S. (2018), 'Review: Ear for eye at Royal Court', *Exeunt*, 3 November. Available online: http://exeuntmagazine.com/reviews/review-ear-eye-royal-court/ (accessed 20 November 2020).

Hancock, D. (2019), *The Countercultural Logic of Neoliberalism*, London and New York: Routledge.

Harris, Z. (2015), *How to Hold Your Breath*, London: Faber & Faber.

Hartl, A. (2021), *Brecht and Post-1990s British Drama*, London: Methuen Drama. Available online: www.perlego.com/book/2106871/brecht-and-post1990s-british-drama-dialectical-theatre-today-pdf (accessed: 30 May 2023).

Hartman, S. (2007), *Lose Your Mother: A Journey along the Atlantic Slave Route*, New York: Farrar, Straus and Giroux.

Harvie, J. (2003), 'Nationalizing the "Creative Industries"', *Contemporary Theatre Review*, 13 (1): 15–32.

Harvie, J. (2018), 'Boom! Adversarial Ageism, Chrononormativity, and the Anthropocene', *Contemporary Theatre Review*, 28 (3): 332–44.

Hayden, S.-L. (2019), 'seven methods of killing kylie jenner at the Royal Court Theatre', *Lucy Writers*, 25 July. Available online: https://lucywritersplatform.com/2019/07/25/seven-methods-of-killing-kylie-jenner-at-the-royal-court-theatre/ (accessed 7 January 2021).

Heise, U. (2015), 'What's the Matter with Dystopia?', *Public Books*, 1 February. Available online: www.publicbooks.org/whats-the-matter-with-dystopia/ (accessed 3 March 2021).

Hemming, S. (2018), 'Director James Macdonald on the rise of "slow theatre"', *Financial Times*, 5 January. Available online: www.ft.com/content/000b9402-f084-11e7-bb7d-c3edfe974e9f (accessed 30 January 2021).

Hess, A. (2015), 'Popping the question: A brief history of asking celebrities, "Are you a feminist?"', *Slate*, 14 January. Available online: https://slate.com/human-interest/2015/01/are-you-a-feminist-a-brief-history-of-todays-most-popular-celebrity-interview-question.html (accessed 17 November 2020).

Hickson, E. (2016), *Oil*, London: Nick Hern.

Hickson, E. (2018), *The Writer*, London: Nick Hern.

Hirsch, A. (2010), 'Clybourne Park: The jokes' not funny if only middle-class white people laugh', *The Guardian*, 18 September. Available online: www.theguardian.com/commentisfree/2010/sep/18/clybourne-park-royal-court-race-gentrification (accessed 20 November 2020).

Hiscock, A. (2022), *Shakespeare, Violence and Early Modern Europe*, Cambridge: Cambridge University Press.

Hoffman, A. J. (2015), *How Culture Shapes the Climate Change Debate*, Redwood: Stanford University Press.

Holdsworth, N. (2014), '"This blessed plot, this earth, this realm, this England": Staging Treatments of Riots in Recent British Theatre', *JCDE*, 2 (1): 78–96.

Holdsworth, N. (2020), *English Theatre and Social Abjection*, Basingstoke: Palgrave Macmillan, 2020.

Howes, S. et al. (2021), 'Women Who Kill: How the state criminalises women we might otherwise be burying', *Centre for Women's Justice*, n.d. Available online: https://static1.squarespace.com/static/5aa98420f2e6b1ba0c874e42/t/602a9a87e96acc025de5de67/1613404821139/CWJ_WomenWhoKill_Rpt_WEB-3+small.pdf (accessed 2 November 2021).

Hoydis, J. (2020), 'A Slow Unfolding "Fault Sequence": Risk and Responsibility in Lucy Kirkwood's *The Children*', *JCDE*, 8 (1): 83–99.

Hughes, J. (2011), *Performance in a Time of Terror: Critical Mimesis and the Age of Uncertainty*, Manchester: Manchester University Press.

Hutchinson, D. (2015), 'Vicky Featherstone: "Critics are Harder on Women"', *The Stage*, 29 September. Available online: www.thestage.co.uk/news/2015/vicky-featherstone-critics-are-harder-on-women/ (accessed 22 May 2020).

Iannello, K. P. (1998), 'Third-Wave Feminism and Individualism: Promoting Equality or Reinforcing the Status Quo?', in L. D. Whitaker (ed.), *Women in Politics: Outsiders or Insiders? A Collection of Readings*, 313–21, Harlow: Longman.

Iball, H. (2008), *Modern Theatre Guides: Sarah Kane's Blasted*, London and New York: Continuum.

Ibsen, H. (2020), *A Doll's House*, ed. S. Duncan, trans. M. Meyer, London: Methuen Drama.

Ishkanian, A. (2014), 'Neoliberalism and Violence: The Big Society and the Changing Politics of Domestic Violence in England', *Critical Social Policy*, 34 (3): 333–53.

Jasanoff, S. (2011), 'Cosmopolitan Knowledge: Climate Science and Global Civic Epistemology', in J. S. Dryzek, R. B. Norgaard and D. Schlosberg (eds), *The Oxford Handbook of Climate Change and Society*, 129–43, Oxford: Oxford University Press.

Jhally, S., creator (2017), *Advertising at the Edge of the Apocalypse*, Northampton, MA: Media Education Foundation.

John, G. (2011), 'The People, the State and the Media', keynote address, Media and the Riots conference, 26 November, London: London College of Communication.

Jones, A. (2019), 'Alice Birch on her impossible new play, Succession and adapting Sally Rooney for TV: "I feel sick"', *iNews*, 16 October. Available online: https://inews.co.uk/culture/arts/alice-birch-blank-donmar-warehouse-succession-story-editor-normal-people-351442 (accessed 7 January 2021).

Jowit, J. (2010), 'Sharp decline in public's belief in climate threat, British poll reveals', *The Guardian*, 23 February. Available online: www.theguardian.com/environment/2010/feb/23/british-public-belief-climate-poll (accessed 26 October 2023).

Kapuściński. R. (1965), *The Shah of Shahs*, trans. W. R. Brand and K. Mroczkowsa-Brand, London: Vintage.

Kelly, L. (1998), *Surviving Sexual Violence*, Cambridge: Polity.

Kelly, L. (2005), *Fertile Fields: Trafficking in Persons in Central Asia*, Grand-Saconnex: International Organization for Migration.

Kelly, L. (2016), 'The Conducive Context of Violence against Women and Girls', *Discoversociety*, 1 March 2016. Available online: http://discoversociety.org/2016/03/01/theorising-violence-against-women-and-girls/ (accessed 20 January 2021).

Kene, A. (2018), *Misty*, London: Nick Hern.

Kirkwood, L. (2012), *NSFW*, London: Nick Hern.

Kirkwood, L. (2016), *The Children*, London: Nick Hern.

Kitto, H. D. F. (2011), *Greek Tragedy: A Literary Study*, London and New York: Routledge.

Kluwick, U. (2011), 'Talking about Climate Change: The Ecological Crisis and Narrative Form', in J. S. Dryzek, R. B. Norgaard and D. Schlosberg (eds), *The Oxford Handbook of Climate Change and Society*, 502–16, Oxford: Oxford University Press.

Koch, D. E. and S. Matsuzaka (2019), 'Trans Feminine Sexual Violence Experiences: The Intersection of Transphobia and Misogyny', *Affilia: Journal of Women and Social Work*, 34 (1): 28–47.

Kott, J. (1990), *Shakespeare Our Contemporary*, trans. B. Taborski, London: Routledge.

Lease, B. (2018), 'What on earth is happening in Poland? on Klątwa, protest, and a new regime', *Contemporary Theatre Review*, 28 (2). Available online: www.contemporarytheatrereview.org/2018/lease-what-on-earth-is-happening-in-poland (accessed 12 February 2019).

Lee-Jones, J. (2019), *seven methods of killing kylie jenner*, London: Oberon.

Leiter, B. (2016), 'The Case against Free Speech', *Sydney Law Review*, 38 (407): 407–39.

Lewenstein, R. (2016), *Fucking Feminists*, in S. Parrish (ed.), *Women Centre Stage: Eight Short Plays By and About Women*, 43–56, London: Nick Hern.

Lewis, R., M. Rowe and C. Wiper (2016), 'Online Abuse of Feminists as an Emerging Form of Violence against Women and Girls', *The British Journal of Criminology*, 57 (6): 1462–81.

Lipscomb, V. B. (2016), *Performing Age in Modern Drama*, Basingstoke: Palgrave Macmillan.

Lonergan, P. (2020), '"A Twisted, Looping Form": Staging Dark Ecologies in Ella Hickson's *Oil*', *Performance Research*, 25 (2): 38–44.

Love, C. (2020), 'From Facts to Feelings: The Development of Katie Mitchell's Ecodramaturgy', *Contemporary Theatre Review*, 30 (2): 226–35.

Lukowski, A. (2018), '"A Very Very Very Dark Matter" review', *Time Out*, 25 October. Available online: www.timeout.com/london/theatre/a-very-very-very-dark-matter-review (accessed 25 May 2019).

Lustgarten, A. (2015), 'Refugees don't need our tears. They need us to stop making them refugees', *The Guardian*, 17 April. Available online: www.theguardian.com/commentisfree/2015/apr/17/refugees-eu-policy-migrants-how-many-deaths (accessed 26 March 2020).

Lustgarten, A. (2016a), 'Introduction', in *Plays: 1*, ix–xiii, London: Methuen Drama.

Lustgarten, A. (2016b), *Lampedusa*, in S. Atkinson (ed.), *HighTide Plays: 1*, 257–91, London: Bloomsbury, 2016.

Lynn, C. (2015), *Lela & Co.*, London: Nick Hern.

Macmillan, D. (2016), *Lungs*, in *Plays One*, 133–228, London: Oberon.

Manavis, S. (2018), 'The Big Bang Theory is a plague on society – we should rejoice its overdue end', *New Statesman*, 23 August. Available online: www.newstatesman.com/culture/tv-radio/2018/08/big-bang-theory-plague-society-we-should-rejoice-its-overdue-end (accessed 19 July 2020).

Marcus, S. (1992), 'Fighting Bodies, Fighting Words: A Theory and Politics of Rape Prevention', in J. Butler and J. W. Scott (eds), *Feminists Theorize the Political*, 385–403, London: Routledge.

Marranca, B. (2017), 'The Imagination of Catastrophe: Caryl Churchill's Natural History Lessons', *PAJ*, 116 (1): 1–6.

Marsh, H. (2016), 'Terrorism, fear and cultural divides: The "unsayable" is said in the RSC's Festival of New Writing', *A Younger Theatre*, 3 August. Available online: www.ayoungertheatre.com/terrorism-fear-and-cultural-divides-the-unsayable-is-said-in-the-rscs-festival-of-new-writing/ (accessed 27 March 2021).

May, T. (2017), 'Independence – 20 years on', Bank of England conference, 28 October, transcript from 'PM speech at 20th anniversary of Bank of England independence event', *gov.uk*. Available online: www.gov.uk/

government/speeches/pm-speech-at-20th-anniversary-of-bank-of-england-independence-event (accessed 23 April 2020).
Mbembe, A. (2019), *Necropolitics*, trans. S. Corcoran, Durham, NC and London: Duke University Press.
McDonagh, M. (2018), *A Very Very Very Dark Matter*, London: Faber & Faber.
McDowall, A. (2015), *Pomona*, London: Methuen Drama.
McGlynn, C., E. Rackley and R. Houghton (2017), 'Beyond "Revenge Porn": The Continuum of Image-Based Sexual Abuse', *Feminist Legal Studies*, 25 (1): 25–46.
McGreenery, C. E. et al. (2010), 'Hurtful Words: Exposure to Peer Verbal Aggression is Associated with Elevated Psychiatric Symptom Scores and Corpus Callosum Abnormalities', *The American Journal of Psychiatry*, 167 (12): 1464–71.
McGuigan, J. (2009), *Cool Capitalism*, London: Pluto.
McMillan, J. (2011), '2011 Arts Roundup', *The Scotsman*, 29 December. Available online: www.scotsman.com/arts-and-culture/theatre-and-stage/2011-arts-roundup-joyce-mcmillan-theatre-1649397 (accessed 25 March 2021).
Megson, C. (2018a), '"Can I Tell You about It?": England, Austerity and "Radical Optimism" in the Theatre of Anders Lustgarten', *JCDE*, 6 (1): 40–54.
Megson, C. (2018b), '"What I'm Aspiring to Be Is a Good Dramatist": Alecky Blythe in Conversation with Chris Megson', *JCDE*, 6 (1): 220–33.
Minamore, B. (2019), 'Better, bolder, further to go: The decade in black British theatre', *The Guardian*, 27 December. Available online: www.theguardian.com/stage/2019/dec/27/better-bolder-further-to-go-the-decade-in-black-british-theatre (accessed 25 March 2021).
Minnaard, L. (2020), 'Lampedusa in Europe; Or Touching Tales of Vulnerability', in M. Boletsi, J. Houwen and L. Minnaard (eds), *Languages of Resistance, Transformation, and Futurity in Mediterranean Crisis-Scapes*, 145–62, Basingstoke: Palgrave Macmillan.
Mirčev, A. (2018), 'Dissensual Politics of Performance', *Contemporary Theatre Review*, 28. (2). Available online: www.contemporarytheatrereview.org/2018/mircev-dissensual-politics-of-performance/ (accessed 12 February 2019).
Mirpuri, A. (2016), 'Racial Violence, Mass Shootings, and the US Neoliberal State', *Critical Ethnic Studies*, 2 (1): 73–106.
Moore, J. W. (2017), 'The Capitalocene, Part I: On the Nature and Origins of Our Ecological Crisis', *The Journal of Peasant Studies*, 44 (3): 594–630.
Morrison, L. (2016), 'The Children: Q&A with playwright Lucy Kirkwood', *Royal Court Theatre* (YouTube), 7 December. Available online: www.youtube.com/watch?v=68eFaUKABMc (accessed 30 January 2021).
Morton, T. (2018), *Dark Ecology: For a Logic of Future Coexistence*, New York: Columbia University Press.
Moser, C. O. N. (2001), 'The Gendered Continuum of Violence and Conflict: An Operational Framework', in C. O. N. Moser and F. C. Clarke (eds), *Victims, Perpetrators or Actors? Gender, Armed Conflict and Political Violence*, 30–52, London: Zed.

Nancy, J.-L. (1991), *The Inoperative Community*, ed. P. Connor, trans. P. Connor et al., Minneapolis: University of Minnesota Press.
Nancy, J.-L. (2005), 'Image and Violence', in *The Ground of the Image*, trans. J. Fort, 15–26, New York: Fordham University Press.
Nanz, P. I. (2000), 'In-between Nations: Ambivalence and the Making of a European Identity', in B. Stråth (ed.), *Europe and the Other and Europe as the Other*, 4th edn, 279–310, Bern: P.I.E. Peter Lang.
Naylor, R. et al. (2016), 'Arts Council England: Analysis of Theatre in England', *Arts Council*, 13 September. Available online: www.artscouncil.org.uk/sites/default/files/download-file/ACE_Theatre_Analysis_BOP_FINAL_REPORT_Feb_2017.pdf (accessed 10 November 2020).
Nevitt, L. (2013), *Theatre & Violence*, London: Palgrave Macmillan.
Nixon, R. (2011), *Slow Violence and the Environmentalism of the Poor*, Cambridge, MA: Harvard University Press.
Nuccitelli, D. (2016), 'The inter-generational theft of Brexit and climate change', *The Guardian*, 27 June. Available online: www.theguardian.com/environment/climate-consensus-97-per-cent/2016/jun/27/the-inter-generational-theft-of-brexit-and-climate-change (accessed 28 January 2021).
Obordo, R. and H. Rahim (2016), 'Ethnic minorities ask: "How did Great Britain become Little England?"', *The Guardian*, 28 June. Available online: www.theguardian.com/world/2016/jun/28/ethnic-minorities-ask-how-did-great-britain-become-little-england (accessed 20 March 2021).
O'Riordan, R. (2016), 'Director's Note', in K. Chandler, *Bird*, ii, London: Nick Hern.
O'Toole, F. (2018), 'The In-Betweener', in L. Hall (ed.), *A Very Very Very Dark Matter* production programme, London: The Bridge Theatre.
ONS (2021), 'Three-quarters of adults in Great Britain worry about climate change', *Office for National Statistics*, 5 November. Available online: www.ons.gov.uk/peoplepopulationandcommunity/wellbeing/articles/threequartersofadultsingreatbritainworryaboutclimatechange/2021-11-05 (accessed 26 October 2023).
Paavolainen, T. (2017), 'Fabric Philosophy: The "Texture" of Theatricality and Performativity', *Performance Philosophy*, 2 (2): 172–88.
Parr, A. (2018), 'Our Crime against the Planet and Ourselves', in B. Evans and N. Lennard (eds), *Violence: Humans in Dark Times*, 55–64, San Francisco: City Lights.
Pettifor, A. (2017), 'Brexit and its Consequences', *Globalizations*, 14 (1): 127–32.
Phelan, M. (2016), 'From Troubles to Post-Conflict Theatre in Northern Ireland', in N. Grene and C. Morash (eds), *The Oxford Handbook of Modern Irish Theatre*, 372–88, Oxford: Oxford University Press.
Phelan, P. (1993), *Unmarked: The Politics of Performance*, London and New York: Routledge.
Pierce, C. M. (1970), 'Offensive Mechanisms', in F. Barbour (ed.), *In the Black Seventies*, 265–82, Boston: Porter Sargent.

Price, T. (2014), 'Introduction', in T. Price and K. Wasserberg (eds), *Contemporary Welsh Plays*, xvii–xx, London: Bloomsbury.
Price, T. and K. Wasserberg (2014), 'Preface', in T. Price and K. Wasserberg (eds), *Contemporary Welsh Plays*, xii–xvi, London: Bloomsbury.
Quinn, B. (2018), 'Royal Court dropped Tibet play after advice from British Council', *The Guardian*, 4 April. Available online: www.theguardian.com/stage/2018/apr/04/unseen-letters-shed-light-on-royal-court-censorship-row-british-council (accessed 16 February 2019).
Raczka, L. (2013), 'There Has Possibly Been An Incident', *Exeunt*, 24 September. Available online: http://exeuntmagazine.com/reviews/there-has-possibly-been-an-incident-2/ (accessed 15 November 2020).
Raczka, L. and Barrel Organ (2015), *Some People Talk About Violence*, London: Oberon.
Radosavljević, D. (2017), 'An open letter to David Hare', *Exeunt*, 1 February. Available online: http://exeuntmagazine.com/features/open-letter-david-hare/ (accessed 15 April 2021).
Raine, N. (2018), *Consent*, London: Nick Hern.
Rappaport, E. (2018), *A Thirst for Empire: How Tea Shaped the Modern World*, Princeton: Princeton University Press.
Read, A. (2013), *Theatre in the Expanded Field: Seven Approaches to Performance*, London: Methuen Drama.
Rebellato, D. (2013), 'Tim Crouch', in D. Rebellato (ed.), *Modern British Playwriting 2000–2009*, 125–44, London: Methuen Drama.
Rebellato, D. (2017), 'Of an Apocalyptic Tone Recently Adopted in Theatre: British Drama, Violence and Writing', *Sillages Critiques*, 22 (1). Available online: doi.org/10.4000/sillagescritiques.4798 (accessed 20 March 2020), 59 paragraphs.
Rebellato, D. (2018), 'Nation and Negation (Terrible Rage)', *JCDE*, 6 (1): 15–39.
Reid, T. (2012), 'Anthony Neilson', in A. Sierz (ed.), *Modern British Playwriting: The 1990s*, 137–62, London: Methuen Drama.
Reid, T. (2019), 'The Dystopian Near-Future in Contemporary British Drama', *JCDE*, 7 (1): 72–88.
Remshardt, R. (2016), 'Seneca Our Contemporary: The Modern Theatrical Reception of Senecan Tragedy', in E. Dodson-Robinson (ed.), *Brill's Companion to the Reception of Senecan Tragedy*, 282–302, Leiden: Brill.
Richards, K. S. (2017), '*Oil* (Review)', *Theatre Journal*, 69 (4): 582–3.
Richardson, A. V. (2020), *Bearing Witness while Black*, Oxford: Oxford University Press.
Ridley, P. (1997), *The Pitchfork Disney*, in *Plays: 1*, 2–96, London: Methuen Drama.
Rimbach, J. A. (1982), 'The Judeo-Christian Tradition and the Human/Animal Bond', *International Journal for the Study of Animal Problems*, 3 (3): 198–207.
Robehmed, N. (2019), 'At 21, Kylie Jenner becomes the youngest self-made billionaire ever', *Forbes*, 5 March, Available online: www.forbes.com/sites/

natalierobehmed/2019/03/05/at-21-kylie-jenner-becomes-the-youngest-self-made-billionaire-ever/?sh=501b24a72794 (accessed 13 January 2021).

Samara, E. (2021), 'Resisting Theatre: The Political in the Performative', in J. Rudakoff (ed.), *Performing #MeToo*, 50–67, Bristol: Intellect.

Santmire, H. P. (1970), *Brother Earth*, Nashville, TN: Thomas Nelson.

Schaag, K. (2020), 'Plastiglomerates, Microplastics, Nanoplastics: Toward a Dark Ecology of Plastic Performativity', *Performance Research*, 25 (2): 14–21.

Schneider, R. (2001), 'Performance Remains', *Performance Research*, 6 (2): 100–8.

Seaton, S. N. (2016), '*Fall of the Kingdom, Rise of the Foot Soldier*', in E. Whyman (ed.), *Making Mischief*, 1–70, London: Oberon.

Shalson, L. (2017), *Theatre & Protest*, Basingstoke: Palgrave Macmillan.

Sierz, A. (2001), *In-Yer-Face Theatre: British Drama Today*, London: Faber.

Sierz, A. (2011), *Rewriting the Nation: British Theatre Today*, London: Methuen Drama.

Sierz, A. (2012), 'Theatre in the 1990s', in A. Sierz (ed.), *Modern British Playwriting: The 1990s*, 28–87, London: Bloomsbury.

Sierz, A. (2017), 'Dark Times: British Theatre after Brexit', *PAJ*, 39 (1): 3–11.

Sierz, A. (2018), 'British Theatre after Brexit: One Year On', *PAJ*, 40 (3): 60–70.

Snyder, L. (2020), 'Storytelling in Apocalyptic Times: Anne Washburn's *Mr Burns, a Post-Electric Play*', *JCDE*, 8 (2): 282–94.

Sobczyk, N. (2019), 'How climate change got labeled a "crisis"', *E&E News*, 10 July. Available online: www.eenews.net/stories/1060718493 (accessed 8 January 2020).

Sofer, A. (2013), *Dark Matter: Invisibility in Drama, Theater, & Performance*, Ann Arbor: University of Michigan Press.

Solga, K. (2009), *Violence against Women in Early Modern Performance: Invisible Acts*, London and New York: Palgrave Macmillan.

Solnick, S. (2020), 'How theatre is tackling the biggest issue of all: The future of our planet', *iNews*, 14 October 2016 (updated 14 July 2020). Available online: https://inews.co.uk/culture/theatre-tackling-biggest-issue-future-planet-25687 (accessed 12 November 2020).

Solnit, R. (2014), *Men Explain Things to Me and Other Essays*, London: Granta.

Sommerstein, A. H. (2010), *The Tangled Ways of Zeus: And Other Studies in and around Greek Tragedy*, Oxford: Oxford University Press.

Sondergard, S. (1985), 'The Dramaturgical Intention of Cruelty in the Cornish *Ordinalia*', *Mediaevalia*, 11 (1): 169–86.

Sontag, S. (2004), *Regarding the Pain of Others*, London: Penguin.

Steger, M. B. and R. K. Roy (2010), *Neoliberalism: A Very Short Introduction*, Oxford: Oxford University Press.

Stenham, P. (2019), *Hotel*, in *Plays: 1*, 307–75, London: Faber & Faber.

Stephens, S. (2014), 'In praise of Chris Thorpe', *Warwick Arts Centre*, 19 May. Available online: www.warwickartscentre.co.uk/news/2014/05/in-praise-of-chris-thorpe-by-simon-stephens/ (accessed 16 February 2019).

Stephens, S. (2015), *Three Kingdoms*, in *Plays: 4*, 12–152, London: Methuen Drama.
Stephenson, H. and N. Langridge (1997), 'Sarah Kane', in H. Stephenson and N. Langridge (eds), *Rage and Reason: Women Playwrights on Playwriting*, 129–35, London: Bloomsbury.
Stewart, H. and R. Mason (2016), 'Nigel Farage's anti-migrant poster reported to police', *The Guardian*, 16 June. Available online: www.theguardian.com/politics/2016/jun/16/nigel-farage-defends-ukip-breaking-point-poster-queue-of-migrants (accessed 13 March 2020).
Stowell, S. (1992a), *A Stage of Their Own: Feminist Playwrights of the Suffrage Era*, Manchester: Manchester University Press.
Stowell, S. (1992b) 'Rehabilitating Realism', *Journal of Dramatic Theory and Criticism*, 6 (2): 81–8.
Stråth, B. (2000), 'Introduction: Europe as a Discourse', in B. Stråth (ed.), *Europe and the Other and Europe as the Other*, 4th edn, 13–44, Bern: P.I.E. Peter Lang.
Stratton, J. (2019), 'The Language of Leaving: Brexit, the Second World War and Cultural Trauma', *Journal for Cultural Research*, 23 (3): 225–51.
Suzor, N. et al. (2019), 'Human Rights by Design: The Responsibilities of Social Media Platforms to Address Gender-Based Violence Online', *Policy and Internet*, 11 (1): 84–103.
Swan, S. H. and S. Colino (2021), *Count Down: How Our Modern World Is Threatening Sperm Counts, Altering Male and Female Reproductive Development, and Imperiling the Future of the Human Race*, New York: Simon & Schuster.
Sweet, J. (2017), 'David Hare', in *What Playwrights Talk about when They Talk about Writing*, 52–69, London: Yale University Press.
Szerszynski, B., C. Waterton and W. Heim (2003), 'Introduction', in B. Szerszynski, C. Waterton and W. Heim (eds), *Nature Performed: Environment, Culture and Performance*, 1–14, London: Blackwell, 2003.
Tan, C. (2016), 'Review: The Children at the Royal Court', *Exeunt*, 25 November. Available online: http://exeuntmagazine.com/reviews/review-children-royal-court/ (accessed 28 January 2021).
Taylor, D. (1997), *Disappearing Acts: Spectacles of Gender and Nationalism in Argentina's 'Dirty War'*, Durham, NC and London: Duke University Press.
Taylor, J. D. (2013), *Negative Capitalism: Cynicism in the Neoliberal Era*, Portland, OR: Zero.
The Black Public Sphere Collective, eds (1995), *The Black Public Sphere*, Chicago: University of Chicago Press.
Ther, P. (2016), *Europe since 1989*, trans. C. Hughes-Kreutzmüller, Princeton, NJ: Princeton University Press.
Thompson, J. (2019), 'Vicky Featherstone interview: "I've never once counted how many women are in any season I've announced"', *Evening Standard*, 1 May. Available online: www.standard.co.uk/culture/theatre/vicky-

featherstone-interview-royal-court-theatre-new-season-a4130621.html (accessed 27 May 2020).
Thorpe, C. (2013), *There Has Possibly Been An Incident*, London: Oberon.
Trueman, M. (2016a), 'London Theater Review: "Oil" at the Almeida Theater', *Variety*, 18 October. Available online: https://variety.com/2016/legit/reviews/oil-review-play-almeida-theater-1201890902/ (accessed 20 January 2020).
Trueman, M. (2016b), 'Katie Mitchell on Cleansed', *National Theatre* (YouTube), 7 March. Available online: www.youtube.com/watch?v=5LizhtwXP8A (accessed 10 April 2020).
tucker green, d. (2018), *ear for eye*, London: Nick Hern.
Turner, C. (2017), 'King's College hires "safe space marshals" to police controversial speaker events on campus', *The Telegraph*, 26 October. Available online: www.telegraph.co.uk/education/2017/10/26/kings-college-hires-safe-space-marshals-police-controversialspeaker/ (accessed 2 July 2019).
Turner, C. (2018), 'Bristol University students seek to ban "Terf" speakers who question transgender status of women', *The Telegraph*, 1 March. Available online: www.telegraph.co.uk/education/2018/03/01/bristol-university-students-seek-ban-terf-speakers-question/ (accessed 2 July 2019).
Vansina, J. (2010), *The Kuba Experience in Rural Congo, 1880–1960*, Madison: University of Wisconsin Press.
Veldestra, C. (2018), 'Bad Feeling at Work: Emotional Labour, Precarity, and the Affective Economy', *Cultural Studies* 34 (1): 1–24.
Velikonja, M. (2013), 'Eurosis', in A. Drace-Francis (ed.), *European Identity: A Historical Reader*, trans. O. Vukovic, 255–7, Basingstoke: Palgrave Macmillan.
Verma, R. (2018), interview with M. Upadhyaya, 'It Was Standard to See Signs Saying, "No Blacks, No Dogs, No Irish"', *Each Other*, 29 November. Available online: https://eachother.org.uk/racism-1960s-britain/ (accessed 16 May 2020).
Vermeulen, P. (2017), 'Future Readers: Narrating the Human in the Anthropocene', *Textual Practice*, 31 (5): 867–85.
Vorozhbit, N. (2017), *Bad Roads*, trans. S. Dugdale, London: Nick Hern.
Wallace, C. (2006), *Suspect Cultures: Narrative, Identity and Citation in 1990s New Drama*, Prague: Litteraria Pragensia.
Warden, C. (2012), *British Avant-Garde Theatre*, Basingstoke: Palgrave Macmillan.
Watson, A. (2021a), 'Theatre's Dark Matter: Pinter's "Staging" of Systemic Violence and its Influence in Contemporary British Theatre', in B. Chiasson and C. Fallow (eds), *Harold Pinter: Stages, Networks and Collaborations*, 139–56, London: Methuen Drama.
Watson, A. (2021b), 'Neoliberal (Dis)Possession in Rose Lewenstein's *Cougar*', *Theatre Notebook*, 75 (3): 201–15.

Watson, A. (2022), 'Contemporary Catastrophes: 2010s British Climate Crisis Theatre and Performativity', *Contemporary Theatre Review*, 32 (2): 140–61. Available online: doi.org/10.1080/10486801.2022.2047035 (accessed 24 August 2022).

Watson, A. (2023), 'Population Concerns, Reproductive Justice, and Gendered Perspectives in Florence Keith-Roach's *Eggs* (2015), Vivienne Franzmann's *Bodies* (2017) and Maud Dromgoole's *3 Billion Seconds* (2018)', in E. Angel-Perez and A. Rousseau (eds), *The New Wave of British Women Playwrights*, 11–33, Berlin and Boston: De Gruyter.

Welton, E. (2020), 'Welcome to *The Jungle*: Performing Borders and Belonging in Contemporary British Migration Theatre', *Theatre Research International*, 45 (3): 230–44.

Wenzel, J. (2006), 'Petro-magic-realism: Toward a Political Ecology of Nigerian Literature', *Postcolonial Studies*, 9 (1): 449–64.

Whitehill, C. (2016a), 'On Writing for a Different Gender', *Exeunt Magazine*, 3 August. Available online: http://exeuntmagazine.com/features/writing-different-gender/ (accessed 19 November 2020).

Whitehill, C. (2016b), *Mr Incredible*, in A. George, M. Burt and T. Wilson (eds), *Plays from Vault*, 51–90, London: Nick Hern.

Whitehill, C. (2016c), *Mr Incredible*, London: Nick Hern.

Whitehill, C. (2017), '"Female Playwrights" Have a Rubbish Time – The Industry Needs a Reset', *The Stage*, 13 September. Available online: www.thestage.co.uk/opinion/opinion/camilla-whitehill-female-playwrights-have-a-rubbish-time-the-industry-needs-a-reset (accessed 19 November 2020).

Whiteley, D. (2016), 'Dunwich: The storms that destroyed "lost town"', *BBC News*, 21 February. Available online: www.bbc.co.uk/news/uk-england-suffolk-35549952 (accessed 28 January 2020).

Whyman, E., ed. (2016), *Making Mischief: Two Radical New Plays*, London: Oberon, 2016.

Williams, R. (2002), 'A Lecture on Realism', *Afterall: A Journal of Art, Context and Enquiry*, 5 (1): 106–15.

Willis, E. (2019), '"Acting in the Real World": Acting, Methodologies, Power and Gender', *Theatre Research International*, 43 (3): 258–71.

Wilmer, S. E. (2018), *Performing Statelessness in Europe*, Basingstoke: Palgrave Macmillan.

Wolfe, C. (2018), 'Is Humanism Really Humane?', in B. Evans and N. Lennard (eds), *Violence: Humans in Dark Times*, 117–26, San Francisco: City Lights.

Wong Davies, A. (2019), 'Jasmine Lee-Jones and Milli Bhatia: "Why do we have to inherit structures in order to make stuff?"', *Exeunt*, 3 July. Available online: http://exeuntmagazine.com/features/milli-bhatia-jasmine-lee-jones-interview/ (accessed 8 January 2021).

Younge, G. (2019), 'Streets on fire: How a decade of protest shaped the world', *The Guardian*, 23 November. Available online: www.theguardian.com/

culture/2019/nov/23/decade-of-protest-occupy-wall-street-extinction-rebellion-gary-younge (accessed 10 November 2020).
Younis, M. (2017), 'Introduction', in R. Edmund, *Black Lives, Black Words*, iv–vi, London: Oberon, 2017.
Yusoff, K. (2018), *A Billion Black Anthropocenes or None*. Minneapolis: University of Minnesota Press.
Zaroulia, M. and P. Hager, eds (2015), *Performances of Capitalism: Crises and Resistance: Inside/Outside Europe*, Basingstoke: Palgrave Macmillan.
Zeldin-O'Neill, S. (2019), '"It's a crisis, not a change": The six Guardian language changes on climate matters', *The Guardian*, 16 October. Available online: www.theguardian.com/environment/2019/oct/16/guardian-language-changes-climate-environment (accessed 8 January 2020).
Žižek, S. (2008), *Violence*, London: Verso.
Žižek, S. (2012), *The Year of Dreaming Dangerously*, London: Verso.
Zola, É. (1881; 2001), 'Naturalism on the Stage (1881)', in T. Cole (ed.), *Playwrights on Playwriting: From Ibsen to Ionesco*, 5–14, New York: Cooper Square.

Index

#MeToo 2, 11, 31, 128, 148, 160, 169
  see also fourth-wave feminism
1980s 14, 105, 112, 149–50
1990s 14–16, 25, 105, 148–9
2011 England riots 68, 71–3, 179

ableism 7, 61–2, 95
Adiseshiah, Siân 25, 42–3
  with Jacqueline Bolton 76, 82–4
affect 16, 20, 29–30, 39–40, 43, 55–6,
    62, 68, 83, 91, 93, 101–2, 108,
    127, 129–30, 170–1
ageism 97–100, 162
Alabanza, Travis
  Burgerz 22, 161, 167, 169–74
  other work 169
Althusser, Louis 51, 58, 178
Ancient Greek theatre 7–9, 16, 52, 54,
    115, 117, 126, 128
Angelaki, Vicky 4, 88, 90, 105, 112,
    117–18
Anthropocene 87
  see also Capitolocene
Anthropocentrism 94, 98
apocalyptic 21, 26, 28, 30, 96, 104–12,
    117, 119–20, 122, 131, 159
Arendt, Hannah 20, 27–9, 32, 34,
    40, 42
Artaud, Antonin 9, 12, 15
Aston, Elaine 25, 43, 148–57, 182
  with Mark O'Thomas 114–15
Austin, J. L. 45, 50–1, 173, 178

Balibar, Étienne 20, 47–8, 58, 60,
    62–3, 83, 171, 178
Balme, Christopher 21, 68–70, 74, 87,
    116–17, 137, 179
Barrel Organ 20, 45–6, 51–7
  see also Lulu Raczka

Bartlett, Mike 105, 107
Bartlett, Neil 108, 180
Beckett, Samuel 12, 25, 43
Benjamin, Walter 23–4, 27–8, 40,
    42, 91
Berry-Hart, Tess
  Cargo 126, 137
Bhatia, Milli
  Dismantle This Room 166
  'My White Best Friend (And
    Other Letters Left Unsaid')
    135, 166
  *seven methods of killing kylie
    jenner* 161–6
Billington, Michael 60–1, 96, 99–100,
    117, 130
Birch, Alice
  playwriting 161, 164
  Anatomy of a Suicide 151
  [BLANK] 160
  Revolt. She said. Revolt again.
    158–9
  with RashDash, *We Want You To
    Watch* 159
Black identity 76–84, 136–42, 162–6
Black Lives Matter 2, 31, 49, 67–8, 76,
    78, 84, 169, 177
Black public sphere 78–82, 166
Blythe, Alecky 71–3
Bond, Edward 13–16, 27
Bourdieu, Pierre 21, 50–1, 53, 56, 58,
    61–2, 178
Brecht, Bertolt 14, 16, 25, 29, 43, 48,
    107
Brexit 4, 6, 20–1, 92, 99, 103–8,
    112–13, 117–22, 123–26,
    134–43, 181–2
British-European relations 21, 103,
    113–21

British identity 93, 103, 113, 123–4, 134–43, 169
Butler, Judith 20, 64, 176
  with Athena Athanasiou, *Dispossession* 111
  performative identity construction 99
  Excitable Speech 50–8, 61, 163
  Frames of War 39–40, 173
  Gender Trouble 2, 99, 124
  Notes Towards a Performative Theory of Assembly 67–8, 72, 79, 85
  Precarious Life 38, 179
  The Force of Nonviolence 68, 79–80

capitalism 13, 87
Capitalocene 87–8
Cameron, David 104, 179
Camus, Albert 12, 108, 180
capitalist realism 105–12, 122, 158, 172
censorship 14–15, 70–1, 179
Chandler, Katherine
  Bird 21, 105, 151–6, 167, 170, 183
  Before it Rains 153
  Parallel Lines 153
  Lose Yourself 153
  Thick As Thieves 153
Churchill, Caryl 4, 77, 150, 157
  A Number 25
  Cloud Nine 90
  Escaped Alone 20, 23–43, 48, 56, 62, 64, 72, 96, 98, 100–1, 106–7, 157, 172
  Far Away 25, 31, 35, 96
  Fen 25, 90
  Glass. Kill. Bluebeard. Imp. 25
  Here We Go 100–1
  Light Shining in Buckinghamshire 25
  Love and Information 25
  Owners 14, 25
  Serious Money 25
  Top Girls 14, 25, 90, 92, 105, 148, 152, 154, 182
class 71–2, 101, 104, 110, 112, 127, 137–8, 142, 148, 152, 167
classism 7, 14, 71, 103, 122, 135, 137, 148
climate crisis 20–1, 34, 71, 85, 87–102, 105, 113, 167, 169–71, 175, 180
climate crisis theatre 85, 87–102, 180
colonialism 6, 11, 46, 59–64, 81, 90, 92, 95, 110, 113, 124, 126, 131, 162, 165
consumerism 13, 92–3, 98–9, 128, 130
continuum-thinking 21–2, 143, 146–7, 150–7, 163, 166–7, 170–4
Cornford, Tom 130, 133–4
COVID-19 virus/ pandemic 4–5, 108, 175, 177, 183
Cracknell, Carrie
  A Doll's House 11
  Oil 89–93
Crouch, Tim
  The Author 15, 17, 173–4
  Total Immediate Collective Imminent Terrestrial Salvation 170
Crimp, Martin
  Dealing With Clair 105
  Attempts on Her Life 105, 109, 159

dehumanization 19, 38–9, 47, 71, 111, 117, 120–6, 137, 143, 165
De-Lahay, Rachel 124, 135
  Routes 137
  'My White Best Friend (And Other Letters Left Unsaid)' festival 166
Dennis-Edwards, Emma 138, 141
  Funeral Flowers 139
Derrida, Jacques 106–7, 178

Diamond, Elin 149–50, 157–60, 164
  See also, realism-without-truth
disposability 21, 33, 47, 79, 98–9, 111, 182
Dolan, Jill 35, 37, 106, 149–51
Duffy, Carol Ann 137, 158
dystopia 21, 25, 29, 34, 77, 104–13, 118–20, 122, 131

Early Modern Theatre 9–11, 15–16, 35, 108, 131, 135–6, 167
Eddo-Lodge, Reni 124, 139–42
European identity/ Europeanness 21, 60–1, 74, 91, 95, 103–4, 113–22, 123–34, 136–8, 143, 169, 181–2
European theatre 6, 8–13, 103, 113–22, 125–6, 128, 136, 138, 179, 181
Euroscepticism 103, 123, 137–8
Evans, Brad and Henry A. Giroux 16, 20, 23–4, 26, 31–3, 42, 64, 98–9, 105, 176

Featherstone, Vicky 2, 114
  Bad Roads 114
  How to Hold Your Breath 128–34
  on censorship 70
  on female representation 131
  on MeToo 2
Finburgh Delijani, Clare 4–7, 40–1
feminism 14, 16, 90–2, 147, 157–9, 163–4, 182
  Fourth-wave feminism 145, 147–8, 182, 167
  in theatre 128, 145, 148–52, 157–67
Fisher, Mark 105, 107–8, 172
Fitzpatrick, Lisa 17–19, 150, 177

Galtung, Johan 13, 48, 178, 180
Gardner, Lyn 77, 109, 113, 115, 122, 130, 136, 138, 183
ghosts 59, 92, 110, 128, 152, 154–5

Girard, René 58, 60–1, 83, 98, 111, 165
Global North 87–9, 91, 93–5, 99, 125, 135, 179
Gluhović, Milija 113, 120, 124, 126
Grace, Fraser 109, 135
Great Recession 4, 105–6
Greig, David 182
  The Events 74
  The Suppliant Women 126
Goddard, Lynette 76–7, 165
  with Marissia Fragkou 82

Habermas, Jürgen 68–9, 81, 113
habitus 40, 53–4, 61–4
Hare, David 115–17, 120, 122, 136
Harris, Zinnie 182
  (the fall of) The Master Builder 128
  A Doll's House 11
  How to Hold Your Breath 21, 113, 123, 128–34, 151
  Meet Me at Dawn 128
  The Duchess [of Malfi] 128, 152
  This Restless House 128
Hartl, Anja 4, 14, 25, 29, 32, 48, 106–7
Harvie, Jen 98–100, 114
hegemonic masculinity 2, 11–12, 17–19, 147, 155, 158–9, 167
Hickson, Ella
  Oil 21, 89–95, 99, 102, 105, 112, 148, 151
  on climate crisis theatre 89, 107
  other work 89
  The Writer 89, 160–1, 164, 166
Holdsworth, Nadine 71–2, 135–6, 138–41
homophobia 7, 148, 161–4

Ibsen, Henrik
  A Doll's House 11, 154
  The Master Builder 11, 128
  The Wild Duck 180
individualism 25, 30, 33, 39, 98–9, 128, 152, 154, 174

in-yer-face theatre 14–16
Iraq War 7, 15, 19, 51, 66, 125
Irish theatre 6, 58, 179, 182

Kafka, Franz 58, 62, 108
Kane, Sarah 4, 77, 113, 115, 119, 150, 157, 182
  Blasted 110, 118, 129, 149, 151
  Cleansed 116, 145–7, 182
  Phaedra's Love 15, 18, 116, 177
Kelly, Dennis 105, 178
  Osama the Hero 15
  Girls & Boys 19
  The Gods Weep 108
Kene, Arinzé 138, 141
King, Dawn
  Foxfinder 96
  Brave New World 108
Kirkwood, Lucy
  Chimerica 73, 96
  Mosquitoes 96
  NSFW 96, 151–2
  The Children 21, 94, 96–102, 149, 170, 180–1
  The Welkin 96, 101

Latif, Nadia
  Fall of the Kingdom, Rise of the Foot Soldier 135–42
  Homegrown 70–1
Lee-Jones, Jasmine
  seven methods of killing kylie jenner 22, 77, 138, 158, 161–7, 170–1, 183
Leigh, Eve 109, 162–3
Lewenstein, Rose
  Cougar 110, 112, 181
  Darknet 109, 163
  Fucking Feminists 159
  Now This is Not the End 151
London 6, 29, 59, 71–2, 107, 109–10, 114, 116, 136, 139, 177
Lonergan, Patrick 91–3
LUNG Productions
  E15 71, 75

Lustgarten, Anders
  A Day at the Racists 127
  If You Don't Let Us Dream, We Won't Let You Sleep 109–10, 127
  Lampedusa 21, 123–34, 155, 171
  on European theatre 115, 117–18
  Shrapnel: 34 Fragments of a Massacre 127–8
Lynn, Cordelia
  Lela & Co. 19, 23, 110
  Sea Creatures 101

Macdonald, James
  Cleansed 115–16
  Escaped Alone 25–43, 96, 98
  Here We Go 100–1
  slow theatre 100–1
  The Children 94–102
Macmillan, Duncan
  1984 108
  2071 31
  Lungs 88
Majumdar, Abhishek
  Pah-La 70, 72
Marranca, Bonnie 26, 30–1, 33–4
May, Theresa 104, 117, 132, 158
Mbembe, Achille 125, 132
McDonagh, Martin
  A Skull in Connemara 58
  A Very Very Very Dark Matter 21, 46, 58–64
  Hangmen 23, 179
  The Beauty Queen of Leenane 58
  The Cripple of Inishmaan 61
  The Lieutenant of Inishmore 58
McDowall, Alistair
  Brilliant Adventures 111
  Pomona 21, 110–12, 118, 122, 143, 175, 181
  X 111
media 32
  film 29, 58, 61, 107, 111, 175, 178
  print 117, 152

Index

television 5, 45, 54, 175, 177–178
social 49, 65, 67, 78, 81, 147–8, 161–7, 183
Mediterranean refugee crisis 21, 29, 102–3, 113, 118, 123, 125–34, 129, 143
Megson, Chris 71, 115
mental health 7, 25–6, 33–4, 46, 51–7, 79, 83–4, 105
Mitchell, Katie
    2071 31
    Atmen 113
    Cleansed 116, 145–7, 181–2
    Miss Julie 11
monologue theatre 1–3, 17–19, 23, 110, 123–34, 138, 169–74, 178
Morton, Timothy 89–95, 98
Mullarkey, Rory
    Cannibals 110
    Pity 109, 179
    Wolf from the Door 106, 109
Murphy, Joe and Joe Robertson
    The Jungle 126–7, 129, 133–4

Nancy, Jean-Luc 20, 39–42, 74, 81, 118, 120, 126, 132
national identity 20–1, 103, 135, 154
National Theatre 96, 110, 137, 145
naturalism 11, 16, 100–1, 157–8
neoliberalism 4, 20–1, 23, 33–4, 39, 71–2, 90, 99, 102, 103–23, 125–35, 138, 140–3, 147, 150, 152–3, 155, 157, 159–60, 163, 166, 167, 169–72, 175, 181
Nevitt, Lucy 18–19, 26, 42, 47, 64, 149, 157, 177
Nixon, Rob 88–93, 95, 99–101, 172, 181
nonviolence 21, 67–8, 72–6, 79–80, 84–5, 179

O'Riordan, Rachel 153–6
Othering 21, 48, 120, 123, 125, 157, 171

Owen, Gary
    Iphigenia in Splott 138
    Violence and Son 179

Paavolainen, Teemu 47–9, 53, 58, 61, 83, 85, 89, 172
Parr, Adrian 88, 91–3
perception 16, 24–5, 28, 37–43, 45, 47, 56, 60, 72, 84, 88–9, 95–6, 101–2, 105–7, 111, 151, 172–3
performativity 2, 18–22, 20–1, 42, 45–64, 68, 74–6, 78–9, 82–5, 87–94, 96, 98–103, 106–11, 113, 115, 120, 124, 127, 130, 132–3, 139–43, 145–50, 153–60, 163–7, 169, 171–6, 178
plural performativity 67–8, 169, 173–4, 176
perpetrator/s 1, 19, 62, 83, 146–7, 154
Pinnock, Winsome 124, 165
Pinter, Harold 13–14, 35, 77, 97, 178
Plato 37, 40, 111
police brutality 65, 68, 77–9, 180
posthumanism 88, 92–6, 101, 180
Post-war British theatre 12–14
Prebble, Lucy 105–6
precarity 72, 79, 96, 105, 107, 133, 154, 156
protest 20–1, 27, 65–85, 112, 161, 179
public sphere 11, 21, 51, 68–76, 81, 85, 87, 117, 134, 142, 150

queer performance 158, 161, 169–74

Raczka, Lulu 20
    A Girl in School Uniform (Walks into a Bar) 52
    on *There Has Possibly Been An Incident* 74

other work 51–2
Some People Talk About Violence 20, 45–6, 51–7, 105, 170
Ravenhill, Mark
  The Cane 13
  Shopping and Fucking 15, 105
  Product 105
realism
  anti-realism / surrealism 12, 15, 115–19, 121, 179
  capitalist 105–11, 122, 158, 172
  fluid realism 150–7, 182
  kitchen-sink / social realism 14, 136
  magic realism 21, 89–90, 93, 102, 105, 129, 151, 154, 155
  patriarchal realism 90, 149–52, 154, 157–8
  realism-without-truth 157–65
  traditional 14, 16, 60, 90, 100–1, 107–8, 116, 149–50, 152, 154
revolution 21, 27, 68, 70, 73, 80, 84, 106, 112, 136, 141, 143, 159, 174, 179
Rebellato, Dan 6, 15–16, 30, 103, 106–7, 111–12, 115–19, 128, 137, 142, 159, 175
Reid, Trish 15, 106–7, 115, 117, 129–30, 138–9, 162–3
reviews, reviewing 20, 63, 93, 96, 117, 162
Richardson, Alissa V. 65, 76–84, 139, 146, 163, 172, 180
Ridley, Philip
  The Pitchfork Disney 15–16
ritual 2, 46, 47–8, 53, 58–62, 63, 83, 98, 111, 162, 165, 170, 173
Royal Court
  International Department 21, 113–15, 118, 120
  Theatre 2, 6, 23, 25, 31, 70, 76–7, 81, 94, 96, 113–15, 128, 133, 161, 166, 177, 180–1, 183

Royal Exchange Manchester 11, 110, 114, 153, 169
Russia 110, 114, 125, 181

Samara, Effie 19, 70, 81, 174
Scotland/ Scottish theatre 7, 113, 123, 128, 152, 182
Seaton, Somalia Nonyé
  Fall of the Kingdom, Rise of the Foot Soldier 21, 77, 109, 123–4, 135–43, 170–3
  other work 135
Seneca 9–10, 15
Shakespeare, William
  influence 7, 131, 135–6
  King Lear 10, 108
  Macbeth 10
  Titus Andronicus 10, 15
Shalson, Lara 65–9
Sierz, Aleks 5, 14–15, 137–8
Skinner, Penelope
  Linda 23, 150
Slovo, Gillian
  The Riots 71–3, 75
Smith, Stef
  Girl in the Machine 109
  Human Animals 96, 107
  Nora: A Doll's House 11
Solga, Kim 10–11, 34–5, 37, 167
Solnit, Rebecca 21, 145–6, 160, 182
Sontag, Susan 20, 29, 32, 35, 39, 42, 73
state-of-the nation theatre 115, 136
Stenham, Polly 105
  Hotel 110
  Julie 11
Stephens, Simon
  A Doll's House 11
  Carmen Disruption 117–19
  Motortown 15
  on Chris Thorpe 73
  Pornography 105, 109
  Three Kingdoms 21, 113, 116–22

Strindberg, August
  Miss Julie 11–12
surrealism 15
structural/systemic misogyny 1–2,
  6, 10, 19, 23, 28, 90, 117, 122,
  129, 145–67, 180
structural/systemic racism 13, 20–1,
  28, 32, 34, 58, 61, 76–85, 103,
  122–43

Teater NO99 21, 116
Theatre of the Absurd 10, 12–13, 16
Thorpe, Chris
  *There Has Possibly Been An
  Incident* 21, 73–6, 85
transphobia 20, 146, 169, 172
trauma 28, 34–5, 41, 76, 79, 84, 113,
  120–4, 126, 133, 135, 138, 143,
  151, 161, 177
Trump, Donald 71, 135
tucker green, debbie
  ear for eye 13, 21, 76–85, 138,
    140–1, 171
  hang 76
  random 76
  stoning mary 76
  truth and reconciliation 76

Verbatim theatre 19, 71–2, 114, 137
violence
  (ultra)subjective 2, 17, 32, 47–8,
    57–8, 60, 61–3, 79, 82, 84, 92,
    139, 142, 148, 152, 161, 163,
    165, 167, 169–71, 175
  (ultra)objective 32, 47–8, 62–3,
    83, 169, 171
  divine 24, 40, 42
  gender-based (GBV) 1–2, 11,
    17, 21, 52, 105, 145–67,
    169–74
  gendered 28, 35, 145–7, 157
  images of 5, 29, 39–40, 105, 116

language/symbolic 1, 15, 21, 29,
  32–4, 50–7, 62, 92, 100, 163
normalized 24, 28, 31–2, 42, 170,
  173
offstage 1–3, 8–9, 12–13, 35
psychological 12, 35, 163–4, 178
racist 12, 20–1, 32, 76–85, 124,
  135, 138, 142, 166, 171
sexual 1, 10, 17–19, 146–9, 153–4,
  157, 177
slow 88–95, 99–101, 172
spectacular 9, 15–19, 29, 32–3,
  36–7, 40–2, 47, 72–3, 167, 169,
  170, 176–177
systemic 1–23, 32–40, 42, 45–9,
  52, 57–64, 68, 72, 76–8, 82–5,
  88, 92, 96, 111–12, 127, 135–6,
  139, 145–8, 152, 155, 158, 160,
  163–7, 171–6
structural 2, 8, 10, 13, 18, 21, 41,
  43, 48–50, 58, 60–1, 68–9,
  78, 81, 83, 95, 103–6, 123–4,
  130–1, 133–43, 146–7, 153,
  160–1, 164–5, 167, 169–77,
  180
taxonomical 13, 57, 88, 94–102,
  147
terrorism 83, 109
war 7, 15, 19, 65–6, 93, 113

Wales/Welsh theatre 7, 10, 152–3
Whitehill, Camilla
  Mr Incredible 1–2, 17–19, 177
  on gender equality in theatre 6,
    19, 142
Williams, Roy
  Sucker Punch 139
  The Death of England 136–7
Wolfe, Cary 88, 93–6, 98–9, 147

Žižek, Slavoj 16, 20, 32–3, 35, 40,
  42–3, 47, 50, 64, 72, 139

www.ingramcontent.com/pod-product-compliance
Lightning Source LLC
Chambersburg PA
CBHW052110300426
44116CB00010B/1606